ECHOES
FROM FAR
LANDS

www.mascotbooks.com

Echoes from Far Lands: stories on cultures, farming, and life

I have tried to recreate events, locales, and conversations from my memories of them. In order to maintain their anonymity in some instances I have changed the names of individuals and places. I may have changed some identifying characteristics and details such as physical properties, occupations, and places of residence.

For more information, please contact:
Mascot Books
620 Herndon Parkway #320
Herndon, VA 20170
info@mascotbooks.com

Library of Congress Control Number: 2019910251

CPSIA Code: PRV1119A
ISBN: 978-1-64543-174-9

Printed in the United States

To Squadron Leader Ridley Bradford, RAF
who gave his life for my country and lent me his name

ECHOES FROM FAR LANDS

stories on cultures, farming, and life

RIDLEY NELSON

TABLE OF CONTENTS

FOR STARTERS

One crowded hour...is worth an age without a name.

– Thomas Osbert Mordaunt

Five years ago, taking a break from weeding a row of smothered onions, I stretched out on the sofa in my basement and reached for the nearest protruding book. It was an Australian anthology of poetry that I had bought long ago in a country town called Wagga Wagga. It fell open at Judith Wright's poem "South of My Days." I was reminded of her lines about old Dan, "Seventy years of stories he clutches round his bones. / Seventy years are hived in him like old honey." It occurred to me that I, too, felt hived full of stories, and, as it happened, about seventy years' worth, too. So, unable to hold them in any longer, I started writing.

I have lived in England, Egypt, Australia, Kenya, Tanzania, India, and America and have travelled to about ninety-five countries. I worked for two commercial companies, one in England and one in Australia, for a British overseas aid program, and for the World Bank. Nearly all of this work was in support of agriculture and rural development, most of it in developing countries. I have avoided writing about the performance of rural development projects, too dry and a different genre, but I do draw from many encounters with farming and pastoralist people from around the world.

This is not a traditional memoir, at least not in the sense of tracing an examined life towards some sort of denouement. It is a mix of memoir, travelogue, essay, and polemic. But to me, that really is life—a dog's breakfast, sometimes one that has been stepped in. In this vein, I have allowed the flow to carry me into eddies. After all, writing is the process of uncovering one's ideas, like the little girl who, when pressed, answered crossly, "How can I know what I think till I hear what I say?"

I make no claim that what I record is unique. You only have to sit on a concrete floor with fellow travelers waiting for a delayed flight in a departure shed somewhere in Africa to know that every expatriate who has spent time overseas can trade unusual yarns until the cows come home, or at least until a speck on the horizon resolves itself into your aircraft. The same would be true of every travelled African or Indian expatriate who has attempted to fathom the strange ways of our West.

I have referred occasionally to forebears, but I have not written about the generations following me, except in one or two places where a recalled event linked to a family member. This is not family history. It is for them to tell their own stories.

It has been said that memoir is the art of inventing the truth.[1] I have tried to re-create events, places and conversations as I recall them, but I doubt that any will be entirely accurate. Some stories will have grown with the telling, picking up snow as they rolled downhill. Over time, the boundary between image and reality blurs. Research suggests that our memory is closest to our recollection of the last telling of an event. I suppose I am stuck with that manufacturing defect.

My theme is that you can only understand yourself and the ways of your tribe if you can begin to understand the ways of other tribes, neither complicated nor unique but increasingly important, I believe, in our divided world. I hope I have avoided allowing this theme to pull the rug out from under a good yarn but, in any case, there is a strong cultural role in storytelling. Research, particularly with hunter-gatherers, has shown that storytellers were, and still are, the main channel for conveying ideas, ethics, and emotions essential for cooperation and survival.

When I reach the final chapter, I let fly a bit, indulging in an exploration of meaning and truth. I build the ideas in this book, but especially that chapter, around two aphorisms: The first is from Professor Raymond Tallis, the British polymath, neuroscientist and cultural critic who, when asked about the meaning of life, replied, "I don't know about the meaning of life, but the purpose of life is to gather together as many meanings as possible and to explore and enrich them. Meaning changes: it is not prescribed."[2] The second is from the eccentric Scottish biologist D'Arcy Wentworth Thompson (1860–1948)[3] who strolled the gray streets of St. Andrews in gym shoes with a parrot on his shoulder and who would drill into his students, "Everything is the way it is because it got that way." At the time, he was exploring the reasons for the shapes found in the animal kingdom such as faces, starfish, and appendages. But I have taken the liberty of broadening this towards cause and effect more generally, trying to understand why people, animals and plants behave as they do.

Now let me come clean: This is not a confessional. I cannot claim to have been molested by a deviant stepfather or to have had parents who were alcoholics, although, come to think of it, they did knock back their fair share of gin. Nor was I abandoned in a shopping bag on the steps of a village church. The most promising handicap I can offer is that, as with many English military brats, I was sent to boarding school at the age of barely seven. Perhaps I bear terrible scars from this; if so, let's hope they show through.

Certainly, I will share my feelings. I will share my reactions as a child on seeing an aircraft explode above me. I will share the euphoria of driving a tractor alone at night on the boundless plains of New South Wales. I will share the spooky intuition I felt as a hop disease inspector. I will share the adrenalin surges of trout fishing among lions and elephants in Africa. But I will not be washing my dirty linen in public. (Or really my clean.)

There are chapters with observations on individual countries, although I put the countries of Africa together because it seemed to work better.

None of the stories from countries are balanced or representative of those countries then or now. You cannot do justice, or for that matter injustice, to a country in a few pages, and certainly not through a handful of odd, droll or unusual encounters, observations, and musings.

I like to think of this book in another way, too—as a collection of stories and ideas told by a very ordinary pilgrim through life who, in earlier times, might have tagged along with Chaucer's bawdy band on their pilgrimage along the South Downs to Canterbury. Which reminds me, please forgive what your culture or upbringing may find unsavory. These things surface inevitably from reporting on witnessed life.

ENTER STAGE RIGHT

**Your children are not your children. They are the
sons and daughters of Life's longing for itself.**

– Kahlil Gibran

Soon after the start of the Second World War, my father, Eric
Nelson, a Royal Air Force officer of Scots descent, then a Squadron Leader,
was posted to Australia to help the Royal Australian Air Force establish a
base to train bomber pilots and gunners.

My father's father was a Royal Navy Admiral who had started his
career in the earliest Holland Class submarines that had a crew of eight.
"Yes, they went down rather better than they came up," he would remark
from his armchair with a wry smile. Later, during World War I, he fought
at the Battle of Jutland as the Second Engineer on the superdreadnought
HMS *Warspite*.

The Number 1 Bombing and Gunnery School[4] (No. 1 BAGS) that my
father commanded was at Evans Head near Lismore, on the northern coast
of New South Wales. There was a headland jutting out into the sea that
could be bombed inaccurately by the trainees with some safety for humans;
less, I presume, for kangaroos and lobsters.

It would be an understatement to say that these were turbulent times. My mother's diary describes the events in Europe soon after they reached Australia:

> *In six short weeks the Germans have walked through Holland, Belgium and France.... A few weeks ago, we would have laughed if we had been told that Paris would fall within three weeks of the Germans entering Belgium and Holland, but such are the facts and the British people are left to carry the torch of civilization alone—Please God may they not fail...*

Soon she was writing:

> *The retreat from Dunkirk will live in everyone's memory for the magnificent courage of the Royal Navy who, aided by boats of every shape and size even including Thames barges, managed to rescue 360,000 men from the shores of Dunkirk....*

When people today moan to me that things are bad, I metaphorically give them a kick up the backside and tell them about what my mother wrote here in her diary. Now *that,* I say, was a time when you could have legitimately complained that things were bad. The world was turning upside down. People just soldiered on.

In 1940, Australia was half a world away from the main action, but by the end of 1941, with Pearl Harbor on December 7, war had taken a giant stride towards Australia's doorstep. My birth on the 7th of January 1942, in Lismore, made me, I suppose, an "Aussie pommy" or a "pommy Aussie." (Pommy is the mildly derogatory Australian term for a Brit—more derogatory obviously in the hyphenated but now archaic version "pommy-bastard," although even this was little more than a good-natured jab. The label "pom" may have come from Prisoner of His Majesty, the convict history. But it is more likely to have come from "pomegranate" due to the complexion of British immigrants, first making "pomegranate" out of "immigrant"—the Aussie facility for cockney rhyming slag—and then subjecting it to a contraction to "pommy," and then to "pom.")

When the telegram proclaiming my arrival reached my grandparents in wartime London, their response went something like:

CONGRATULATIONS WONDERFUL NEWS STOP BUT
STRONGLY SUGGEST RECONSIDER NAME

My parents brushed this aside. The name *Ridley* came from my father's closest friend, to whom this book is dedicated, Ridley Bradford. He was killed early in the war, on April 30, 1940, in a Wellington bomber of No. 37 Squadron. He took off with his crew from RAF Feltwell in England on a raid on the port town of Stavanger in Norway. They were last reported engaged with enemy fighters off the Norwegian coast. His aircraft, and whatever remains of him and his gallant crew, lies under the sea somewhere southwest of Stavanger. I honor them for their sacrifice.

A few days after I was born, my mother wrote in her diary:

War News. Very bad in the Pacific. Japs taken Tarakan, rich oil island of the Dutch Indies and they seem to be making good progress in Malaya and the Philippines. One has to turn to the Russian front for consolation where there is steady progress. I guess the Germans are having a time. The Middle East is going satisfactorily too and General Rommel is slowly but surely being told where he gets off.

All of us born onto this planet are preposterously improbable. From the Big Bang onwards, we are perched on top of an Everest-sized pile of rolled dice. Any event, from a small divergence in a Big Bang ratio of particles, to the untimely death of an ancestor in a bullock cart accident in 1262, would have changed our existence entirely or eliminated us from the game. My return to England in a convoy, leaving Australia in November 1942, was one of the earliest rolled dice in my own post-birth layer of the pile, a hazardous wartime voyage, in the end taking nearly six months. Being less than a year old, I have no recollection of it, other than through my parents' stories.

We traveled on the first leg to South Africa on a Free French coal-burning ship, the 9,600-ton SS *Desirade*. Sailing alone across the Indian Ocean, the ship had a fire in the coal bunkers for the entire voyage. In those days, fires in coal bunkers were not uncommon; the Titanic had set sail with a fire in a bunker that was finally extinguished by the Atlantic Ocean with the help of an iceberg. The SS *Desirade* is reported to have been capable of thirteen knots, but I believe we were steaming at a dangerously slow eight knots, perhaps due to the fire. The fire was combatted by shutting down the hatches and starving it of oxygen. Every morning at breakfast my parents would ask the imperturbable French captain how his fire was coming along. Every morning, he would shrug and reply, "Ah, comme ci comme ça." But we eventually made it through the dangerous approaches into Durban.

After many weeks of waiting, we left South Africa on the more dangerous leg aboard the SS *Nestor*, a 14,500-ton passenger ship sailing initially alone and then later in convoy. Built in 1913, the *Nestor* had the highest funnel of any British passenger ship of its day, some eighty feet. This made it healthier for passengers in peacetime sunning themselves on the deckchairs, but distinctly unhealthy in wartime for the safety of the ship. All a German U-boat commander needed was that one telltale wisp.

After leaving South Africa, our ship was diverted to the island of St. Helena, Napoleon's imprisonment island, to pick up the survivors of a sunk passenger ship named the *City of Cairo*.[5] The story of that sinking, and the fate of the passengers and crew on the life-boats that made it to that tiny spec, St. Helena, and those that overshot or were never seen again, is told in a harrowing book called *Goodnight, Sorry for Sinking You: The Story of the S.S. City of Cairo*, by Ralph Barker (1984).

With these new passengers, our ship was crowded, but the original *Nestor* passengers were able to benefit from the influx of experience on how to survive for weeks at sea in an open lifeboat on a couple of ounces of water a day. Wherever they went on the ship, passengers carried their life-jacket and a "skedaddle bag." This contained whatever they felt they might need in the event of a hasty exit onto lifeboats. Apparently, in addition to water, Horlicks tablets were popular skedaddle bag contents—a type of malt-based energy tablet—but they fell out of favor when some of the *City of Cairo* survivors described how their throats had been so dry and raw from dehydration that getting them down might cause damage.

My mother made me a small kapok life jacket since there were none on board to fit a one-year-old. Kapok is a buoyant dispersal fiber from a tree seed. Halfway through the voyage, as we approached the more dangerous waters, my father decided that they had not properly tested it. They filled a bath to the brim, strapped me into it, and lowered me in. I sank like a holed plastic duck. There was a hasty redesign and more kapok was stuffed in.

With a last stop in Sierra Leone, the convoy initially avoided the U-boats by zigzagging up through the North Atlantic. But on the night of March 29, 1943, in the Bay of Biscay off Spain, two U-boats found us.[6] Five of the thirty-six ships were torpedoed in a period of an hour; four of them went down, but one stayed afloat. Our ship was one of the lucky ones.

My father, as the senior military officer in the convoy, although not a navy officer, was asked to be present on the bridge during the night action against the submarine attack. My mother was waiting anxiously in a lounge near her muster station behind the bridge with me in her arms, both of us wearing our lifejackets. The *City of Cairo* passengers were praying, "Please God, not again, not again."

Depth charges were being dropped by the convoy ships, but these were random potshots. There was, by that time, sonar technology to spot subs below the surface, but it was of little use for finding them surfaced at night.

The position of the U-boats, or even the number, was not known. At one point during the action, my father heard over the crackling radio, "Apples! Definitely Apples!" This meant U-boat debris had been spotted. But, in fact, the records show that no submarine was hit.[7]

I was recently looking through the list of those in our convoy who were lost. The youngest, from the sinking of the SS *Empire Whale*, was Ordinary Seaman James Lamport, aged seventeen, from South Shields in England. I salute him for taking my place. I made it out of this attack to lead a full life. His was cut short. By his age of seventeen, I was awkwardly enjoying teenage dances, drinking pints of Worthington E in village pubs, and wondering what glory or brickbats life would hold for me. He never got beyond a first shot.

We reached Liverpool early in April. I had learned to walk on the heaving deck of the *Nestor*, a skill that had to be quickly unlearned once I was on dry land. My mother's faded cine films show that, for the first weeks, I found solid earth under foot very difficult with its infuriating stability. Perhaps this was one of my earliest sub-conscious lessons—that even the seemingly solid physical world could be unpredictable.

Throughout the final two weeks that our convoy had been funneling painfully slowly into the choke points around Britain, my grandfather, an Admiral, was anxiously following our progress. He had been recalled out of retirement to the Admiralty in London and was able to follow our plotted position and the positions of known or suspected U-boats. Every evening when he returned to their home in Hampstead prepared for the nightly bombing raids, my grandmother would ask him as casually as she could muster how our convoy was progressing. He would tell her everything was fine and there was nothing to worry about. These were the necessary fibs of wartime.

My father's Australia posting was followed back in England by a year and a half towards the end of the war commanding a Lancaster bomber squadron, No. 103 Squadron, at Elsham Wolds, in Lincolnshire. As the boss, he was only allowed to fly one mission a month. He came through those missions unscathed. His chances of achieving that over his length of command were a bit under 50%; his successor just before the end of the war failed to return from his first mission. At an average of 3% losses per raid, Bomber Command's air war for the crews was a grim roulette, as it was, of course, for those on the receiving end.

OF CAMELS, "FAGS," BEAKS, AND GROISE

**Where you will sit when you are old
shows where you stood in youth.**

– African Yoruba proverb

Soon after the war, when I was four, came a posting for my father to Egypt. This was my first dip into another culture, inevitably colored by the British influence and control over the Canal Zone and all that that entailed. We lived on an RAF base at Fayid, near the Great Bitter Lake. It was nestled on a parched stretch of desert with low mountains to the east. The blown *simoom* sand found its way into everything, especially children's eyes. Our perpetually smiling gardener, a teenage boy named Mohammed, became my friend, although no doubt warily because of his position and mine. He showed me how to sow maize and how to tell when it was ripe to pick. Looking back, I think he sowed my initial interest in agriculture.

We would sometimes take picnics to the Suez Canal which, when constructed in the 1860s, had created the Great Bitter Lake out of a saline depression—possibly the location of the Exodus and the parting of the waters. We would watch the ships nose their way north and south through the desert, from a distance looking like woodblock toys dragged on a string through a toddler's sandpit.

We caught my first pet there, from a tree. He was a greenish-yellow, swivel-eyed chameleon, well up to species standards on camouflage but woefully short of social skills. He was joined later by two guinea pigs, but they soon became a morning snack for the neighbor's dog. Later, we had a very small pet stray donkey, Moses, stunted from birth due to poor nutrition. He wandered the house and garden freely, once horrifying a visiting British dignitary's wife who had been ushered into the living room by a servant while he went to find my mother. She found the donkey curled up asleep on the sofa. Everyone came running to her shriek.

It was in Egypt that I first became suspicious about Father Christmas. One Christmas Eve during an afternoon walk, I watched him stagger out of the bar of the officer's mess tipsy, stumble up the steps of a DC3, take off over the desert, and an hour or so later land back at the base to *Ho, Ho, Ho* his way down the steps and hand out gifts—all straight from the North Pole. Apart from seeing him board, I think I was already vaguely aware that a DC3 could never make it from Egypt to the North Pole and be back in the time it had taken me to put on my party costume and walk to the mess hall.

"Mummy, Mummy," I shouted, tugging at her sleeve, "I just saw Father Christmas leaving the…"

"No you didn't darling," she cut in with a loud voice, then more quietly, "Shush, don't spoil it for the others." She stuffed a large slice of chocolate cake in my mouth.

On a visit to Cairo, I found the Cairo Museum scary. I think we were given a private tour of the storage rooms. There were many black and shriveled mummies that had burst out of their wrappings at the head and feet, revealing grinning mouths with missing teeth and, at the lower end, dark brown curled toes, poorly manicured. I remember wondering whether any "willies" had broken out, but I didn't spot any.

Later, at the pyramids, perched on top of a knock-kneed camel well past its prime, family photos remind me that I bawled my eyes out. I remember the reason: I had asked a close friend of my father, "Uncle Tony, what's that shoe hanging there?" (There was a brass shoe mascot hanging from the camel's neck.)

"Oh, that's all that was left of the last little boy that rode it," he said with a grin.

The quick reassurance from my mother that he was joking fell on deaf ears. I had boy-eating camel nightmares for a week to add to the ranks of grinning-mouthed mummies.

We lived in a comfortable bungalow, but Egypt was very hot for much of the year and there was no air conditioning. The best one could do on a hot night was to lie below a creaky ceiling fan, flap the sweat-soaked top sheet by hand, and lay a wet facecloth on one's stomach or face. Morning brought building heat rather than relief.

On returning to England from two-and-a-half years in Egypt, as I turned seven, I was sent to an English preparatory school, Vinehall, in Sussex. *Preparatory* meant preparatory for the later "public" school. The age range was seven to thirteen. I think I had a mild attention problem in those days. My father would sometimes remark to me when he saw me procrastinating or being indecisive, "Come on, come on, you're pissing about like a fart in a colander!" An English expression, the image being… well, you get it!

When I mention my early boarding age to Americans. I sense that I am being given the once-over for the inevitable psychological defects. Some of them hint that my parents must have been heartless dolts. Certainly, I was not a particularly happy little tyke in the first few terms, but there were reasons for their decision. My father could expect to be posted to a new base every two-and-a-half years, some possibly overseas. For educational stability, early boarding was the accepted path for military officers' sons;

15

less so for daughters who, in those days, I'm afraid, were considered the less essential investment.

I cried myself to sleep for the first few weeks. Long-distance telephone calls were expensive, so I had few calls home. In any case, the theory was that phone calls simply exacerbated homesickness and that it was better that a boy just suck it up and get on with school and sports without mummy reminding him every few days that he was missed terribly.

In our free time, we were free to roam at will over the partly-wooded school grounds looking across a valley of cow pastures and chestnut trees to the site of the Battle of Hastings, where, in 1066, King Harold got one in the eye from William the Conqueror's archers—the last time England was invaded. Climbing to the top of the huge chestnut trees was one of the big dares. One very windy day, three of us reached to the topmost branches at over a hundred feet, to a point where the branches were barely five inches across. The wind was swaying them twenty feet from side to side. It was exhilarating beyond anything I had ever experienced. We were whooping and shouting and challenging each other to go higher. For an hour, we clung there like chattering monkeys trying to avoid the tiger below. It was surprising that none of us fell, at least not very far. The possibility of death didn't occur to us.

We were tribal and feral. We had our camps in the woods. We were free to light wood fires and bake potatoes into barely edible charcoal lumps that were hard to tell from the charred logs. We played in the woods at cowboys and Indians with our toy revolvers, only there were no Indians; only imaginary ones. Nobody wanted to have just a bow and arrow. How could bows and arrows stand up to a six-shooter? We became adept at using cover. We were lion cubs preparing for life on the savanna.

Latin was a required subject from a very young age. Our Latin teacher was fierce and demanding. If there was any lack of attention or poor class results, he would fly into a rage and go purple in the face. One sure indicator of his fury was when his right-hand fingers started probing a hole in his right buttock, where there was said to be a buried piece of shrapnel earned in the trenches of the First World War. There were school jokes and dramatic demos by the acknowledged clowns about how his bum had come to be sticking up above the trenches to intercept this shard of flying steel. It was said that the offending projectile could not be removed because it would have been too risky to some vital nerve or artery. The wound apparently troubled him greatly when his blood pressure was up.

I hated Latin. My mother didn't help my poor standing with the Latin teacher by remarking airily to him during a Parents' Day visit that she never quite understood why a "dead language" like Latin was of any use. That was a nail in my coffin that he couldn't let go: "Nelson, frankly I don't give a damn what your mother thinks about dead languages," he'd say. "*You'll* be a dead language if you don't buck up."

In the end, at the age of thirteen, I passed my entrance exams for my "public school" with marks surprisingly well above expectations, even in Latin.

Confusingly, a public school in Britain is a private school, fee-paying, and in my day, tending towards snobby upper-class pretentions, perhaps less so today. There were some quaint traditions at Haileybury. It had once been the training college of the British East India Company, which, with little supervision from the British government, had largely run India for many years up until 1858, the year after the Indian Rebellion, then known by colonial Brits as the Indian Mutiny. Boys in the first year were referred to as "governor," a sarcastic reference inherited from the East India College where the pinnacle of a career would have been to become a Governor in India or some other colony. A school prefect might shout, "Governor Nelson! Get yer stinking rugby socks off my bloody locker!" He was free to add, "…you miserable little grub," or some such term of endearment.

In the first year, every boy was a "fag." I have found in America that announcing casually at dinner with my wife and friends, "I was once a fag," draws immediate attention, even the occasional dropped fork. "Fagging" was, I think, universal in such schools at that time. A "fag" worked during his first year for one of the "prefects" in the "house," a senior boy. Your main duties were buying bread for your prefect at the tuck shop during the morning break, putting out his rugby clothes before sports, and spit-and-polishing his shoes. You were essentially a personal slave, but one that could not be mistreated. At the end of the term ("semester" in America), a "fag" was tipped about twenty shillings, good pocket money in those days when beer was about two or three pints to the shilling.

The teachers were referred to as "beaks." You were expected to "tick" a "beak" if you passed one in the quadrangle, in the same way that you might salute a military officer. This meant raising the index finger of your right hand as you passed with a little wrist and elbow bend. The beak ticked you back.

In my last two years, I was a school prefect and then head of my house. Being a prefect allowed one to wear a distinctive black and white spotted tie and carry an umbrella, which most prefects did rain or shine, as you might bear a ceremonial mace. This looked absurd at a summer cricket match with not a cloud in the sky, but you carried it anyway. It was your badge of office. It was also your weapon. It was handy for poking "nervy" little governors who got out of line as you might lunge with a fencing rapier. How quaint can be the trappings of power but, one soon learns, how insidious.

The Dining Hall at Haileybury was a fine structure. It was said to be one of the largest shallow unsupported domes in England at the time of its construction. The food was institutional to the standards of the day. There were dishes such as beef stew, boiled potato and cabbage, and a thin, brown Windsor soup and hunks of cut bread like weathered chalk. The fare was mostly edible, provided one was hungry enough, which we usually were. One mother of a prospective student on a tour of the kitchens had peered into a caldron containing a bubbling mass of recalcitrant beef stew and remarked, "Ah, I see this is where you wash the rugby clothes!"

On the dining tables, there were saucers heaped with cylindrical pats of butter about half an inch thick, referred to as "groise"—a corruption of grease. The word might be applied as in, "Governor Nelson, sling the bloody groise up this way, yer greedy little bugger." Some earlier generation of boys had discovered that, if flicked hard enough from a tensioned knife with the handle firmly wedged under the solid oak table supports, a circular pat of groise could be launched with enough velocity to stick onto the ceiling—at least the lower parts of the ceiling around the edges of the dome. To achieve this feat took considerable skill and dexterity—I suppose the equivalent in rocketry of achieving orbital velocity. The ceiling had become a temporary parking lot for numerous pats of yellow groise at varying stages of maturity. They would go rancid and dry out until the day came when, like an autumn leaf, they would throw in the towel and fall to earth. The landing site might be some unfortunate boy's soup, an unlucky head, or the wooden floor where it would lie in wait to put our "Toby," the waiter who served us, on his back with a loaded tray of plates.

In the final three years, you graduated to a small study; some for four boys, some for two. This was an improvement on the fifteen-boy common rooms of the early years. Beneath one of the studies I shared there was a low space reached through a trap door in the floor hidden under a thread-bare carpet. It was a small, low hideout room about four feet high in the rubble of the building foundations. A crude bare-bulb light had been precariously connected by a budding, but evidently not quite fully flowered, schoolboy electrician to an electric power distribution box which protested with angry sparks when inadvertently bumped. From old mathematics exercise books down there, it seemed there had been a history of site habitation that stretched back to at least 1910, some fifty years earlier at the time. There were broken bricks, schoolwork exercise books, and cigarette butts, showing all the archeological strata of generations of occupation. It was sobering to realize that some of the torn pages carrying those earlier dates were the scribblings of boys who, upon leaving school at the age of eighteen, had, within months, given their lives on the Western Front. If I remember correctly, eleven hundred boys from Haileybury had died in the two World

Wars, seventeen had been awarded Victoria Crosses, the highest British and Commonwealth award for gallantry. For a school of about five hundred boys, these were gaping holes in two generations. Looking back, we never treated our inherited hideout with the reverence it deserved.

The lack of girls left us all hopelessly short of the social skills needed for wooing the opposite sex with any civility. Public school students entering university were at a disadvantage against those from co-educational schools. Our main contact with girls outside the school holidays was voyeuristic. The barely nubile daughters of teachers would be shamelessly ogled as they paraded past the study blocks. Sometimes they would enlist a school friend to share in the adoration. Half-open study windows would be crammed with faces and hissed ribald comments would carry across the quadrangle. There were titillating rumors of furtive dalliances in the thickets of nearby Golding's Wood attributed to the generally acknowledged experts in these matters whose home lives had somehow given them a head-start over the rest of us.

One year, the school military Cadet Corps went to Catterick Army Camp in Yorkshire for a week of army training exercises. It was a bleak, windswept place on the moors. We slept in canvas army tents arrayed in ranks of numbered rows. I can still bring back the reek of old, damp canvas laced with unwashed bodies and the tang of urine.

The toilet block had the capacity to seat about forty in the one shed of cubicles, although it was rarely fully occupied with strainers except just after the morning *Reveille* bugle call. For some reason, the cans in this drafty crapatorium were often emptied close to peak seating times. They were emptied by hand into a trailered disposal tank that slopped sickeningly as it trundled along outside, drawn by a camouflaged army tractor. Each can was pulled out by hand through a trap door at the rear of the cubicle, emptied out, given a shot of Jeyes Fluid disinfectant, and shoved back under the wooden seat. I once found myself sitting on the throne during an emptying run. I heard the trap door behind me open with a bang and an ablutions squad private shouted, "Hold on mate. Lift 'em up!" You hung on as best you could and were well advised to heed his advice because the can fitted snugly under the wooden seats; there was risk of a pruning action. As you hung on, you heard the glutinous splash behind the cubicle and then the can was shot back under you with a cheery, "There ya go mate, bombs away." For a sixteen-year-old from a family with quite comfortable air force accommodation, this was a new excretory experience. I suppose it was good grounding for later encounters with various unsavory facilities in India, Australia, and Africa—of which we'll explore more as we go along.

At the end of my years at Haileybury, I passed my exams and got my choice of university to study agricultural science. But in order to start taking this degree, all students were required to complete a year working on a farm. I chose to do this in Australia.

A POMMY JACKAROO

**Ten little Jackaroos at riding wished to shine,
One rode the Corkscrew colt, and
then there were nine.**

– A. B. Banjo Patterson

A jackaroo is a young trainee farmhand with social pretensions. He needs to be able to stay on a skittish stockhorse and do anything and everything around the property except sleep with the boss's daughter or, if he has any sense, the overseer's girlfriend. He does it all for a pittance in pay; in the 1960s, five pounds a week. He gets three meals a day including all-you-can-eat lamb chops and variable, sometimes spartan, sleeping quarters. But there is usually ample whisky, gin, wine and beer on the house with the boss and his family in the evening. Most jackaroos are intent on owning their own property or managing one. A *jillaroo* is the female version.

Despite being Australian-born, having been brought up as a pom, and with an unmistakable pommy accent, I had a bit to live down. We had always had a horse at home, so the riding was not a problem. But jackarooing was a new world. As a macho challenge for a young man who needed to get his hands and a few other parts dirty, it was not a bad option. For ruggedness, it might not top crab boats on the Bering Sea, but it would be well up there.

The first property I worked on, Kielli, near Mortlake, in the Western Districts of Victoria, was owned by Ken and Joan Palmer, a great couple who bred pedigree Hereford cattle. Their son David was a fine first mentor.

The stud Hereford bulls on the farm, especially the best bull calves destined for the Sydney Royal Show, were pampered like royalty. From a young age, they had the arrogant gaze of the privileged. They seemed to sense that they were not going to end up as steak any time soon. They were weighed every Monday morning. If a weight gain was low, the boss and the head stockman, Martin Rowan, adjusted feed mixes or fretted about a possible health problem. Each animal had a different menu of feed components written on a chalk board. Feeding was art as much as science; a good stockman operates partly on intuition. The stalls were knee-deep in fresh straw bedding. The bulls were shampooed regularly with Sunlight shampoo and groomed like Hollywood poodles. They were the princes of the cattle world.

But I recall one dinner when Ken Palmer went a step too far on behalf of his bulls. He announced over a juicy steak that he was thinking of putting air conditioning in the bullpens. Joan, his wife, put down her knife and fork and blew a gasket. "You mean we humans don't have air conditioning, but the bloody bulls are going to?" The rest of the meal was frosty enough to have air conditioned the house for a week. The idea was not broached again while I was working there.

Barbecues are an Australian specialty. But in my first week as a jackaroo, I was taken aback by my boss's technique. We went outside the back door and he handed me a one-foot square cookie tin, an Australian Arnott's biscuit tin, along with a hinged wire mesh cooking clamp and a couple of issues of the *Melbourne Age* newspaper. We squatted on the flagstones.

"Ridley, most people have fancy barbies. Unnecessary. This is how we do it here." He tore up the newspaper into individual pages, no doubles.

"Prefer the *Melbourne Age* meself," he said with a wink, "But if yer desperate, the *Sydney Morning Herald* will do!" We filled the biscuit tin with the balls of paper, keeping about the same amount spare to add later, and closed the clamp down on two steaks.

Ken lit the paper balls with a match. "Keep turning the steaks over like this, so both sides are done evenly." He took a swig of his double scotch. He lowered his voice as if imparting a cult secret. "The trick is that the dripping fat keeps the paper burning longer than you would think." He handed the clamp to me and stood up. "All yours mate, keep it turning. Take mine medium rare. I'll ask the others."

How much newsprint we consumed in our weekly barbeques I wouldn't like to guess, but the results were superb. The steak would cook fast and a little charred.

Some weekends on Friday after work, we would head to the pub in the small town of Mortlake. At that time in the state of Victoria there remained a bizarre vestige of drinking regulation, an Australian partial prohibition. The pubs closed at six in the evening. It was known as the "Six o'clock Swill." The incentive to imbibe large quantities over a very short period was obvious to anyone except, presumably, the state parliament of Victoria and some influential, steely-faced teetotalers.

We would arrive at the pub about ten minutes short of closing time. The uninviting bar, with no pretense at décor, would be packed shoulder to shoulder with a mob of jostling men just off from work. No women. The four of us would fan out inside the doorway like a pride of hunting lions. We would try to work our way across the slop-soaked sawdust to the bar, negotiating a forest of work-ripe Aussie singlets. The first of us to make it there and catch the eye of a barman would signal his success to the others and order about sixteen beers. The rest of us would realign ourselves in the crowd into a fragile human chain. Wisely, the beer was dispensed in plastic tumblers rather than glasses. We would pass them over the heads of the men, spilling slops on anyone who was not cooperative, while doing our best to protect those who were.

Outside on the pavement, we would sit with our feet in the street gutter, four beers each protected between our boots. We would down them in twenty minutes, since the police would come along and clear away late drinkers. By six-thirty, it was a drunken and unruly mob that staggered off, some to continue drinking at home. Soon after this, the law was changed and the state of Victoria shifted to more civilized hours in line with the other states. The drinking sprint had finally graduated to the drinking mile.

When shearing time came around, I worked with the shearers as a rouseabout (sometimes referred to as a *roustabout*) picking up shorn fleeces. A shearing shed, and the maze of yards and races that feed the sheep to it, hums like a bothered beehive. It is a loosely scripted opera of sheep, men, and dogs, performing against a backdrop of lanolin-greased wooden walls with an orchestra of percussion shouts piercing the drone of shears. The shearers, from four up to eight in bigger sheds, sway like classical violinists, but with no conductor, each playing to his own score.

As a rouseabout, you need your wits about you. Shearing is a processing line that can grind to a halt with the slightest hiccup. The moment the last of a fleece falls from the shears to the floor, clinging together like a loose skin, the rouseabout finds the two hind leg portions, folds the fleece over twice into an S-shape, with a final fold inwards, carries it to the skirting table, and throws it upwards and forwards. If well lofted, it floats down spread out like a tablecloth, the outer side of the fleece up. If not, it collapses in a heap and you get dirty looks from the skirters at the table who must unscramble it.

Here, it is classed by the wool-classer into its fineness grade and "skirted" around the edges to remove dirty wool from the belly and backside portions. Then it is tossed into the wooden bin for its class before later being pressed, using a ratchet levered press, into 300 pound bales. Big brutes to roll around by hand or load onto a truck.

A rouseabout must be aware of the stage reached by every shearer so he can be ready to dart in and pick up the fleece the moment it is finished. Four shearers would be the most you could handle alone. Apart from picking up, you keep the shearing floor swept of wool pieces and bring the tar pot if a sheep is cut. If his last fleece is still on the floor when the shearer comes backwards out of the pen dragging his next sheep on its rump, and if you are still there gathering it up, he is entitled to heel you down the chute where the shorn sheep slide to the yards below. If two or three shearers finish at the same time, you have overload. You kick the fleeces out of the way and retrieve them later. I never did get kicked down the chute, but I came close one morning, when I was running on three cylinders with a pounding hangover and a mouth like a kangaroo's armpit.

Bringing in the hay was several weeks of boot camp. We used an old flatbed farm truck that would not have looked out of place on an antique lot. The truck at Kielli had no name as other farm trucks I have met did, but it was invested with all sorts of unprintable names when it played up. When equipment or a task went awry, a common cry of frustration on the farm was, "Yer wouldn't bloody read about it in books!" Books, it seemed, were the source of all deviance, including the deviance of obstinate trucks, kicking cows, stupid sheep, mean horses, temperamental balers, and wayward sump oil.

We loaded hay bales using two men with pitch forks and a third on top of the truck stacking. Unless the paddock was very uneven, we generally had no driver. On the steering column of the truck there was an engine governor, a lever connected by wire to the accelerator cable. This set the engine speed, at least approximately and depending on the mood of the engine on the day.

With two men to a bale, the forward pitcher nearest to the truck door would set the engine speed lever, put the truck in first gear, hop out and slam the door, leaving the window open. As it drove off pilotless, he would hop on the running board, lean in, tweak the steering to follow the line of bales and race to his pitching lane. At the end of the row, the forward pitcher would hop on the running board again, turn the lurching truck around, and set it on course for the next row.

You had to keep up with the truck, otherwise the whole rhythm was thrown off. When it wandered off-course, you would race to the cab to straighten it up. Trying to control a heavy bale on the end of a pitchfork, two men with arms at full stretch, alongside the swaying stack on the truck was a test of strength and balance. If you slipped, you could fall under the rear wheels—no driver to hit the brakes.

The temperature was often over 90 Fahrenheit. We poured sweat all day, drinking copiously from an old canvas water-bag hanging like a giant scrotum from the front bumper. As one of my mates once remarked, "Nothing better on a hot day than cool water tasting of moldy canvas and bloated water-tank possum." Actually, I thought the water from a water-bag had a fine flavor; there were hints of a peaty single malt.

At Easter time, I travelled with our show bulls and cows from Kielli to the Sydney Royal Show, the largest Australian agricultural show of the year, the showplace for prize stock. The bulls were housed in huge hangar-like sheds at the iconic Sydney showground. For each stretch of twenty stalls, there was a storage room for feed, hay, and grooming equipment. This included our essential stock of Sunlight shampoo. (I myself used a cheap bar of soap on my hair, but I borrowed the bull's shampoo if I needed to get fancied up.) Each one of my charges was worth far beyond any assets that I myself owned at that time. One of our bulls won a top prize and sold for, if I remember correctly, eight thousand guineas—big money in those days.

I slept on the flat top of the storage shed under the main shed roof.

There was a wooden sleeping enclosure there for stockmen with a wall about waist-high and a crude vertical access ladder nailed to the shed wall. It wasn't wise to stand upright to change your pants with the procession of show visitors walking past twelve feet below admiring the bulls. For a mattress, an old military-type canvas bag (palliasse) was provided by the showground administration which you stuffed with straw and laced up at one end. There were no pillows, so I stuffed one leg of some old jeans with bunched-up straw and tied some bailer twine at each end to make a primitive bolster. I had a battered suitcase in which I kept all my worldly possessions, including my Australian godfather's then sixty-year-old stock whip, a black dinner jacket, dress shirt, black tie, dress shoes, and working clothes. The smart clothes lay at the bottom, separated by a threadbare towel, then came layers of used socks, working shirts, and assorted underwear in various states of unwash. I think I must have used an early version of a laundromat up the road. The social dimension to working as a jackaroo meant that you could look filthy from mucking out bull stalls by day but going to a big event like the Cattleman's Ball at The Wentworth Hotel, you wore black tie and dinner suit.

One evening, I was brushing my teeth in the cattle lines ablutions block when I thought I heard bagpipes. As a Scot by ancestry, the pipes have always triggered a primordial stirring. Walking back to the shed, I strained to hear them. Like foghorns, it is difficult to tell which direction they are moving. The cattle had stopped chewing, then all their heads turned as a young man entered the shed and slow-marched down the main aisle playing the pipes.

"Well, I'll be buggered. See that, mate?" asked a fellow jackaroo from across the aisle. The piper wore no kilt, just cattlemen's "moleskins" of thick, tight-woven cotton. Sometimes a lone piper can sound thin, but this sound filled the great shed. The corrugated iron roof had haunting acoustics. He halted at the crossing of two aisles, marching in place. The cattle were straining in their halters to see this wailing, straight-horned beast. A crowd of stockmen gathered. He was playing "The Skye Boat Song." Being young and far from home for the first time, I found myself swallowing hard. As all travelers learn, the strings of home tug more sharply in youth. After two more airs on the pipes, another jackaroo pushed through the crowd and whispered into the piper's ear. They called for two pitchforks. I brought them from my shed. They laid them at right angles on the straw-littered aisle. The piper started up again and the new bloke launched into a traditional sword dance. He was another Scot and, as we soon saw, an accomplished dancer.

After a couple of minutes, he flung off his elastic-sided boots. The curves on the ends of the forks and the arched handles lay higher off the floor than traditional Scots swords; he needed the extra spring. The piper changed gear to a faster phase of the dance, upping the tempo. The crowd cheered. The dancer stayed with it, arms held high, setting and turning, sweat flying.

An unshaven giant of a stockman from a famous Queensland stud was watching beside me, transfixed. As the last bar of the reel faded and the soaked dancer and his piper took a bow, a cheer went up. "Stubbies" of VB and Castlemaine XXXX beer materialized from the sheds and the evening blossomed into a wild, impromptu party. Passing city girls who had come for the evening showground events joined us. Dancing among bulls was a new experience for them—as, it seemed, were jackaroos.

Our prize bull, young Midgeon Lord, looking regal in his glossy coat, was a favorite with the girls. He had followed the strange happenings wide-eyed. The Sydney Show had been as new to him as it had been to me. In a day or so, he was up for auction with idyllic years ahead dutifully serving his maidens. He would never nuzzle or lean into me again. He was about to join the big boys.

From Sydney, I headed inland north-west over the Blue Mountains and down into the plains. There was an opening for a jackaroo at Sinclair Hill's property at Berwicks, Willow Tree, near Quirindi, in New South Wales. It lay on the edge of the Liverpool Ranges. He was Australia's top polo player, a few years later making a handicap of ten, the highest you can get. The dirt road to the property forded Big Jack's Creek and Little Jack's Creek that could flash-flood dangerously with rain up in the hills. With rain forecast over the ranges, the advice was to stop, open the window and listen for the roar. "Don't worry mate," said my fellow jackaroo, David, "You'll hear her coming. Ye'd be deaf as a post not to!"

David was a "bonzer bloke." By muscular Australian standards he was slight, but he was tough and wiry. He wore a sweat-stained, broad-brimmed hat with a piece missing from the brim, a casualty of a stampede in the cattle yards. As we all did, he wore the elastic-sided boots—what we referred to with an appropriately exaggerated Aussie accent as, "The high-heeled boot with the hand-stitched toe"—although, in fact, very few of us wore the high-heeled version; it was not well-suited to working in a shearing shed or tossing hay bales.

Sinclair Hill was a larger-than-life character, famously aggressive on the polo field, riding opponents off the line of the ball with more raw power than any player I have ever seen. He was described by another Australian polo player, Chris Ashton, this way: "After the Almighty made Sinclair, He surely broke the mold. Sinclair's chutzpah and showmanship was to polo in England and Australia in the 1960s and '70s what Muhammad Ali was to boxing…"[8]

Sinclair rode skilled ponies[9] that came to the game via the stockhorse route—no better training for a polo pony. On his visits to England on the international circuit, he had coached Prince Charles; Prince Charles' sons, Prince William and Prince Harry, later jackarooed for him on one of his Queensland properties. At work he was tough and demanding of his men, and, in some people's opinion, utterly exasperating. But he was widely respected on the farm because he could out-perform and out-muscle any of us at the tasks he set. He was a hands-on boss. He was also a great source of dryland farming knowledge where the trick is to conserve every drop of moisture by shallow tilling to prevent weeds, leaving a friable dry soil mulch barrier over the cracking clay soil below which, if not tilled, could crack open wide enough to swallow a horse's leg and breath out the precious moisture.

At this property, I improved my skills in killing sheep, looked after polo ponies, became competent at castrating lambs "the old-fashioned" way, learned how to brand cattle, and worked many weeks of twelve-hour night shifts driving a tractor. Our single, big tractor ran twenty-four hours a day, pulling a plow or a seed drill for growing wheat. For weeks it was never turned off. Explained Sinclair, "It's an efficient way to run machinery, provided labor costs for night work are not too high, because much of an engine's wear is during warming up."

Generally, I took the night shift, from six in the evening to six in the morning. David took the day shift. He brought me my dinner on a heaped plate at eight in the evening. I wolfed it down sitting on the tractor with the engine still running and then set off again. There was no time to lose; the acreage was in the thousands.

There is something spiritual about being out on the plains driving a tractor without a cab through a hoar-frost night under the great wash of the southern stars. It's a time to contemplate meaning and life or, for a young man, less weighty matters like the opacity of women. The sound of a diesel engine changes from its daytime thrump. It engulfs you like a cocoon, pressing in on you, bouncing off the hills and the trees and the great curve of the universe. The throbbing runs from your hands on the wheel down through your chest and pelvis to the ends of your toes. But despite the engine noise, you can still hear a gum leaf fall on the tractor hood; there are layers in night sound.

The tractor headlights become a beckoning ghost scouting ahead, lamp held high. The scattered stands of gum trees creep up behind you like the Great Birnam Wood of Macbeth advancing stealthily to Dunsinane. Across the black earth, there are eyes. Some move rhythmically; these you know are set above a grinding jaw—a kangaroo seeking out the newly-sprouted wild oats from the first rains. Some eyes change brightness like a variable star—a small animal warily on the move, probably a possum, trying to hunt and eat quickly while avoiding the night owl. Sometimes the eyes seem human and hostile; an aboriginal spirit, perhaps, scowling at this disturbance of a Dreaming Track from the age when the world was sung into being.

To keep warm, I wore the farm's communal World War II flying suit. Judging by the odor, it had been worn by countless jackaroos through many seasons since its last visit to a tub, if indeed it had ever seen suds since its last Lancaster raid over Hamburg.

Driving the night shifts left little chance to sleep in the daytime on my open verandah. The daylight streamed in, other jackaroos came crashing through the screen door, and there was the occasional urgent errand to town for the boss for a spare part. I was averaging about four hours sleep.

One night on the tractor, I nodded off. I awoke to find myself a few yards short of a dry creek gully about twenty feet deep. I had veered off course by a hundred yards. There were no roll bars on the tractor. You would have to jump for it if you awoke soon enough. I stopped by the edge of the gully, shaken, got down, and slept for thirty minutes on the plowed ground with my head by the tractor wheel, leaving the engine running. If you turned it off, I had been warned that the boss up at the homestead two miles away would awaken to the hollow silence of the valley and come rattling down the hill in the Land Rover to find out what was holding things up. The timing of sowing is critical in dryland areas; every day's delay costs money. He had reason for impatience.

As the hours wore on, and the constellation of the Southern Cross obediently tracked round, three in the morning was the most difficult time. It was long since dinner and human banter and three hours to change-over time and breakfast, an eerie no-man's-land hour. Some nights around that time, I would drift into a meditative trance.

Sometimes I would get stuck in a cycle of trivial thoughts. Is there some alien insect-like "jackaroach" up there sowing psychedelic mushrooms on a cold Martian night?…Does a monkey have a soul? If not, when were souls first dished out?…That girl in the pub from out Cobar way who looked you straight in the eye and said, "I suppose you know I'm the best ride in the North West," maybe she said "rider"? Naah. Face it, you idiot, you blew it…Did Big Jonesy really do it with that new girl in town on the back seat of that abandoned VW?

But sometimes, more weighty musings would break in. Who, or what, was mischievous enough to set me down here in the first place? Was it just a silly prank? Generally, I concluded that it was unlikely that my existence was the result of some numinous ninny with a strange sense of humor playing with matches. But regardless of the logic of my presence, was I expected to change the world, and, like T. E. Lawrence, "To write my will across the sky in stars"? Or was I just some two-penny screw meant to hold together some unremarkable widget? Perhaps I was just a zany spirit, free to ride the next wave any way I liked until I fell off ignominiously into the beach foam.

Mostly I arrived at the view that it was improbable that there was no reason at all for my existence, because so far there seemed to have been reasons for everything—not just random, ricochet reasons but real, consequential reasons. And if there was a reason, did it necessarily require a god and therefore faith in a something or a someone? Or could belief just call for the exercise of reason in the search for one's own constellation of truths? But if there was some purpose for my existence, then presumably there was something larger that mankind should be seeking. That seemed frighteningly burdensome, loaded with awkward responsibility.

More than fifty years later, I still wade these turbid waters. I'm not sure that I am closer, but I think I am clearer, if that makes any sense. I come back to these questions in the final chapter.

But wait, I'm still out there driving a tractor. The end of a night shift, whether it had been numbingly dull or enlivened by reverie, would be signaled by a faint hood of light to the East, shouldering aside the spent stars. Tiredness would give way to anticipation. David would soon be charging down the dirt track in the Land Rover to take over. Energy would return. Breakfast up at the house would be ready, cooked lovingly by our wonderful caretaker lady, four lamb chops, three or four orange-yolked eggs from the scrawny chooks laying carelessly in the machinery shed, seven rashers of bacon, two slabs of crumbling doorstep bread, home-baked, and sweet, smoky tea in a stained enamel mug. Whacko Bluey! Lovely Gravy!

If you have a weak stomach, you may want to skip this section.

There is a skill to killing a sheep quickly and cleanly. The technique I learned was to straddle the sheep, hold the muzzle up in one hand and, with a sharp knife, cut quickly through the neck at the throat just deep enough for the head to be snapped far enough back to break the spinal cord at the neck. There is a spurt of blood which you try to stay clear of. You also try to keep it off your leather boots. Blood damages leather—the work of the enzymes. Some of the older hands would stab a thin-bladed knife straight into the heart which called for precision aim. Either way, with the right technique, the sheep is dead within a couple of seconds.

The day before my first sheep kill, I had not been sure how I would handle it, although I had never had a problem with the sight of blood. As it turned out, I was more shocked that I *wasn't* shocked by watching the sheep take its last breath. For a moment, I even worried that my parents had bred an unfeeling little shit. But killing things was a part of farming; it was to be my profession.

Once a sheep has been killed, the carcass is hauled up, head down, for skinning, using a rope pulley attached to a wooden rod hooked through cuts behind the tendons of the hind legs. The butchering, the gutting and the cutting up, like a deer, involves slicing it down the stomach, extracting the guts, and punching off the skin with a closed fist, much easier while the carcass is still warm. It is then cut up into pieces for the fridge or freezer. We were expected to check the liver for the white blotchy signs of hydatid cysts—a type of tapeworm that can infect humans. A positive would be a reject carcass.

Castrating lambs, tail docking, ear clipping, the Mules operation and a worming drench—a worm medicine—are done at "lamb marking" time, one of the busiest times on a sheep station. The lambs are caught from a packed yard of ewes (mothers) and lambs. For castration and tail docking, a male lamb is caught by an assistant and held by the hind legs, tail towards the operator, rump on the sheepyard rail. For readers who need the full technical—I did warn you—you take the top of the scrotum in the left hand between thumb and forefinger and the tip of the tail in the back part of the same hand. You cut the top off the scrotum with a knife pulling towards your stomach, carrying through with a single stroke to also cut off the tail an inch or two from the base. For efficiency, it is supposed to be one continuous knife stroke; not easy. You squeeze the two balls up out of the bag with finger and thumb of both hands, enough to get your teeth clamped over them, raising your head and curling your right forefinger around the cords to secure them from behind. You end up with two warm lamb's balls dangling from your mouth with the cords sticking to your increasingly bloody chin. Why use the teeth? Lamb's balls are slippery and hard to grip with the fingers.

On the morning of my Castration-for-Beginners introductory session, one of the old hands warned me after my first clumsy attempts, "Keep yer elbow in mate or yer'll lose yer bloody family jewels! And keep yer bloody knife sharp—sharp tools always make work easier and safer."

I nodded, glancing down at my corroded knife that was indeed very bloody. He meant that I should keep my elbow close in to my stomach to stop the knife from coming too far back towards my crotch. A blunt knife would increase the risk because I would have to pull harder, especially the last part of the stroke severing the tough tail. I was assured by the team through a crescendo of guffaws that many a pommy jackaroo had been, "Sent back home to his mummy short of a ball or two and with a very squeaky voice!" While such a slip of the knife seemed to me, from the lamb's perspective, an entirely appropriate comeuppance given the activity we were engaged in, I assured them that I had no intention of returning home with fewer "family jewels" than I had left with. I quickly sharpened my knife.

After castration, the next operator in the line carried out the Mules operation, known as *mulesing*. This involved cutting away the wrinkled skin around the backside of the lamb with sharp shears. Mulesing tightens up the folds of wool-bearing skin that can retain moisture from urine or rain. Merinos have been bred to have wrinkled skin, which is good at the front end for increased wool-bearing skin area but not so good around the backside. Continually moist folds at the rear often result in fly-strike; the flies lay their eggs in the folds and, when they hatch, the "fly-blown" sheep is slowly eaten alive by maggots, a nasty end if not caught soon enough. There has been criticism of the cruelty of mulesing but I won't get into the debate or the alternatives. Too long a story.

After this two-minute whirlwind, the lamb is put down on the ground to find its mother out of many hundreds. They always find her and, from my observation, very few, if any, die from this two-minute trauma.

Later that year, I moved north to a job at Terlings, near Moree, in the north of New South Wales, not too far south of the Queensland border crossing near Goondawindi. It was owned by Sinclair Hill's father, Leslie Hill. It was about 35,000 acres of flat land known from the name of the native vegetation as Brigalow-Belah country.

There were about fifty horses on the place, although I was never quite sure if anyone really knew because the boss often gave a different number than the overseer. The better of these horses were destined to become polo ponies for Sinclair. Starting as stockhorses mustering sheep and cattle was ideal training for polo; they could turn on a dropped penny or stop dead on their haunches chasing a polo ball or a nimble steer. The challenge for the rider was that the most experienced horses sensed, before you did, when and which way they should turn. This could result in a parting of the ways. I once got catapulted into a barbed wire fence and wished I had been wearing a thicker shirt.

There were uncounted kangaroos on the property, I would guess many hundreds. They were a major pest. One adult kangaroo eats approximately what two sheep eat, and they can burst through sheep-netting fences and destroy crops. Leslie Hill allowed (in fact encouraged) "roo shooting," done by spotlighting at night, but at the insistence of his wife, he kept as a sanctuary the homestead paddock—about five hundred acres around the house—where shooting was prohibited. The kangaroos, despite their reputation for being quite dim, seemed to have familiarized themselves with this local regulation; they would even run against the guns to reach the safety of the sanctuary paddock.

There were also feral pigs that destroyed crops and messed up water points. It was possible to run down a modest-sized wild pig if it came far out onto the plowed block to nibble fresh weed growth. With their short legs, there was a chance that they would tire sooner on rough, lumpy, plow than a fit human with some rugby skills. We would carry a thick wheat bag on the tractor to stuff a live pig in; you always carried a bag anyway, to help beat out bush fires.

The idea was to drive up as close as possible to a pig that had become complacent about tractor noise, stop the tractor dead, leap off, and race after it. A rugby tackle would bring it down kicking and squealing, but you had to quickly get the bag over its head. You could get hurt and you would never tackle a big boar. I never got one, but another bloke did. They put it in a sheep yard and fed it on grain for about ten days before killing it. This diluted the strong gamey flavor.

Shooting pigs was the less strenuous alternative, but not necessarily the least risky. I was once mustering sheep with two other men. A young man named Bill, I think, was mustering with another team in a nearby paddock. We had been instructed to put the two mobs of sheep together and move them several miles to fresh pasture. Bill saw a wild pig come running out of the bushes ahead of him and drew his revolver. But the sudden movement of drawing it, or perhaps the movement of the pig, spooked his horse and it crab-jumped sideways. Bill instinctively clutched at the reins to stay in the saddle, but in doing so, squeezed the trigger.

There was a shot. Someone shouted, "Bill's got a pig!" They found Bill lying on the ground with blood coming from the top of his right thigh. He raised himself on one elbow and announced with some embarrassment, "I think I shot meself!" Someone said, "Yea Bill, I think yer bloody did, mate!" At this point, I led some horses back to the yards while someone rode to get a Ute.

They ripped up a shirt and started to get a tourniquet around the upper part of his thigh, which helped stem the bleeding, although surprisingly he was not bleeding heavily. Still lying on the ground, Bill said, "I can see where the bullet went in, but I'm buggered if I can see where it came out." This led to a search for the exit hole until someone reminded them, "It doesn't bloody matter where it came out. We need to get him to the bloody hospital!"

In case any bones were broken, they strapped his leg to an old fence post with some stirrup leathers and lifted him into the back of the Ute. They set off, pedal to the floor, into town. As Bill told the story the following evening in hospital, he was lying in the back of the Ute, along with assorted shovels and crow bars, with his leg strapped to the fence post, gunning down the dirt road to Moree. The post, to which Bill's leg was firmly attached, was bouncing up and down about a foot with every pothole. It took the boys in the front several miles to realize that the loud banging in the back was not the loose shock absorber or the fencing gear but Bill hammering with his fist on the cab, shouting, "Slow down, yer bastards! Slow down, yer bastards!"

From his hospital bed the next day, he was proudly displaying the .38 caliber bullet that the doctor had taken out of his leg. It had a dent in one side of the trailing edge from hitting either a piece of saddlery before it entered or perhaps a bone as it passed down his leg. The bullet had gone into the top of his thigh and traveled all the way past his knee without serious bone or cartilage damage and had come to rest under the skin of his calf. A couple of weeks later, he was back mustering sheep. But from then on, he was more careful about pulling a revolver on a pig when mounted on a jumpy horse.

Some of the horses were very skittish. Every Monday morning's fresh batch could mean an impromptu rodeo. There seemed to be no record of which ones had been ridden how long ago, or by whom. You didn't know whether your assigned horse had been ridden a week or two back or many months back unless someone happened to recognize it. "Hey, isn't that Looney Blue? Jeez, rather you than me, mate!" It was a lottery that could determine how easy your week would turn out to be and how much interaction you would have with the ground.

One week, I was assigned a horse that seemed almost unbroken. (Either that or it bore a grudge against poms.) On this occasion, I broke the cardinal rule by not completely closing the yard gate before mounting. It was always wise to mount a new horse prepared for fireworks.

Immediately I swung up into the saddle, it leaped forward, did a couple of huge buckjumps, nose between its legs, and took off around the yard, bucking viciously. I did reasonably well for one-and-a-half circuits, but it finally threw me against the high rails. Spotting the gate ajar, it charged for the gap, barged it open, and took off into the home paddock, reins and stirrups flying. On reaching a barbed wire fence it took off too late, or perhaps too early, and ripped a gash in its stomach about eight inches long. We eventually managed to round it up. It was wild-eyed and soaked in sweat and foam.

We stitched it up with some difficulty using an old bush trick, pushing ordinary sewing pins through both sides of the wound and drawing the two sides together by wrapping strong cotton twine tightly round each pin, drawing the wound together before tying it off—no vet needed. For ten days, I dressed the stitched wound daily with antibiotic sulfanilamide powder. It healed quickly. Taking the "stitches" out was just a matter of pulling the pins, although getting close enough was still tricky with a nervous horse unaccustomed to being in a stable.

The pub in Moree was the jackaroos' watering hole on Friday nights after work. There would be an evening of rowdy drinking, sometimes preceded by a visit to the nearby open-air movie house across the road with about fifty folding canvas seats. Many patrons who went to the movies couldn't handle the ten-minute interval while the next spool was loaded. They would nip over to the pub. I only ever saw the first half of films during my time in Moree.

In those days, to drink beyond ten thirty, New South Wales law required you to sign a book to certify that you were a "bona fide traveler" requiring that you had come from more than twenty-five miles away. This law was a nod to the travel distances of big property country. The book at the Moree pub was falling apart and stained with beer slops. You filled in your name and address. A glance down the columns showed names like *Mickey Mouse* from Disneyland, *Blue the Spew* from Outatown, and *Blunder the Chunder* from East Wheredyathink—chunder being the vernacular for throwing up. Once the barman had passed the book around and seen you sign it, he had done his bit. From then on, it was between you and the cops. They never showed up when I was there.

One character at the pub was a flasher of remarkable skill. With a beer in his left hand and the thumb of his right hand tucked casually inside his elastic belt, he would sidle up to a stranger and engage him in conversation with the usual, "Owyergoinorrightmate?" He would launch into a discussion about cattle prices, the merits of Queensland beers or some recent political scandal. After several minutes, without even a flicker of warning, he would snap his pants down to reveal himself and snap them back into place with a lightning movement, accompanied, if you listened carefully, by a disconcerting slap. His speed on the draw would have done him credit in an American Western. The whole sequence could not have taken more than a second.

The stranger, depending on how many drinks he had on board, could never be quite sure what he had just witnessed. Our flasher would continue the conversation without breaking sentence. After about ten minutes, when the stranger had regained his composure and concluded that it must have been his imagination, our flasher would repeat the performance. From the end of the bar, we jackaroos would watch this boorish show with, I confess, equally boorish delight. I never saw a victim who seemed quite sure what was going on. But, in the end, most of them would sidle away looking uncomfortable. Our man's skill was as much in the deadpan expression and the unbroken flow of conversation as in his riveting manual dexterity. He was a maestro of his peculiar craft.

Once the pub closed for the evening, and the last of the "bona fide travelers" along with the many less bona fide had been encouraged to leave or been tossed out, there would be a stockwhip-cracking contest in the main street. Stockwhips are the Australian cattle drovers whip, usually about six or seven feet long.[10] The best could crack above their head into all three corners of a triangle without a break.

I was not in that class, although I could crack doubles reasonably well and I was not bad for accuracy, having once cracked a cigarette out of a mate's mouth; not too hard actually, after a couple of ranging cracks, just a light flick. The crack of the stockwhips in the street in the middle of the night was magnified by the echo off the buildings. There were complaints from town residents trying to sleep. But this was the jackaroos' tribal ceremony; the police never broke it up while I was there.

PASSAGE TO ENGLAND

...I saw the porpoises' thick backs
Cartwheeling like the flywheels of the tide,
Soapy and shining...

– Seamus Heaney, *Shore Woman*

After a year working as a jackaroo, having spent a fair share of my meagre five pounds a week on beer, travel and the odd date, I didn't have enough saved for a passage home. So with help from a family friend who was a wool buyer and exporter with contacts with shipping companies, I was offered a working passage back to England on the SS *Townsville Star*, a 10,700-ton merchant vessel of the Blue Star Line.

I have always had a love-hate relationship with the sea. I had long felt that, as an Englishman with the illustrious name of Nelson, I was somehow born with the sea inside me. But chronic seasickness usually ensured that whatever was inside me would end up outside me, even on a light swell. So I embarked on this one-month voyage with some misgivings, along with many cartons of Kwells.

As a token wage, I was paid the princely sum of one shilling for the whole month at sea, enough to buy a pint of bitter at the first English pub I stopped at after disembarking. Once underway, anything on the ship that didn't move, or wear trousers, or didn't require being suspended over the side, I painted. We were carrying a full load of frozen meat to England, about 160,000 beef carcasses, so there was no reason to stop except to refuel in Singapore; the Brits were anxious for their steaks. The ship was manned by Australian and British officers with a Chinese crew, mostly from Hong Kong and Singapore. I worked alongside the merchant marine cadets who were training to become officers.

The first week we had rough weather so, true to form, I was "shooting tigers" all over the ship. The First Officer and the senior marine cadet developed a strategy that worked quite well. Whenever it was rough, I was assigned the job of painting toilets. Toilets became my specialty. I was your toilet man. There were disadvantages as well as advantages to this trade specialization.

The advantage was that my head was never more than a few feet from a bowl. The disadvantage was that I was closeted in an airless space with no visible horizon beyond the water slopping in the bowl, and I was breathing acrid toilet odor along with noxious paint fumes. All my toilets ended up with layer upon layer of semi-gloss. The First Officer came up to me one day with a grin and a wink and said, "Have to say mate, toilet stalls have never looked better. Could eat me bloody breakfast in them!"

One of my responsibilities was to look after a black Labrador being shipped from Australia to England. He had a kennel on the deck at a spot that caught a breeze but was protected from the sea spray in rough weather. I fed him and walked him around the deck to do his business and to get his exercise. It took me a while to train him to be comfortable crapping in the rust-red drainage scuppers below the railing, the easiest place to flush away poop. There was no dog food on board, so I was instructed to feed him Chinese food from the kitchens.

When it came to his dinner time, I would go down to the kitchen with him and the assistant chef, always bubbling with mirth, would ask, "What you doggie wanna today? He wanna Beef Lo Mein? He wanna Peking Duck? What he wan? All velly good chow. Make doggie velly big, velly stlong."

The Labrador seemed delighted with his new fare. One of the assistant chefs used to say that my charge would make an excellent dish to give the Chinese crew a bit of variety. He said that if one morning he was gone from his kennel I would know where to look. He said he would type out a new item on the menu, but he had difficulty pronouncing *Labrador* and thought he wouldn't be able to spell it. He returned to his woks cackling with laughter. Despite walks two or three times a day around the deck, games with the crew, and with two couples travelling as passengers, our Labrador put on a few pounds during the voyage.

When the weather was hot, dry and windless, which meant wind from astern to compensate for the ships forward speed, the kitchen staff would spread out their dried sardines on the deck to air. They were silver-yellow and crusty like scabs with gaping mouths and small, black accusing eyes that seemed to be asking, "Whose dumb idea was that last turn?"

The crew ate them stir-fried over white boiled rice with red chili. Kept in the hessian sacks, they were inclined to sweat in the tropics unless they got aired occasionally. Our Labrador soon took to them, so I had to keep him away. There seemed to be an etiquette about how these drying sardines were treated by those walking along the deck. You never walked on them with shoes. If there was no way past on the starboard side, you went around on the port side. But if, like some of the Chinese crew, you went barefoot, it seemed to be acceptable to walk over them provided that, when you got to the other side, you brushed off any that were still clinging to your sweaty soles.

Many days there were dolphins playing around the bow. I would hang over the rail and watch, mesmerized, by their oil-slick speed, their ostentation, and by the smooth, arched surfing speed they could maintain. One day I spotted one with a scar behind its head. It stayed with us for over an hour because I returned from a painting stint and there it was, still in the same spot in the formation. Precision flying. Much later in the voyage, between Wales and Ireland, we were to see lazily arching porpoises, the same species that I had sometimes seen when fishing or sailing the South Devon estuaries.

At our refueling stop in Singapore, our only stop on the voyage, we were advised by the First Officer before we went ashore that we were to be back on board by four in the morning, but that the vessel would no longer be at anchor in the main harbor area. The ship was moving around to the west side of the island, to a refueling pier at Tanjong Penjuru. We were warned that, if we were late, the vessel would leave without us. The First Officer added, "We might wait a bit for an officer, but we won't wait even a minute for the lowest of the low...or even the merely low." He seemed to be looking at me when he said that last part. As a working passage man, he and I both knew where I fell in the pecking order.

I had been invited to dinner in Singapore by an RAF family couple. But he was away at an official event, so I dined with his wife, who'd known me since childhood. He had spent over three years in Japanese prison camps after the fall of Singapore in 1942. After dinner, I went downtown to hang out until two in the morning at a place by the harbor where the marine cadets had said we would meet to share a taxi back to the ship. They didn't show up, having secured a free lift, earlier, back to the ship. I went to a local bar shack and had rather more drinks than I had intended before giving up waiting. I wandered over to a taxi rank. I told the first taxi driver my destination; he shook his head. He didn't seem to have a clue where Tanjong Penjuru was. I went to the next; a shrug. The third, fourth and fifth were the same. I began to think that I had got the name wrong.

With visions of the ship leaving without me, panic was starting to build. I tried variants of pronunciation. I tried writing it down. I was running out of ideas when a rough character in a heavily dented taxi across the road waved me over. He nodded resignedly when I told him my destination. It dawned on me that the others knew where it was but didn't want to go there late at night with little chance of a return fare.

We set off at a crazy speed, driving out of the city and onto a dirt road. Then he suddenly screeched to a stop, turned right and plunged into an oil palm plantation on a dirt track. This seemed to me a highly improbable route to one of the main refueling piers for Singapore, so I started to have visions of ending up chained to a post as a bargaining chip for a Chinese mafia big shot. Still quite drunk, I found myself murmuring inanely the first lines of Rupert Brooke's "If I should die, think only this of me…" But as I finished the second verse, we emerged abruptly out of the plantations at a long, flood-lit pier. To my relief there she lay, the good ship *Townsville Star*. And I still had an hour and a bit to go.

As I was walking up the gangplank, a young Australian engineer who had been on duty in the refrigeration holds was rushing down, peeling off his overalls to grab my taxi. He muttered. "Thanks, mate! Gotta get down the road for a Short Time." It seemed to me he was taking a big risk of missing the ship. But he must have completed his Short Time in a very short time because he made it back, with minutes to spare, before we were nudged out by two portly tugs.

An hour or so later, a few miles down the straits, there was a roar that shook the ship. An RAF twin engine Canberra light bomber flew straight at us over the water from the stern at fifty feet and after passing over the ship did a couple of wing waves before banking steeply to the south, gaining height under full-throated power. I waved—inconspicuously I thought. It was the husband of the lady I had had dinner with the previous night. The Captain saw me wave and came down from the bridge to where I was getting some paints out.

He asked, "Was that a friend of yours?" I nodded sheepishly and said, "Yes, he's the RAF boss in Singapore." He said, "Scared the bloody pants off me. I imagine he's got so many bloody gongs on his chest that he can hardly stand upright!" I said, "Yes, a few, he was a POW of the Japanese for over three years. Captured at the fall of Singapore."[11] After that, my stock on the ship with the officers rose a bit.

Some days later at sea, in the Indian Ocean, we abruptly ran into a powerful localized storm. The seas built fiercely within minutes. Three of us had been rolling paint on the foredeck and we were too slow cleaning up and putting our paint and rollers away. We ended up having to take refuge in a storage locker in the forecastle because it was too dangerous by then to make it back to the main part of the ship, with waves sweeping the foredeck. It was dark in the locker with one feeble wire-framed light and it reeked of tar, rope and paint. We were heaving up and down what seemed like a hundred feet with each wave. The ship creaked and juddered and I donated my lunch to a coil of frayed mooring rope. After about an hour, the storm abated as quickly as it had come. Between waves still breaking across deck but less frequently—and after some hand signals from the First Officer below the bridge to get our timing synchronized with the over wash—we legged it back to the main part of the ship.

After twenty-eight days at sea, we nosed into Liverpool docks. At the top of the gangplank the Captain, thanking me for my services, pressed the one shilling coin for my token wage into my hand and whispered, "Now don't spend it all at once, young man!"

Back in England, I marveled at the vivid greenness of the small, hedged farm fields after the golden yellows and the great fenced "paddocks" of the Australian bush, any one of which could have swallowed twenty English farms.

So here I skip four years at university for the sake of pressing on. They were glorious years of immaturity, punctuated by clumsy or fatuously optimistic amorous adventures, misspent evenings singing rugby songs in Kentish pubs, and the occasional frantic spurt of academics.

CHICK SEXING
AND HOP INSPECTING

**_For some art experts, having "the eye" is
like having faith: you can't explain why
you have it or how you have it._**

– Author Susannah Clapp in _With Chatwin_, 1997[12]

In my youth and at university, I took summer jobs on farms. One
of them operated a poultry unit where I assisted with the sexing of day-old
chicks. The peculiar skill of chick sexing has featured in debates about the
nature of intuition. It turns out that peering into chicks' bottoms has almost
psychic qualities.

Chicks need to be sexed within a day or two of hatching. The tiny
male and female features visible in their multi-purpose orifice become
less easy to differentiate once the bird starts eating and crapping. There
is great commercial value in getting the sex right as soon as possible, ide-
ally above 99%, because you don't want to feed a chick for several weeks
that you thought would lay eggs only to discover that it can't. The skilled
chick sexer completes two years of training. It may seem a long time for
becoming a specialist in an organ that is about the size of a pinhead, but
the observable differences are minuscule and they vary between individu-

als. An operator still gains precision through practice for many more years. The skilled sexer seems to develop a sixth sense, an intuition, in spotting the problematic ones.

On the farm where I worked, our balding, hook-nosed, chick sexer, with rampant eczema—the image of a battle-scarred cockerel—gave me some chick sexing lessons: The day-old chick is held in the left-hand and squeezed to express any feces. The sexer then spreads open the vent (cloaca) with a thumb and finger. This exposes what is called the "bead," a tiny blob. Typically, a male will have a convex bead and a female concave, or just flat. But there is a percentage of male and female chicks where the rule of convex-versus-concave simply doesn't work. Their organ deceives. There is no time to have a cup of tea, call your mother, shift the light, or mull over the options; a sexer needs to keep up a rate of about five hundred an hour.

As Joshua Foer noted in his book, *Moonwalking with Einstein*,[13] there is an intuition element that chick sexers just cannot explain. The man I worked with sometimes just couldn't explain why a difficult one was male and not female or vice versa; he simply ran out of anatomical minutiae and the words to label them. He offered instead a strangely avian twitching shrug. "Just bloody *is,* mate," he would intone, "Just bloody is." In his opinion, the best sexers were the ones who had peered into the most chicks' bottoms. Made sense.

Today in the U.K., there is a shortage of chick sexers, despite not-bad pay. The problem is partly the length of training. But I suspect also it is because the work calls for extraordinarily sustained concentration. I wonder whether the millennial generation, with their frenetic multi-tasking, are suited to such intensity of focus on a single, miniscule organ minute after minute for eight hours a day, quite apart from whether they would consider it a job they would want to admit to over a pint of ale down at the Rose and Crown.

I became even more intrigued by the chick sexing phenomenon when I took a summer job inspecting hops in the county of Kent, the English home of hop-growing. Again, a little background.

Hops grow upward, along wire and twine supports, on an intricate fixed hop garden framework about twenty feet high. The climbing vine is called a *bine*. Sometimes the bines reach twenty feet. (The one in my garden in Virginia this year is at twenty feet already by the first week in June and still groping vainly for more height). There is a devastating hop disease called *verticillium wilt*, a lethal fungus of hops that is spread by diseased plant and/or soil material.

The fungus causes yellowing and tiger-striping on the leaves. It can remain viable in the soil for over a decade. If diseased plants are not caught in the early stages and destroyed cleanly and thoroughly, tractor cultivation down the rows, or wind-blown leaves, or even birds with soil or vegetation on their feet, can transfer the disease to uninfected plants. It's a dreaded plague for growers with good hop soils.

The more diseased hops I encountered, the more I realized that spotting *verticillium wilt* in its earliest stages was as fuzzy as the chick sexing thing. Seeing diseased plants at different stages of infection every day, I became increasingly adept at spotting the very earliest signs. Soon, I was getting a strange feeling that there was an unseen hand guiding me. I seemed to be spotting it when there were no describable symptoms.

Fortunately, there is a reasonably reliable backup test to confirm the disease—not to be conducted unless you are almost certain, because of the risk of disease transfer, you need to sterilize hands and knife with formaldehyde. If you peel back the bark of the stem low on the bine, the tissue in a diseased bine is just starting to show a very slight brownish tinge. I was finding that I could not explain to my colleagues what visible features on a plant had tipped me off.

A British north country co-worker, puzzling over a plant I had identified and confirmed as diseased, exclaimed, "Bloody 'ell! What gave away that 'un? That's fookin' spooky!"

"There's just something not right about it," I said, waving my arms vaguely.

I was never sure if it was a close-up difference in one or two leaves or a standing-back difference in the whole plant. Perhaps it was a bit of both. I felt like a mother noticing that her child is coming down with something but unable to describe the symptoms to the doctor.

But that wasn't all of it. I noticed that my mind drew unusually intense gratification in spotting very early cases, as though my brain was rewarding me for practicing some ancient magic not quite of this world. I got a high out of it.

Whether I would be able to resurrect this skill if I went into a hop garden today I have no idea; I haven't looked at a diseased hop plant for half a century. I suspect it's not quite like riding a bicycle.

I have come across other people who have derived similar satisfaction from observational skills, so I don't claim that chick sexers and hop inspectors are unique or that they have a monopoly on intuition. It's the same phenomenon as having "The Eye" (that author Susannah Clapp writes about, and that I reference at the beginning of this chapter) with, say, antiques or artwork. Many experts cannot explain why they think a painting or artifact is what they say it is. They just *sense* it. In her book about Bruce Chatwin, Susannah Clapp reports him as a young boy saying to his father in bewilderment, "I don't know *how* I know. I just *know*."

No doubt this human attribute of intuition will be picked apart by science one day and digitized. In fact, to some extent, it already has been. It is being done in several observational fields through fluorescence imaging techniques and huge computing power that can handle multi-dimensional, complex data, can apply machine learning, and can track changes over time. A pity, really. It would be nice to think that there is still a halo of the inexplicable in a few corners of our increasingly evidentiary world. But wherever Artificial Intelligence takes us, I doubt a computer will get the same visceral kick out of "intuition" that I did.

ON ENGLISHNESS—PUBS, CHURCHES, AND TRIBAL CEREMONY

Into my heart an air that kills
From yon far country blows:
What are those blue remembered hills,
What spires, what farms are those?

— A.E. Housman, *A Shropshire Lad*

For me, there have always been three features of quintessential Englishness: The pubs, the village churches, and the tribal ceremony.

The public house has been the forum of the English village for about a thousand years, from even before the Magna Carta. Ye Olde Trip to Jerusalem, a pub in Nottingham that I used to frequent many years ago, is one of the oldest, claiming an origin back in 1189, but if you want to go purely by documented records, then 1751. Ye Olde Fighting Cocks at St Albans claims the year 793, but again, 17th century, if you want to see it in writing. One sips one's pint of bitter in such places with reverence, and, if you are tall, bent or sitting.

But in recent years the pub has slipped from its pre-eminent position in village life. With drunk-driving penalties and the fact that most clients do now drive rather than walk, bicycle or crawl, pubbing habits are not what they were. The evening pub crawl around a circuit of quaint rural villages has largely died. To survive these changes, pubs have shifted from beer, whisky, and gin to a wider range of drinks and to posher grub. Pubs have become eating establishments with a serious drinking sideline, rather than drinking establishments with a casual nibbling sideline.

English pubs have been exported to every inhabited continent. I have drunk in English pub replicas in Bangalore, Hyderabad, Singapore, Ho Chi Minh City, Kuala Lumpur, Cape Town, Nyeri, Songea, Bangkok, Djakarta, Sydney, Washington D.C., and many other cities, towns and villages around the world, all, in their own way, memorable. But the décor, the aroma, the accents, the toilet wall graffiti, and the native ribaldry never quite make the transition, despite heroic efforts such as the pub in Bangkok with a blazing wood fire for ambience and air conditioning blasting flat out to combat heat stroke.

During my days as a student, I knew an old character in the English county of Kent. He was about seventy, short, slight and wiry. He had a hooked, drink-red, nose and sunken eyes that seemed not quite a pair. One was a little higher than the other, as if added as an artist's afterthought. He had been a coal miner. He bred whippets for racing, a miner's thing from way back.

One evening in 1964, he took me on a pub crawl around the miners' pubs. They were a rowdy bunch, quite combative, some with a chip on their shoulder, perhaps a reaction to my out-of-place accent, although a simpler hypothesis would have been inebriation.

At our second pub, he introduced me to an old friend with a wizened face and rounded shoulders who had retired from mining some years earlier. They talked of old times, which mines had closed, who had moved where, and who had died. His nose sported a cluster of blackheads, as though some Lilliputian hunter had fired a cartridge of miniature buckshot into it. Water was clearly not his favorite liquid, nor soap his favorite solid. But I was told he had been a fine miner and always looked out for his mates, especially when things below got dicey.

I noticed an old lady in her eighties hunched over a half-full mug of ale. She wore a threadbare tweed skirt and an old, stretched woolen cardigan with a hole making good progress at her drinking elbow. My guide greeted her as a long-lost friend with his cockney, "Gawd, blimey!"

They talked of old times, of who had sons still working the mines, of who had divorced or married. He took me aside as I was buying a round and hinted that she had been a, *wink-wink*, "popular lady" with the mining fraternity in her day. Then he leaned closer to me and whispered that she had a four-masted barque in full sail tattooed across her bottom. I spluttered into my pint.

He insisted on asking her to show me this piece of artwork. There was a storeroom down a passageway at the rear of the pub which he said was suitable for an exclusive private viewing, that is, if I didn't mind the brooms and empty beer kegs. Her eager nod made it clear that she was more than ready to oblige—for a pint or two, of course.

I took a long—a *very* long—draft of my pint of bitter, set it down slowly, and politely declined. I bought her a pint anyway. She grinned, displaying a missing tooth, pulled back the sleeves of her cardigan, and winked at me across her beer. My guide said I was missing a unique opportunity and that I would never see the like again. I assured him that I didn't doubt the uniqueness of the artwork, but I whispered in his ear, "Sails must be hanging limp as a square rigger in the doldrums." He grinned and patted my shoulder.

At about the same period, I used to visit a pub called the Ringlestone Arms on the downs above Harrietsham in Kent. It dated from 1533 and was run in the early 1960s by two old ladies, the mother, Florence Gasking, aged about eighty-five, and the daughter, Dora, about sixty-five. We students used to call the place *Dirty Dora's*, although I don't recall that she was particularly dirty, in either sense of the word other than the occasional choice expletive. But, in blatant contravention of the local licensing laws, they opened and closed whenever they chose to, letting in those they felt like letting in, and sending packing those they didn't like the look of. For some of the most favored friends, there was said to be a secret door knock code, but I never graduated to that.

Usually I was able to get in because I had been able to explain that my father had been, and still was, in the RAF. Florence and Dora had run a pub during the war near the famous Battle of Britain fighter station at Biggin Hill.[14] The lost pilots that had frequented their pub still haunted them twenty years later, their lives were peopled by the ghosts of lost airmen.

One evening, I failed to convince them to open the door. I showed up with five student mates, but my well-rehearsed pitch through the locked door didn't work, perhaps because they were quite deaf. We were told bluntly to buzz off. It was an eerie night with no moon. The wind was moaning in the twisted beech trees along the lane. The pub sign was squeaking plaintively. One of the girls was scared and wanting to leave. There were no lights inside or out. I knocked for a second try, thinking they had not understood. Suddenly a window flew open and there was Dora, eyes blazing, probably clutching her shotgun although it was too dark to see, telling us to bloody well f...off and leave them alone! We gave up and went to drink less audaciously in Maidstone town.

But the nights when we *did* get in were well worth the rejections. In those days, the pub had no electricity, just oil lamps. The bar was hazy with the smoke of poorly-trimmed wicks and unattended logs on the open fire. They stocked no draught beer, simply bottled beer and a limited range of whisky and gin. There were rarely more than ten patrons; those who had somehow run the blockade. The low level of light and the selectivity of entry seemed to call forth church-like conversation. As naturally rowdy students, this was a challenge to sustain for three hours but nobody was game to break the spell. This was hallowed ground; getting in at all was an honor not to be squandered.

The toilets were outside along the side of the building. This was awkward because the front door was always locked. This meant that whenever anyone wanted a leak, Florence would have to get her big lamp and lead you to the door, swinging her heavy key chain. We always agreed in advance to coordinate bladders and relieve ourselves as a squad so she didn't have to jump up and down all night. When we were all ready to go, after a series of raised eyebrow signals, we would give her the nod. I always felt like a prisoner in the Tower being led from the dungeon to the place of execution. She would yank back the bolt with a clang and we would meekly file out. She would hang around with the front door ajar waiting impatiently while we were out doing our business.

If I remember correctly, the men's toilet had a trough set in the concrete floor along one wall. I don't think it had a door, at least not one that ever closed. It was usually a foot deep in drifted leaves from the lane. We would all line up in the darkness along what we believed was the correct wall and aim into the leaves. The odor was throat-gripping. Once we had all relieved ourselves, we would file back in and she would bolt the door behind us. There was an ominous finality in the clunk. She seemed to be saying, "That's yer lot for the night, boys." Perhaps she had learned from wartime Lancaster pilots that, on a seven-hour bombing raid, you could always fall back on a champagne bottle if the Elsan mid-fuselage was hard to get to or if you hadn't joined the pissing-on-the-rear-wheel-for-luck ceremony before climbing aboard.

One evening I was talking to Dora about Battle of Britain pilots. My generation of RAF brats knew the names of some of the most famous. One I had known personally was Al Deere, a highly decorated New Zealander and a Wing Leader at Biggin Hill. He had survived nine crash landings, including one north of Dunkirk. Dora had known him well. She suddenly got up and went to a large wooden chest. She opened it. It was full of memorabilia, signed photos, RAF hats left and never collected, and letters in original brown envelopes.

She reached deep into the back and pulled out an old, yellowed check for one pound, eight shillings and sixpence. It was from a fighter pilot whose name I didn't recognize. The day after it was given to them in payment for a bar bill, he was reported missing over the English Channel. She took the check back from me and turned her face away. "Of course, we never cashed it," she murmured as she put it back into the chest with two-handed reverence.

Florence and Dora died long ago. But the Ringlestone Arms is still a pub. It has a restaurant and a website on which there is reference to Florence and Dora. The pub has a resident ghost with a macabre story. There had been a boy poacher a century or so earlier who had been sealed up in a hollow wall space near the fireplace so that the constables couldn't catch him. If caught, he would have been hanged. Poaching was a serious crime in those days. He had been given food and water for weeks through a loose brick in the inside wall. Eventually, when his food and water were no longer being taken, the loose brick had been sealed and cemented. His skeleton is said to be still there in the hollow wall but his ghost is inclined to roam.

The other uniquely English institution, not without social connections to the pub, in fact often across the village green from it, is the church. There is a deep peace in the musty silence of an English village church; a different kind of peace from the great cathedrals which are only conditionally welcoming, with their sculptures threatening hell and damnation. Notwithstanding the odd, menacing gargoyle, village churches seem to me to be more benign. Phillip Larkin, in his poem "Church-going," captures the atmosphere, "Once I am sure there's nothing going on, I step inside, letting the door thud shut…." He finds inside a "tense, musty, unignorable silence."

The first thing that strikes me is the whisky-complex aroma, a blended distillate of old hymn books, matured oak beams, damp stone, musty kneelers, the whole laced with a dash of bird droppings. In winter, there is the added whiff of kerosene from a cheap oil heater, a vain attempt to take the chill off a sparsely attended evensong.

The pew racks hold old hymn books with the odd, displaced page, a fumble perhaps from cold, half-gloved, fingers. And there may be a child's scribble pad slipping out from behind a worn cloth-bound bible. Beside the altar will be a vase of wilted flowers, kindly provided by a Mrs. Brocklehurst—her week for the parishioners to praise—along with the Almighty—her flower arranging talents. Inside, near the door, there will be an ancient stone font, often appearing to be the oldest piece in the church. This brings to mind the parish bulletin that once announced, "From now on there will be a font at the front and rear of the church so that babies can be baptized at both ends."

Around the walls are memorials of the big parish families and those who died in the two great wars. The British Empire speaks from every alcove, men who died in the Indian Mutiny, the Boer War, in Malakand, and on the Somme—the echoes of so many sermons trying vainly to season the bitter pill. Since the British buried their fallen at the battlefield, there will be no gravestones in the graveyard of men killed in action unless there was an RAF crew whose failing Lancaster nearly made it back to the nearby base, but not quite.

My sister, Erica, once lived in an old manor house beside the church in a village near Newark, in England. The house was built in 1507 but was partly burned down in 1771 and restored and rebuilt so there was a "new" wing—yes, the 1770s can be new for England—attached to the old. The church was 15th century onwards. The iron gate to the churchyard and the nearest gravestones were a few paces from her front door.

She had no legal or ecclesiastical responsibility for the maintenance of the church as early lords of the manor would have had, but she wanted to keep it in reasonable shape. Living overseas, disconnected from such English village culture, I was able to feed my shriveling roots by helping a little with the maintenance of the church during my visits.

My first effort was to tackle the small shrubbery that had been sprouting uncontrolled for years high up on the parapet around the base of the spire. Climbing up through the tower with a large shovel was tricky. There was a rickety wooden ladder, probably a couple of hundred years old passing the bell ropes and the huge cast iron bells and through a small door onto the parapet at the base of the spire. Emerging with difficulty, I found about eighteen inches of accumulated pigeon droppings and a number of mature elderberry shrubs about eight feet in height growing in this fine potting medium. I tried to calculate how many years eighteen inches of bird droppings might constitute; over a hundred, I figured. What would the world be like, I wondered, when the next eager *ruin-bibber*, as Larkin called them, clambered up to repeat my manorial manurial task?

The first question before I started digging was what to do with three pigeon's nests, each with young hatchlings waiting to be fed with their next course of grain regurgitation. I considered a swift execution of these pests of farmers' crops but decided to give them a shot at a life. It was difficult to ignore the mothers eying me from a nearby tree.

I cupped my hands under the rudimentary material of each nest of wobbly-necked chicks and laid them on the first opening of bare flagstone that I had dug down to. I ripped out the elderberry saplings and tossed them over the side, a hundred feet down into the graveyard. Once cleaned out down to the flagstones all around, I carefully cupped the three nests and placed them on the stone in approximately the same compass bearing from where I had taken them. I never returned to see how they fared in their less acrid accommodation, but I believe they made it. Watching from the house, I saw the adults visiting over the following days.

It seems to me that a country's reputation in the eyes of outsiders is often several decades out of date. One example is the reputation of English food, which surely has improved enormously since it slowly emerged from the handicap of war rationing. But the English have several cultural traits that have been quite persistent. There is the reserve in social interaction, compared with, say, Australians who come straight out and simply *say it*.

And there remains the class distinction, but less so today. There are the fences the English put around themselves and their "castles," compared to, say, Americans. But it goes beyond hedges to extend to psychological fences. Then there is their quirky Monty Python-esque humor and their slow launch jokes that can build to a punchline over a whole pint of ale. Finally, and unequivocally diagnostic, there is the English absolute no-no—the taking of yourself too seriously. Taking yourself too seriously is responded to by others through "taking the piss,"[15] knocking you off your perch.

Growing up in England, I became particularly conscious of class when staying with my maternal grandmother and grandfather. My grandmother was a small but redoubtable lady who punched well above her lettuce-light weight and drove her duck-egg blue Morris Minor like a go-kart. My grandfather, at six foot four and at peace in his elevated world, a pipe always in his mouth, floated well above her ground-level busyness.

On outings, his eyes, with their thick cataract glasses, seemed eternally fixed on the horizon, probably tunny fishing on the North Sea, his consuming passion. Their fine home in Surrey looked across a wooded valley of cow pastures. There were secret nooks and crannies in the house and garages that could be explored, especially a maze-like attic where long-dead Great Uncle Ted's beautifully crafted model racing yachts with dusty, moth-eaten sails stood in keel-stands, waiting patiently for pond-racing outings that never came.

"Garnie," my toddler name for her when the word "Grannie" got scrambled, was very conscious of her station in life. Going to church on Sundays was as much a social event as worship, although she was certainly a committed Church of England Christian. From her house to the church was a walk of a half-mile along a straight village road. In those days, most people living within a mile or so of church walked. She would be well-dressed, but in dark colors and she would wear her latest fashionable bowl-shaped hat with tight barred duck feathers from Selfridges. She would stride out through the wooden gate of the house clutching her bag, eagle-eyed for prey. My sister and I and my parents would follow close behind, all in our Sunday best.

The first hundred yards might be uneventful but, as it started to become clear which family was walking ahead of us and which behind, the jockeying began. "There are the Simpsons! Come along. Come along, everyone!"

We would all shift into a fast military march as though our regimental band had run amuck. But the uncooperative Simpsons would pause to talk with someone getting out of a car, so we would be left with no option but to overshoot. Then would come the hissed order, "Slow down, slow down, they might catch up." My sister and I would change gear to our slow funeral march, only too familiar from watching endless RAF ceremonial parades.

Trailing behind her, we exaggerated our slow march mercilessly. But by now she would have spied an even more socially desirable quarry ahead, perhaps the Dimblebys of BBC broadcasting fame, who lived down the road. So we would shift into overdrive and leg it down the road like the last of the Israelites before the waters closed behind. All this faulty-clutch acceleration and deceleration had to be accomplished without entirely abandoning decorum. It wouldn't do to appear too pushy.

Once inside the church, there was less freedom to pick pew neighbors. In anticipation of a packed church, the ushers led you firmly to a pew, filling them up from the front. But my grandmother, aided by her small size, was expert at ducking under an usher's outstretched arm if she had spied a *people-like-us* family that we absolutely must sit next to. Once seated firmly beside the prey, there would be the whispered, "What a lovely surprise. Must get together sometime."

It was important to win at least a smile and a nod, or even better, a furtive planning session with diaries as the glaring minister processed down the aisle to the opening hymn.

A formal dinner party at a fine house in England, possibly the seat of an aristocrat or a big local landowner, was a tribal ceremony always worth observing. Many aristocrats were fine families who gave back to their country at least as much as they took, often a great deal more. Many died for their country, including the RAF officer to whom this book is dedicated who would have inherited his father's baronetcy.

Despite the occasional bad egg—in earlier days, often shipped off to the colonies—they made important contributions to the English way of life. One of those contributions was inheriting, maintaining and passing down the fine houses, gardens and parks in the face of increasing taxes and a harsh, new war-depleted world. Another was leaving behind them family sagas of remarkable service and mostly harmless eccentricity. The recent popularity of *Downton Abbey* and other such sagas suggests there is a wide fascination with this lost world and a yearning for being at least a fly on the wall, whether upstairs or downstairs.

However, while there were vestiges, the younger days of my teens and twenties were much more recent than the heydays of the great houses and the trappings of empire. Still, at a typical formal dinner party of the 1960s, the men would be decked out in black-tie dinner jacket, the ladies in cocktail dress or, if attending a ball, long gowns. The evening would begin in a spacious paneled living room, perhaps twenty people. In summer, with the long evenings, double doors would be open onto a manicured lawn with herbaceous borders looking across a *ha ha,* a sunken fence, to a pedigree Friesian cow herd or sleek black Angus steers beyond. A butler would bring drinks, but in lesser houses or smaller parties these would be served by the husband.

Talk might be of the latest outbreak of foot-and-mouth disease in cattle or the latest pheasant shooting or fox hunting exploits—who had fallen at the hedge jumping out of the Cocked Hat copse. But talk might also be of the latest art exhibition or colors in interior design. Or politics. After a couple of rounds of drinks, one would be ushered into a fine dining room to be seated by the lady of the house, spouses always separated.

As seating was being directed, sometimes with the help of hand-scripted name cards, there might be a mildly ribald comment about seating placement. Considerable thought would have gone into the placing of the teenage young. The young of the house might have put in a bid beforehand on who should sit where. For the younger teenagers, a bumping of knees would be the event of an evening and later, alone in bed, the subject of a search for meaning, turning over the ghastly possibility that it had been inadvertent, despite what had surely seemed a flit of a smile.

After a three or four-course dinner—perhaps pheasant pie, beef, or salmon as a main course—the lady of the house, with a quiet cough, would rise and ask the ladies if they would care to move to the drawing room; no option to remain. The men would stand on their departure and then remain at the dinner table for port, for men's talk, for cigars and coffee, only joining the ladies later. Port would be passed always to the left—in yachting terminology, "port to port." Traditionally, the port decanter was not supposed to touch the table as it went around, but I don't recall anyone sticking to that part of the ritual. In some circles, if the port got stuck on the way around, the guest to the left was entitled to enquire impudently of the offender, "Do you know the Bishop of Norwich?" The origin of this gentile sarcasm was that there had once been a Bishop of Norwich who was a port aficionado but who, being well into his nineties and even further into his cups, had tended to nod off, leaving the port run aground in front of him.

After port and cigars, and possibly some mildly bawdy jokes, the men would rejoin the ladies. There would be either a game of charades or some further rounds of gossip or stories until exchanged glances between spouses would trigger the departure of all.

In Victorian and Edwardian England and even up into the 1960s, in the upper and upper-middle classes of society, introductions were very important. To a lesser extent today, they still are. You didn't just *talk* to someone—at least not easily—unless and until you had been formally introduced, unless your credentials and caste had been, so to speak, *verified*.

One example I give you here of the importance of introduction comes from well before my time but to hell with it, it's a story I like! I forget its origin. A young, single English woman was traveling to India on a passenger liner in the 1930s as part of what was known as the "fishing fleet." These were women heading out to British India to find a husband, perhaps in the civil service or the army, preferably not commerce which was considered too "common."

After ten days at sea and some drinking, she ended up in bed one night with one of the dining room stewards, a handsome young Englishman, but of a distinctly lower class. The following morning, when waiting tables at breakfast, he came over to her table, enquired warmly how she was and addressed her by her first name. She froze, drew herself up in her chair, glared at him, and pouted coldly, "In my society, sleeping with someone does not constitute an introduction!"

In the same vein, in my family files there is a letter from an English great aunt describing to her parents a flight in Europe in one of the earliest passenger aircraft, when she was nineteen years old. She writes about feeling "seasick" so a passenger in front of her "opened a window" and she felt better. Then a man she didn't know in the seat across the aisle had, "Acted rather forward" by trying to engage her in conversation.

She wrote, "...so I clasped my hands in my lap and looked straight ahead!" Probably, the poor man was just trying to take her mind off her seasickness. But, you see, they had never been introduced...and she was a very proper young lady.

The English of my parents' generation still displayed vestiges of Victorian primness, but it depended on audience. Sex was not something much discussed in polite company, beyond a few risqué jokes, but attitudes had loosened since Victorian days when discussing even the pollination of a dandelion could raise blushes on a lady's cheeks.

In those days, an engaged young lady asking an aunt for advice about the impending wedding night might have received the admonition, "Oh my dear, just lie quite still and think of the Empire!"[16]

But coming to my own times of the 1960s, as a university student, I once phoned my grandmother on my father's side with some trepidation to ask whether she would let me use their seaside cottage in Devon for a week. To my relief, her initial response was, "Yes dear, I think we can do that. You would have such fun."

After painstaking instructions from her about where the key would be hidden—hanging in plain view on a hook by the front door—how the coin-fed gas meter worked, and how life-threatening the hand-lit gas hot water system was, all of which I knew, I thought I should come clean on who would be in my party. I mumbled, "Grandma, er…just so you know…er…we would be four boys and four girls, all students from my college. Very well-behaved…of course."

There was a painful silence.

"Hello, hello, are you still there?" I asked. Then I thought I heard her conferring with grandfather.

"No…um…that would be…um, fine," she came back hesitantly, followed by an awkward pause, "but no funny business now; no funny business, alright?"

I squeaked out a barely convincing affirmation that, of course, there would be absolutely no funny business. Quickly I thanked her and hung up before she had further visions of their cottage being turned into a den of fornication. We had a great week sailing and drinking in pubs by the harbor. To my relief, she never later made any attempt to grill me about any sort of business we may have conducted, funny or otherwise!

My opinion of my parents' boundaries of propriety changed somewhat when I was about nine. My sister and I pulled out a gramophone record that we had found secreted away in a cupboard slipped into an old Christmas carols album sleeve. Being near Christmas time, we wound up the gramophone, put the 78 RPM record on the turntable, lifted the needle arm, and sat back, waiting for a scratchy "Oh Little Town of Bethlehem." To our shock and then delight, it turned out to be a recording of a famous French farting contestant, Le Prince de Petomane (1857 to 1945), a professional flatulist—a famed farter—who we soon discovered had spectacular control of his plumbing, not to mention his internal fermentations. This particular gentleman's renown in his art medium, I now see from the Internet, has spawned even musicals and movies. Fame can come upon us—or out of us—in many strange ways!

WAGGA WAGGA, GUMLY GUMLY, AND BOOK BOOK

I am compelled into this country.

– Patrick White, *Voss*

I arrived in **Wagga Wagga,** Australia, in 1965, to join a research and development team testing techniques of zero tillage—growing crops without plowing—a widespread farming practice today, but entirely new and untested at that time.

The town is about a five-hour drive south west of Sydney, a mixed wheat and sheep farming area with about 22 inches of rain a year; just enough for cropping. The hottest summer temperature recorded is about 113 degrees Fahrenheit, so rainfall can get sucked out of the ground fast. Wagga Wagga is not too far from the threshold of the drier outback grazing country which extends further inland towards the semi-desert and desert center.

The locals refer to the town as *Wagga* despite the urging of a song by country singer Greg Champion, "Don't call Wagga Wagga Wagga." It lies in the inland Riverina area of New South Wales dissected by the Murrumbidgee River, flat wheat and sheep country with a few low ranges and rocky outcrops.

Wagga was the local Wiradjuri tribe's word for a crow, an onomato-poeic representation of the sound of the crow. So Wagga Wagga, as the plural, means *a place of many crows*. Aboriginal "reduplication"—saying a word twice for the plural—is what has given us such glorious Australian place names as *Grong Grong, Woy Woy, Book Book, Gumly Gumly, Goonoo Goonoo, Gummin Gummin, Greg Greg, Bong Bong, Beggan Beggan, Mitta Mitta, Yabba Yabba, Gunya Gunya* and *Woop Woop*. (The last one is mythical, actually; the equivalent of the American *Boondocks.*)

There are other delightful place names like *Burrumbuttock*, a place I used to visit, out near *Walla Walla*. There are also, by the way, the longer place names in Australia like *Mamungkukumpurangkuntjunya*, the name of a hill in South Australia, meaning *where the devil pees*, although, to reflect the generous verbosity of the original, perhaps it would be better translated in English as *the location where the devil determined to micturate*.

The population of Wagga town today is forty-seven thousand; it was little more than half that size in my day. The three different houses I rented over this period in and around Wagga all had tin roofs and no air conditioning; you could have dried prunes in them during the summer, although the traditional surrounding verandahs helped a little.

Wagga in the 1960s exhibited a distinctly Aussie brand of Wild West machismo. Local farmers came into town for supplies driving their dusty Utes (utility pick-up) with *roo bars* on the front. They strutted the long main street in their R. M. Williams elastic-sided boots and their broad-brimmed hats. They exuded a confidence that grew from being the owner of a big chunk of country and knowing they could build just about anything for the farm if they put their mind to it.

But they were by no means unsophisticated. They could more than hold their own in any city joint in Sydney or London. The businesses serviced them. The pubs plied them with grog. The stock and station agents and auctioneers knew who farmed where, who had run off with whom, who had croaked within the week, and who was in financial strife. There were farm machinery agents with yards full of the latest tractors, harvesters and seed drills. There were travel agents, jewelers, Ute salesmen and lawyers who had refined their techniques for persuading farmers to part with their considerable, if unstable, earnings. Good times came and went with the swings of wool, cattle, and wheat prices, and with the ebb and flow of drought and flood. Nature played a bigger hand than the mayor in running the town.

The practical skills of farmers were extraordinary. The best could snoop around a sophisticated new seed drill on display at an agriculture show, jot down a few measurements, and, with a welder, oxyacetylene cutter, and a heap of angle-iron, sheet metal, and piping, build a functional replica at a third of the sticker price, often with a few improvements.

They could control three hundred sheep with a couple of dogs and a motorbike or stockhorse. They could drive a tractor all day, drink like drains into the night, and climb back on a tractor the next morning, ready to go again. They could come into the homestead smelling of sheep fleece lanolin from a day in the yards, have a quick shower, pull on a dinner suit, and be at the Picnic Races Ball that same evening, sophisticated as any dapper young blade at an English hunt ball—but with twice the balls.

There were young farmers who would fly to Moscow or to Capetown, hire a car, and drive the country on their own, just to broaden their experiences in foreign parts. There were farmers who could invite a "city girl" to what she thought would be dinner at a fancy restaurant, pick her up in a dusty Ute, drive her to the top of the ranges, open a cool box of chicken pieces, cold beer and wine, progress to a bit of activity across the bench seat...and get away with it.

There was an infamous den of bachelors in Wagga who spent as much time as any of us did in the watering holes along the main street, *Romano's* pub especially. They had rented from an old lady a run-down weatherboard house in Gumly Gumly (meaning place of many frogs). It was a little settlement that was being swallowed by Wagga Wagga—the crow swallowing the frog, I suppose.

They named their place Guzzle Gully, a name that they had crudely painted on a splintered plank and nailed to a piece of broken fence post by the gate. This gave them the memorable address: Guzzle Gully, Gumly Gumly, Wagga Wagga, New South Wales. If I remember correctly, after a year or two of, shall we say, inattentive tenancy, they were asked to find somewhere else to inhabit. Rumor had it that the final straw for their hapless landlady had come when one of them tried to demonstrate how some incredible hulk he had seen in a recent movie had been able to walk through walls. Notwithstanding that the house was hardly in good repair, the owner was unimpressed by early indications of a shortcut between the two main rooms.

A few years back, I heard that Guzzle Gully was still standing, but as an abandoned shell, and that, from the state of the living room floor, it appeared to have been taken over by sheep. It seemed to me that, of the two species, sheep may have been the more benign tenants. A more recent informant, my good mate Tony, who passes the place almost daily, sent me a photo. Guzzle Gully is, indeed, still standing, but the front door is now boarded up. So it seems that, in the end, sheep, too, had proven to be less than model tenants.

There were one or two farmers in the hill country to the east renowned for *larrikin* behavior. A *larrikin* is an Australian term for a bit of a hooligan or, more formally, a person who acts in defiance of convention; something of a badge of honor in those days.

One of them, who perhaps should remain nameless, had a widely-envied record. Some of his proudest achievements took place in Russia, travelling, if I remember correctly, with a farmer mate from the same shire. He was convinced they were being spied on by the KGB. At one stay, they were in a once-grand hotel, I think in Leningrad. As was his custom, he had rounded up a couple of English-speaking Russian ladies to join them for vodka in their room on the seventh floor.

At some point in the increasingly convivial evening, one of the fawning young ladies clutched his arm, batted her eyelashes, and asked him, "Can you throw a boomerang?"

"Sure I can throw a bloody boomerang," he growled. He went into the toilet and unscrewed the wooden seat. He took it to the double doors that led onto a small balcony, pushed them open and flung it, boomerang-style, out into the night.

"Will it come back?" asked his admirer. "Of course it'll come back," he replied.

At that moment, there was a loud crash five floors below. There was a strong wind blowing that night and his boomerang had blown back through a plate glass window into the dining room. He and his traveling mate were asked, not very politely, to find other accommodations. But those who heard of his many exploits, which included relieving Russian cement mixers of their wheels at night to retread his deteriorating hire car, regarded him with awe as not merely an important player in the Cold War but as a fully-qualified and fine larrikin bravely upholding the great Aussie traditions of larrikinism.

About 1967, I was living fourteen miles outside Wagga in a rented farmhouse in The Rock postal district, near a tiny settlement called Collingullie, with, as a contrast to Guzzle Gully, the minimalist address: "Sunshine," The Rock, New South Wales.

I shared Sunshine with my friend and work colleague, Lewis Rowell. My mother back in England wrote with concern, envisaging me living in a tin shack beside a large boulder somewhere out on the great red plains. The Rock was indeed a rock, but no mere boulder, towering above the plains by about a thousand feet. It was some miles from the house. I reassured her that my pad, while no palace, was reasonably habitable by the standards of the simple Australian farmhouse and that, in any case, the rent was lower out of town.

The drinking water at Sunshine came from water collected from the corrugated iron roof. It ran into a corrugated iron tank carrying with it from the roof the blown dust from the driveway and sheep paddocks, bird droppings, the lighter fractions of manure from the nearby sheep yards, assorted insects, and the occasional dead possum. Except for the possums, which bloated and floated, these impurities sank into the debris field at the bottom out of harm's way—one hoped. To conserve this roof-tank drinking water through droughts, we had a borehole for our shower water that was too saline for drinking. But in any case, our liquid needs were largely met by other beverages.

Our toilet, our *dunny*, was in an outhouse up a short path from the house. It was a patented, self-contained septic system toilet known as a *Hygeia Dissolvenator*. This was a dysfunctional crapper that post-war rural Australians became all too familiar with. I saw one recently advertised at auction on the Internet as, "Lot 1465 Rare and Collectable Hygeia Dissolvenator. Early Toilet Commode." Who collects such things? It was described on the site as a "formidable early rural toilet." Formidable, I can vouch for.

It was a heinous contraption; a brave shot at a cheap, theoretically odorless septic system fallen well short of its designer's addled dreams. Not to get too technical, but it combined, as a self-contained unit, the toilet can with a wooden seat set into a steel cylindrical septic tank chamber.

The seat was set off-center at the top of the tank and the tank was partly sunk in the ground, connected at the rear to a drain field. Inside the tank, about a foot from the top, there was a circular revolving plate which was set at a slight angle. This revolving plate, designed to seal out the smell from below, was connected to the toilet seat by a ratchet that spun your business out of sight clockwise when you pumped the seat up and down.

Why would I remember clockwise after so many years? Behind the commode, under the steel cylinder, this plate dipped below the surface of the tank contents where your business was supposed to float off or, if it was still clinging at the end of its first circuit, was scraped off by a hidden bar which, in ours, seemed to have corroded. If you were energetic, you could generate quite a speed with the revolving plate and a glutinous gurgling would rise from the underworld. I had met these Hygeia Dissolvenators before at a jackaroos' house where it was inside the house in the bathroom; an architect with not only no foresight but with no foresmell. At least at Sunshine, ours was outside in the yard, in an outhouse where the soft bush breezes were free to do their best.

Some months after we had moved in, the odor of our Hygeia was extending its reach and gripping the throat more savagely, so I consulted a salesman at the hardware store in town. I was told, "What you want, mate, is the Hygeia dissolvenator *crystals*."

So I bought a five-gallon drum of the stuff, drove home, and tipped a large dose into the toilet. The more the better, I thought. Why not? Give it the works! Shortly afterwards, my housemate Lewis came back and a farmer friend stopped by. Lewis offered him a beer. Half an hour later, our visitor went up the pathway to our outhouse for a pee. He hurried back, "There's something very nasty happening up there!"

We followed him up and found an evil, brown froth bubbling over the front of the toilet bowl and advancing down the footpath like some science fiction movie fungus bent on engulfing the planet. As we retreated back down the path, someone muttered, "Yer can't trust bloody poms with shit!"

Rural Australia still had quite a few outside dunnys in the 1960s. One evening about 1968, at the Yerong Creek community hall—a small, one-pub place south of Wagga near The Rock—I was part-way through one of my seasonal talks to farmers. About fifty had turned up. No doubt they had come more for the free beer and snacks we offered afterwards than for any enlightenment from me, although occasionally we added a movie of Australian Rules football or motor racing to entice more in and lighten the fare. Suddenly, one of them, who must have slipped out from the back of the hall unnoticed, came running in and whispered to a farmer in the second row. They both ran out. Then another one ran in and about four more hurried out. By this time, my well-practiced talk was starting to disintegrate. I was wondering if perhaps I had said something indiscrete. Then a farmer ran in more boldly down the aisle waving his arms and shouting, "The dunny's on bloody fire!"

We all ran outside and there, behind the village hall, was the ancient one-holer flaming merrily, emitting occasional jets of sparks and popping sounds. Apparently, the local farmers' fire association had been burning fire breaks along the verges of the roads that day and, as sometimes happens, the fire had smoldered beneath the upturned dry-grass sod of the plowed containment strip and had popped up next to the crapper.

As we all stood around watching, three local farmers brought up the community fire truck. It was an old flatbed mounted with a battered water tank and pump. After several pulls and hiccups, the ancient Briggs and Stratton pump engine burst into life. The farmer standing on the back of the truck gave the blazing dunny a direct shot with the hose. It collapsed in a shower of sparks, leaving the wooden toilet seat on the top of the metal can still ablaze, a defiant single Olympic ring of flame.

We stood and watched for some time, our faces glowing in the flickering firelight. A farmer beside me shook his head as he turned away murmuring, "Sad to see 'er go, 'ad some good times in there!" Not being from Yerong Creek, and never having had the pleasure of using it myself, I had no such nostalgic attachments.

As the fire died down, we all filed back into the hall and I continued as best I could where I had left off. This was not easy for any of us with the distasteful aroma of the roasting dunny contents seeping into the hall on the cooling night air; even less did it help the enthusiasm for the beer and snacks afterwards. Most of the guests left earlier than usual. We even had some sausage rolls left over.

My shared bachelor pad in Wagga, after three of us had moved into town to a small house on Fox Street, did not have much of a reputation for gourmet fare. Women visited, but rarely to eat. Many evenings, we went to the pubs first and then, far too late and ready to gnaw on an old boot, tried to knock some food together using my pressure cooker—the brute force approach to cuisine.

Occasionally, our efforts came out edible, but more often the haste, the lack of a plan, and the random selection of off-the-shelf ingredients, offered up a biblical mess of potage. On one occasion, in our desperation, we stuffed the inside of a whole frozen chicken with uncooked dry rice and herbs, threw in a few vegetables, added some water, and gave it a twenty-minute blast in the pressure cooker.

When we took the lid off, we discovered that the chicken had opened out like a dahlia. The dry rice had done what it was supposed to do; increase in volume by five times. It was surprising there had been no explosion. We ate it anyway, like animals, picking out the splayed bones as best we could and washing it down with what Lewis referred to as the *Chateau Cardboard,* the boxed wine of embarrassingly humble pedigree.

An alternative for evening eating in Wagga in those days was the Ko Wah Chinese restaurant—adequate, but with an unforgivingly stolid numbered menu. Ko Wah also did take-out food and party catering. I once volunteered to collect containers of chicken chop suey, beef lo mein, and rice from them for an end-of-season party at our sailing club by the local lake.

I had started drinking earlier so I was already, in yachting parlance, three sheets to the wind. On my return trip with the food in my very country Holden car, I forgot the humpback bridge that had been mischievously placed on a deceptive half bend over a small creek.

With my trunk (boot) full of rice pots, along with some spare parts and a few herbicide containers, I had wedged the chop suey and lo mein containers in a row across the back seat. I hit the hump doing about sixty miles an hour. The wedged containers remained firmly in place, but the lids and contents, dutifully obeying all three of Newton's Laws of Motion, rose about two feet into the air, moved about a foot forwards and sideways, and came down all over my rear seat and the floor. A few of the more adventurous pieces made it to the roof. The back seat was swimming.

On arrival at the club, my mate the barman came out to help carry. Hissing in horror, he said, "Jeez mate, looks like a dinosaur took a chunder. Quick, no one will know." We shoveled most of it back into the containers using plastic dishes, with help from our bare hands.

Later in the evening, one sailor remarked that the food had been unusually tasty, but his wife complained that it wasn't very hot. Nobody seemed to have found a ballpoint pen and a small notebook that I was sure I had left on the back seat. It took me weeks to get rid of the pieces that had found their way into every nook and cranny of my car and to dissipate the aroma of a morning-after Chinese hash-house.

The Book Book party, thrown annually by the Wagga Wagga Bachelors Club, was legendary across New South Wales and even further afield in outposts like Tasmania. Book Book is little more than a T-junction on the Tumbarumba Road some twenty miles southeast of Wagga. There was a farmer's shearing shed and a gray corrugated iron community hall; in recent years, I hear it had been condemned as unfit for human habitation and demolished. It was surrounded by waving yellow barley grass, sheep, and a few roadside gum trees. A large pit had been dynamited in the ground outside the shearing shed to barbeque sheep. It was not hard to find farmers to donate sheep.

I had the questionable honor one year of being the Book Book party sub-committee member in charge of beer supply. This was a frustrating task for one with an analytical inclination, since nobody had past records of consumption or the numbers of paid-up guests and gate-crashers, nor how many kegs had been bought or returned.

If I recall correctly, I calculated on an average of eight pints per person. This seemed to me to be sufficient since some women never drank beer at all and there was an array of basic spirits and cheap Australian boxed wine. I don't recall coordinating on beer volume with the wine and spirits supply member. That year, to my relief, we didn't run out, although we came uncomfortably close. I returned only one-and-a-half unused kegs to Romano's pub the next day. Running dry would not only have lost the Book Book party its enviable reputation but to have been perpetrated by a pom would have subjected me to years of ribbing, if I had been permitted to live at all.

Inside the Book Book shearing shed, there was the fine aroma of sheep droppings and sheep urine wafting up from below the sheep pen areas which had the usual slatted floors. As the evening progressed, this became increasingly laced with the more hoppy aroma of beer slops. The guests were diverse. Most of the men were from the Wagga area, but there were classy town girls from Sydney and Melbourne who wanted to taste, or re-discover, the bush culture.

The local Wagga-area guests were moderately well-dressed. There were a few "feral westies"—tough young men from further to the west; big, dry, flat country. There were men and women who worked for the local farm supply stock and station agents, the men in light-colored, well-ironed shirts and strides. There were young lawyers and other professionals from Wagga and further afield, some remarkably well-travelled. There were one or two jackaroos who would come deliberately dressed down in dirty moleskins or jeans as though they had just slid off a horse.

We danced to a band and taped music. The dancing was energetic and occurred on a variety of floors. At one of the Book Book parties before my time, they had even managed to achieve a broken leg. Apparently a young farmer dancing with his girlfriend had broken through the slatted shearing shed floor that had been tested beyond its limits by his inebriated stomp.

Australians in outback areas are accustomed to driving long distances for a party. One year on the weekend of the Book Book party, I'd been working for two weeks in the far north of New South Wales. On the day of the party, I set my alarm to wake up at "sparrow"—the Aussie contraction for getting up very early—"getting up at first sparrow fart."

I drove from Tamworth to Wagga Wagga, with a quick business stop in Dubbo, a total of about four hundred and fifty miles, which took about ten hours. After a shower and change of clothes, I went straight to the party. After the next day in Wagga for reparations, I drove back to Tamworth to continue with my work program. Close to a thousand miles, round trip, for a party was a little excessive, even in those days, but it would have been unthinkable to have missed the Book Book bash.

The Picnic Races, followed in the evening by the Picnic Races Ball, was the big party weekend of the year in most rural towns. Originally, the races were simply local horses and riders competing in amateur competition, but by the 1960s, the races had become closer to the British point-to-point, with mostly thoroughbred horses and some close-to-professional jockeys. In Wagga, the ball was a classy affair, men in dinner suits, women in ball gowns. It was held in the corrugated iron Kyeamba Smith Hall, a large barn of a structure like an aircraft hangar.

The décor was rustic, with strings of used silver-foil milk bottle caps hanging down the walls, well-worn lengths of folding cinema seats along the walls, and trestle tables bearing the inevitable cold chicken buffet, a meat dish that could be easily prepared in advance and survive with minimal refrigeration.

Some young men in rural areas in those days were not particularly attentive to their women dates. I may have been one of them. "The woman" or "the Sheila"—although those labels were starting to give way to others more enlightened—was still seen as something of a chattel. Women were increasingly rejecting such treatment, but a few seemed to turn a blind eye.

One year, at the Picnic Races Ball, I started the evening standing at the bar on the beer-absorbent sawdust talking to a young farmer I had just met. He already had a few beers under his belt. We "shouted" each other several rounds leaning on the bar. This was the Great Australian Lean—nearside shoulder low, elbow on the bar, mouth hovering near the glass, one knee against the front panel of the bar, the other leg stretched out straight at right angles like a prop, foot anchored in the sawdust, right wrist bent for maneuvering your glass the minimal necessary inches to your mouth—the ultimate in drinking efficiency.

As we drank, he slipped slowly into incoherence. At least I thought so. He seemed to crumple like a botched meringue coming out of the oven. His shoulders drooped. His jacket hung more loosely. We continued for about an hour before I learned that he had brought a girlfriend with him. He mentioned her name and I realized I had met her once before. I suggested that he might want to go and find her, adding that she might be sitting on the old auction lot folding cinema seats arrayed along the wall, the mustering site for wallflowers.

At my suggestion, he frowned and croaked, "Nah, she'll be right, mate. No worries."

So, we continued our deteriorating exchange. Finally, after about an hour and a half, I announced more firmly, "Sorry mate, really must go and circulate."

He looked at me as if I had hit him between the eyes with a fence post. His eyes crossed but fought their way back to an uneasy compromise, "Wasser madder mate? Can't yer talk ter a bloke?"

I mumbled a final apology and left him to his philosophizing, which I saw he visited on a victim leaning on the bar on the other side of him but with a leftie stance. Walking across the dance floor, I saw his girlfriend with others, precisely where I had predicted. Ungentlemanly, I shirked my duty and looked the other way. She was his problem, not mine.

Even the many who treated their dates with chivalry and respect could give them a rather more agricultural experience than they had been used to up in Sydney—up in the old *Steak and Kidney*, the rhyming slang for Sydney.

Shortly before one of the Picnic Races Balls, I had bumped into my mate Peter in a yard in town. He was hosing out the inside of his Ute, washing down the seats, even stuffing the hose down the back of the bench seat to flush out pieces of hay and other farm debris. I asked him what the hell he was doing.

"Just hosing her out. Picking up a woman in a couple of hours. You going?"

"Yes, I'm going. But how the hell is she going to sit in this swamp in a ball gown?"

"It'll be right, mate," Peter answered. "I'm going to mop it up with this wheat bag. I always leave those rubber floor plug thingies out so she drains. Better sitting on a damp seat than hay and sheep shit, eh?"

"I suppose," I said, "But I think you'll need to dry it out with something better than that."

I caught up with them early in the evening. With a discreet flanking maneuver, I was able to see that his date looked dry enough and had no hay or wheat straw sticking to her dress. Somehow, he had got away with it.

AFRICA
THE LIGHT CONTINENT

However long the night, the dawn will break.

– African proverb

After leaving Australia, and slotting in some post-graduate studies in England back at my old university, I ended up in Africa, living in Kenya and Tanzania. Nineteenth-century book titles promised tales of Darkest Africa, (for example *In Darkest Africa* by Henry Morton Stanley), but, to me, Africa has always seemed the lightest of continents—in the levity of its many peoples, the golden light across the savanna at sunset, and the glow through the beards of the wildebeest cresting a ridge in a breaking dawn. No living thing seems out of place; not a gazelle, not a thorn tree, not a dung beetle. They seem to have been brushed on by a paint-dipped finger. It is a compelling continent. Three of my children, Jaime, Antonia and Sinclair, were born there and saw their first elephant calves, lion cubs and cheetah cubs there; no need for picture books.

But not all has been well with Africa. Since the release from colonialism that left low levels of education and skills, especially at higher levels, and with barely a handful of truly visionary leaders, the continent struggled. Most of what I write is from the immediate post-colonial days, the hopeful but frustrating days of the 1970s, in the development field sometimes called Africa's "lost decade."

While Asia and South America, based on FAO and World Bank data, increased the amount of food produced per person between 1962 and 1984 by about 30% in Asia and about 20% in South America, the production per person in Africa fell by about 10%. This was due to poor policies in agriculture, some questionable economic structural adjustment policies, weak bureaucracies, a continuing malaise left by colonialism including lack of skills, a high population growth rate, drought, debt, and low commodity prices. By 1980, making up quickly for this lost decade had become an almost impossible task. But more recently, the continent has finally started to move, although not uniformly.

TANZANIA IN THE 1970S - TOP-DOWN SOCIALIST PLANNING AND UJAMAA

The political philosophies of the world span from individualist to collectivist.[17] The individualists, to the right of the political spectrum, believe that people will be happiest if they are free to pursue their dreams and not too much is done for those who sink. The collectivists, to the left, believe people will be happiest if there is more give, if people share and look after each other. In Tanzania, in the 1970s, the collectivist concept calling for more planning and, in this case, quite far to the left, was known as *ujamaa,* loosely meaning *familyhood.* At that time, across the northern border, in Kenya, President Kenyatta's crowd-rousing call was *harambee,* meaning *all pull together*—on the face of it a similar idea, but in application very different; Kenya at the time was considerably more capitalist.

The collectivist approach in Tanzania, engineered in the rural areas through the *ujamaa* villagization program, ran into many of the problems familiar from the decline of other such systems like the collective farming of the Soviet bloc. By the early 1970s, forcing households from scattered traditional settlements into planned villages was in full swing. The idea originated from President Nyerere, but with influence from leftist literature. His theory was given an African slant through his argument that Africans had always worked together in groups. This was true, but only in certain respects. Many a night I spent with enthusiastic young Tanzanians, drinking in smoky bars, debating this.

They would say, "Ndugu (Brother) Nelson, *ujamaa* will be good. You will see. African farmers have always worked together communally."

I would come back, "But the wheels of group labor have always been greased with the idea that I work for you if you are going to work for me. Outside the extended family, it's not as different from hired labor as the President seems to think."

"Ndugu, you are wrong. In this region, even, there used to be many labor groups, historically."

"And what if I was a farmer in your group and I didn't show up to work on your land? What then?"

"Well, if there was an excuse, alright, but if not, then you would not be so welcome in my group. Sharing goes both ways."

"Precisely," I would say, "There was an obligation. It was not very different from holding a labor promissory note. But, in any case, traditionally, you kept your own land with the right to cultivate, a right given by the chief or elders."

"Yes, always you kept your land. Land is the most important thing for an African."

"But now people are losing their traditional land rights!" I would remind them.

These debates were difficult to fight to anything but a draw. But whatever the outcome, Tanzanians were always friendly and collegial. We were still a team aiming to score goals; we just had different views on how to position the players and on game strategy, but, increasingly, we were running into differences about the rules of the game too.

I was worried also about the fading belief in the role of prices; I argued that prices for producers and the decline of farm services which raised farm input prices mattered. That debate alone could run five beers.

President Nyerere was a fine human being, in some respects up there close to Nelson Mandela in stature. He was compassionate, committed and totally honest. But in this strategy at that time, his head was in the clouds and his generous heart was not replicable across the population that was supposed to somehow make this social experiment work.

Sometimes, Nyerere was taken for a ride by overly-enthusiastic party cadres out in the districts. The incentives to perform and to please were huge, party promotions were at stake and party position gave access to increasingly scarce resources. Rumor had it that in one district he had been driven past a cultivating village work group, hacking away eagerly with their hoes to open up a new plot to show him what good things were happening on the new farming blocks. Thirty minutes later, he drove past another group but thought that two of the ladies in the group looked familiar. It turned out that the district party people had gathered up the first group, driven them round and ahead of him in a truck, and set them down on another plot he was about to pass! He was not amused by this deception. We heard that some heads rolled!

James C. Scott, in his book *Seeing Like a State*[18] got the Tanzania *ujamaa* picture largely right when, looking back, he wrote, "The modern planned village in Tanzania was essentially a point-by-point negation of existing rural practice, which included shifting cultivation and pastoralism, poly-cropping, living well off the main roads, kinship and lineage authority, small scattered settlements with houses built higgledy-piggledy, and pro-duction that was dispersed and opaque to the state."

Government and party control in the new villages became increasingly oppressive. It stretched even to the type of houses permitted. Apart from severing rural families from their house style born of social and practical needs, the modern houses were hot, claustrophobic and impervious to smoke from a traditional indoor fire. Usually they were much smaller, rectangular instead of the traditional thatched roof round shape, and they were laid out in precision military rows. In one case, I found the remains of an old traditional house that was only two feet out of line on the new planned village grid. I discovered that the family had been required to demolish it and rebuild a new house to the new design exactly on the pegged line. *Ujamaa* villages undermined the character of society. But breaking society seemed to be part of the idea.

"If you go for the full Chinese-type communism," one American communist advisor with experience of Mao's China earnestly tutored me, "You must make it absolutely clear to the populace that there is no going back. No retreat. No choice." Then he added, "Actually, Tanzania hasn't gone far enough. The center needs to do more planning and control." He added ominously, "There are ways."

I was about to punch back, but it seemed fruitless. I could see he would accept no hint of even minor drift towards incentives, freedom, or filthy capitalism. People were pawns to be moved on a board, but according to the rules of a new game, refereed from some place far removed and threateningly on high.

The houses in the new villages were often miles from the farming plots, so damage to crops by birds, monkeys, porcupines and, in some places elephants, often at night, was difficult to prevent. A lot of time was lost in walking to distant plots. My theoretical calculations found that, assuming a three-hundred-household village, about twenty to twenty-five percent of available labor time was likely to be lost in walking from the central housing area to allocated plots on outlying village blocks, about one-and-a-half to two hours a day. This turned out to be quite an accurate projection when later household surveys showed actual walking times.

Following the forced movement into villages and the allocation of land parcels on blocks, there was an emerging food production crisis. This was partly due to the farming disruption and the uncertainty, but was exacerbated by poor rains, weak international prices, and poor economic and pricing policy, effectively putting increased taxes on farmers.[19]

In some parts of Tanzania, the party-dictated crop rotations were unworkable. A maize-cotton-cassava rotation was impossible on three equal-sized village blocks because the most favored cassava varieties stayed in the ground for eighteen months. It could not be harvested in time to make room for the next crop in the cycle. Nobody seemed to care, the party had spoken, and lower ranks were expected to obey. Soon, fertilizer and seed were becoming expensive and hard to obtain as government marketing agency performance declined. The flow of seed from newly-bred crop varieties was insufficient due to lack of plant breeding research and seed multiplication budget. There was some progress with education, health, and village water supply but, in the end, the facilities built mostly by donor-supported rural development projects were often poorly staffed and poorly operated and maintained.

However, one tribe on the slopes of Mount Kilimanjaro, the Chagga, were left largely untouched by this social upheaval due to their independence—some would say intransigence—and due to the complexity of their inter-cropped mountain slope farming systems. The Chagga grew perennial crops such as coffee and banana mixed with maize, beans, and cassava, and they kept several types of livestock. Bananas of many types were their staple food and used in their brewing of *mbege*, their banana beer.

The Chagga farms had ingenious irrigation channels. Such a network system would have been impossible to operate under government-controlled, consolidated farming blocks. So, in these areas, villagization became a regulation-bending game for benighted officials trying to keep pace with the stream of edicts from on high.

I asked one young draughtsman in a government office on the slopes of Kilimanjaro who was busy drawing lines on a map, what he was doing. "Making new villages," he replied, quickly looking up, embarrassed about what he had just said.

I asked him about naming conventions. New village names were being assigned, some with a letter added to delineate a separate settlement. Few villagers were consulted about names (or anything else) but, in any case, little changed on the ground for them, although they were expected to form the required village development committees. So the Chagga were left largely free to ignore the whirlwind of compulsions, which, as a tribe, they were inclined to do anyway.

As it became apparent that the party vision for communal farming was not giving the results hoped for, by the late 1970s into the early 1980s, it was starting to be accepted that farmers should be free to go back to their old land and to farm as they chose. This reversal was not shouted from the rooftops but was dribbled out over time to camouflage the policy reversal. Nyerere eventually, in 1985, stepped aside, still convinced of the principles but chastened by the complexities of application. By this time, much damage had been done to agriculture and to land ownership in the scrambling of traditional land use rights.

In any case, most Tanzanian officials were still not convinced that small farmers could be efficient if properly supported. They clung to the idea that large state-run farms with tractors, the top-down-make-things-happen way to production, was better. But the evidence showed that existing state farms were not doing better at all. They had high costs and poor yields, the meagre produce that entered the local economy trickled out through questionable pathways, and there was little of the claimed demonstration of new farming technologies appropriate for smallholders.

It was during the trough of this economic downturn—as Tanzania's more capitalist neighbor Kenya was growing quite well despite a crippling population growth rate—that a rueful joke was heard in the villages in northwest Tanzania not far from the Kenya border: "Kenya is a man-eat-man society. Tanzania is a man-eat-*nothing* society!"[20]

The town of Dodoma in Tanzania in the mid-1970s was supposed to become the new capital, an African Brazilia, another manifestation of the top-down approach. In the end, it never managed to displace Dar es

Salaam, although it is officially the legislative capital. Parliament is there, and it is expected to continue to grow. The administrative capital is Dar. Unfortunately, Dodoma was a poor site. Being a low rainfall area, it had water problems from the start. The Prime Minister's Office, leading the charge, had bravely set up their head office there, so I and my wife at that time, Anne, were posted there from Kenya. Some Tanzanian officials posted to Dodoma used to keep a packed suitcase behind their desks, ready to head for the airport or train station to return to Dar whenever a pretext could be dreamed up. Who could blame them? That was where their families lived. The good schools were there.

In Dodoma, in 1974, there were few shops or services beyond the usual local market, but there was a promising bakery with crusty brown bread. When I mentioned this welcome find to one of the old-hand expatriates who ran the pharmacy, he put down a pot of pills and looked at me with a frown.

"Oh dear," he said, "You didn't buy the brown bread, did you?" I nodded. He looked at me reproachfully, "Have you looked closely to see why it's brown?" On closer examination back at the house, we realized that what we had thought was wheat germ, wheat husk and other wholesome parts of the grain were, in fact, pieces of insect wing, crushed cockroach, weevils, and assorted floor sweepings.

"Yes," he said when I saw him the next day and confirmed his observations, "I'm afraid the brown bread is just the dirty flour." We switched to the white. Even if the white was by no means pristine, at least questionable matter was less camouflaged—by other questionable matter.

My office in Dodoma was in the German pre-First World War fortified HQ, a modified fort. It still had some of the narrow fortress windows for shooting out of. It was beautifully cool from the thick stone walls; thick enough to withstand a field gun shell. There was still, I think, the remains of an armory under the courtyard.

For health care in Dodoma, there was one of the best-managed and best-staffed small hospitals in Tanzania—Mvumi Mission Hospital—about fifteen miles outside of town. My daughter Antonia was born there. It had excellent staff and was quite adequate for comfort. Now greatly expanded, it remains a vital hospital for the area.

The Roman Catholic White Fathers have for many years made an important contribution to tackling poverty in remote parts of Africa, especially in Tanzania. The name *White Fathers* came from the color of their habits rather than the color of their skin, although at that time most were still white, from Europe.

In the 1970s, I used to meet them often in the districts south of Lake Victoria. They were entertaining characters, with exceptional local knowledge. They had a good grasp of tribal custom, local problems, and of who was who among the political movers and shakers and among the local elders.

One of them once described to me how he was going through the initiation steps for joining a local men's *Sukuma* tribal society. It was a great honor for him to have been invited. This was a dual-purpose society dedicated to beer drinking and practicing traditional herbal medicine. But the beer seemed to be taken more seriously than the herbs. To qualify, he was expected to learn to brew beer and to be familiar with the preparation and uses of about eighty herbal plants. We sat together having a coffee in a hotel in the local town. It was clear he had been an ardent student; after enumerating several of the herbs on his fingers and describing the uses of each, he came to a very special one. He slid his elbows across the grease-hazed plastic table, disturbing a gang of flies, "You wouldn't believe it, there's one herb that cures syphilis. It's incredibly powerful. It will cure a horse." His eyes narrowed, "Sometimes it kills people!"

His initiation requirement, following a test on the identification and uses of the herbs, was to throw an unforgettable beer-drinking party, a mighty booze-up that would be spoken of by the elders for years, if not for generations. The batch of brew for his party had required a large and costly pile of wood. I heard later his party was a grand success, the indicator being that most members were drunk for two days!

The White Fathers spoke both Swahili and the local Sukuma tribal language. But the younger ones, newly arrived, struggled for the first year or two with Sukuma.[21] One young priest, who had arrived three years previously, had been disappointed that his service attendance had dropped off since his first year despite feeling that his fluency and confidence had greatly improved. There seemed to be an inverse relationship between his fluency and the size of his congregation.

Eventually, a lady in his flock admitted to him with much giggling that, during his first year, many of them had been determined not to miss a single church service because his mistakes were their weekly entertainment! What he had interpreted as radiant faces of religious devotion turned out to have been barely controlled mirth. He was later told by an embarrassed parishioner that in one of his sermons he had urged his congregation to, "Go forth into the highways and byways, take the breasts of the young maidens, and burn them in the eternal fire!"[22]

Being originally from Europe, the Fathers liked their wine. They had developed a grape-growing operation and winery at Dodoma, first started, I believe in 1938, but their winery was nationalized by the government in the early-1970s. The quality of the wine up to that time had been drinkable, although by no means an award contender. But from the first vintage following nationalization, the quality sadly declined. However, at this low point for the winery, the forces of supply and demand kicked in. Demand increased considerably because competing alcohol at safety levels above the local hooch was in desperately short supply. With the economic downturn, beer had become hard to find. So wine drinkers, almost entirely still expats at that time, had to swallow whatever discriminatory palates they still clung to, along with the sweet and soulless Dodoma Red. It was better than nothing.

At about this time, a very nicely-printed advertising card appeared on hotel tables in Tanzania. It read:

DODOMA WINE

A TRUE WINE OF THE COUNTRY
PLANTED IN CENTRAL TANZANIA BY
THE MISSION FATHERS. THE ADVENTUROUS
FLAVOUR OF AN AFRICAN SAFARI WITH
A BOQUET AS SUBTLE AS A CHARGING RHINO.

One certainly could not quarrel with the description. But expats were debating who had produced this ad. Some believed that it had been printed on a printing press owned by the White Fathers as a not-too-subtle dig over the nationalizing of their beloved winery—they certainly had the sense of humor to do it.

Today, I believe the winery is doing well. I am not fully up-to-date, but I think it is privately owned and may be starting to match a few of the South African wines for quality. The potential had always been there; it was the execution that had faltered. Never count out African smallholders for quality farm production.

In 1976, when living in Kenya but working in Tanzania, I became stranded in Tanzania in the town of Kigoma for Christmas, away from my family in Nairobi. The weekly flight to Dar es Salaam was canceled and it was too late to catch the night train across country to Dar or get a connecting flight to Nairobi.

Kigoma is a pleasant place on the shores of Lake Tanganyika, the second oldest freshwater lake in the world. It lies in the floor of one branch of the sunken Rift Valley. It has about 1,100 miles of shoreline and a depth of nearly two thousand feet.

I stayed with my good friend Gordon Moore, a British consultant, who was helping to run a rural development project there. He was a jovial character who had worked in Kenya for many years in rural finance, an English farmer on a modest scale, a product of colonial times but entirely at home and reveling in independent Africa.

He lived alone and cherished his independence and he welcomed the challenges facing the project he helped manage. He was out of beer and wine, both of which, by then, were hard to find, even for those who were adept at manipulating the system. I had brought with me my usual offering of gin but, with overconfidence in the alcohol supply, we had drained it the week before after several tiring days visiting villages. It looked like it was going to be a dry holiday.

The day before Christmas, we walked into town and bought a live chicken in the local market. It was a bustling place with rows of corrugated iron stalls selling chickens, fly-covered goat meat, neatly-stacked pyramids of tomatoes, bunches of onions, cheap, used clothes, and piles of leather and rubber tire flip-flops. Back at the bungalow, we chopped our chicken's head off with an axe, plucked and gutted it, and stewed it all afternoon, hoping to induce it into some semblance of tenderness.

After years in the field, Gordon had become skilled in the culinary manipulation of the local fowl, but this one clung defiantly to its athleticism. Accepting that this was our only option, and in the absence of any spirits to lift our spirits, we strolled down to the Kigoma Club on Christmas morning.

The Kigoma Club was a concrete-floored hut with a corrugated iron roof; hot, sparsely furnished, but quite clean. It was the only club in town; the Tanzanian version of a London gentleman's club—men only. We went inside and ordered two *Konyagis*, the very drinkable Tanzanian molasses-based alcohol advertised as being "not a rum and not a gin."

The barman shook his head, *hamna*, there was none. We suggested beer. No, none. After four or five bids from our side, he confessed that he had no alcohol of any sort from any origin, fine, mediocre, or dreadful. I wondered out loud if he had been enterprising enough to bring in any of the local village hooch, dangerous though it was. He shook his head glumly. He didn't want to risk losing his job.

We asked him what he did have. He brightened up and announced proudly, "Coca-Cola, Sir!" We both shrugged. I said, "Better than nothing I suppose, we'll take two." He filled two glasses of water and slid them towards us. Then he crouched down below the bar and a hand came up with one purple tablet and then another. He stood up and, with studied precision, placed a tablet beside each glass.

"What the hell is this?" Gordon said.

"It's Coca-Cola, Sir!...You put the tablet in the water!"

We followed his instructions and a purple froth rose up and spilled over the lips of our glasses before subsiding, spent, into the rust-red concoction. It looked undrinkable. We tasted it, put our glasses slowly down on the bar and looked at each other. Christmas was not looking good.

"Dr. Livingstone, down the road, probably fared better," I said, thumbing in the direction of Ujiji a few miles south, Livingstone's hang-out in the 1870's when the explorer, Henry Morton Stanley, the Welsh journalist, found him—not that he was ever lost!

"Jane Goodall's probably doing better," said Gordon, "I bet she's got some whisky." Her chimpanzee research center at Gombe Stream Reserve was a few miles north up the lake.

I upped his bid, "Even her chimps are probably doing better!" We looked down at our glasses, contemplating the congealing foam.

At that moment, Toni, the Italian who ran the shipping harbor in Kigoma, put his head through the door and shouted in his heavy accent, "Hey, you boys wanna come a my place and have Chianti and spaghetti for Christmas!"

"Yes, please!" we shouted in unison.

We followed Toni to his house. There was Toni himself and three other local couples and, for a brief visit later, if I remember correctly, an American priest popped in who, using a power boat and driver, used to visit his flock in the villages down the lake on water skis—a great opening, Gordon had suggested, to a sermon about Jesus walking on the Sea of Galilee. There was an Irish marine engineer, Patrick, who was putting new turbines into the six-hundred-passenger lake cruising ship, the MV *Liemba*, today the oldest operating passenger ship in the world. Patrick's life was the Liemba.[23] He cared for her as his own flesh and blood.

So, with leverage from Toni's stash of Chianti Classico, along with some bottles later in the evening that were distinctly less classico, we ended up having a fine Christmas surrounded by a bunch of convivial eccentrics.

Sometimes, in the south of Tanzania, I stayed at an old colonial pub in the small town of Songea. One evening our team of five returned there, tired and dusty. We had driven all day, meeting groups and households in villages and on farms. We had had an early breakfast and no lunch, so we were hungry.

We sat down to dinner at a long wooden table in the seedy but functional dining room. The menu was fixed. In other words, there wasn't one. The waiter brought us each a large soup plate overflowing with a non-descript, brownish stew. At first sight, it looked promising, although a little loose for my taste. We all tucked in eagerly. As if under a conductor's baton, we all put down our knives and forks and looked at each other. For a moment, nobody spoke.

Then someone exclaimed, "Oh, God! Soap!" It tasted as though a bar of soap had been cut up and boiled in it. I called the waiter over. He sniffed at it and hurried out to the kitchen. I heard him haranguing two of the women, but one of them was defiant. She shouted back at him that if he would give them more *sufurias* (the large African aluminum cooking pots) for both the cooking and the washing of clothes, these problems wouldn't happen!

Too tired to wait for the kitchen's proposal of a fresh chicken dish— that would have taken an hour, starting with the live fowl strutting the yard with unjustified composure—we ended up at the bar. Our dinner became hands of the small sweet local bananas, raw peanuts, local fire-shelled roasted cashew nuts and rounds of good local beer. One could do a lot worse.

Tanzania had many colonial Railway Hotels located in the small towns on the railway system, some quite large. They were something of an institution, built to service early rail travelers on long trips. In the 1970s, they were adequate places to stay, a few quite good, but they had their idiosyncrasies.

There was an unyielding morning routine implanted in British colonial days. Early morning tea, a British imposition visited upon the length and breadth of the Empire, seemed to have become compulsory. In some hotels, there was just no getting out of it. Personally, I had never had any desire to start my day with a cup of tea—even less when I found that, if you were unlucky with your room number, it would be delivered at about five in the morning.

The system worked like this: Usually, there would be only one "tea man" who did all the rooms; the rest of the staff would be preparing for breakfast service in the dining room. The tea man, recruited, it seemed, for age and experience rather than youth and agility, would start at Room 1 and end at, say, Room 30. Each room took him about five minutes. Puffing and panting, he would carry a large tray with teapot, cup and saucer, milk, sugar and sweet damp biscuits, sometimes up several stairs. After this, he went back down for the next load. If the hotel was nearly full, this meant about two hours of tea service.

I tried everything to fend off this tea assault. Asking the desk in the evening to be spared the chai round rarely worked. Either the message was never passed on to the morning crew or perhaps delivering morning tea had become a compulsive disorder; something they just couldn't help.

One time I pinned a large notice on my door saying in Swahili that I didn't want chai. It failed. As the chai man incorrectly interpreted it, I was upset that my tea had not arrived earlier. He knocked more frantically and apologized profusely for the delay. I began to accept that my anti-tea crusade was futile. And I realized that, even if I had been successful in repelling the tea assault, I was still going to be woken up by the knocks and slamming of doors ahead of me advancing down the corridor like an approaching bomber raid. Surrender was the only option. I could have strangled Sir Thomas Lipton!

SOMALIA AND DROUGHT

In the late 1970s—the good old days, in retrospect—Somalia was a country of proud people tackling enormous challenges with some success. At that time, I was travelling through the pastoral rangeland areas looking into the feasibility of a project to control the Tsetse fly. These are disease-carrying biting flies, like horseflies.

At that time, Somalia was facing an extended drought, as it is again at the time of this writing. The droughts had led the government to try to settle destitute pastoralist families who had lost their livestock onto farming settlement schemes as an alternative living. An Australian consultant was helping them to farm sorghum, a drought-tolerant crop, using a fleet of Somali-supplied Romanian tractors; they might have been Bulgarian, I forget. A colleague once commented to him that he had heard that these Soviet-type tractors didn't have much power. "Wouldn't pull a greased stick out of a dog's arse, mate!" was the colorful Aussie response.

I doubted the future of such farming enterprises for pastoralist Somalis who were not traditionally agriculturalists but, in the end, the program did produce some food and cattle forage, although at considerable cost, and it did create a few jobs.

Along the coast, there was another program to get pastoralists into shark fishing and fish drying—even more of a long-shot, I thought, for a people who knew nothing of the sea, mostly couldn't swim, and never ate fish. However, quite a lot of sharks were being caught, and the meat was being dried in long tin sheds that reeked of rotten fish. Later data suggested that some progress was made in persuading town Somalis to start eating fish partly by banning the sale of cattle and goat meat in the local markets two days a week.

Looking back, the introduction of nomadic pastoralists in Somalia to fishing is what led them towards their later more lucrative profession of piracy. It gave them the skills in boat handling and motor maintenance. And piracy paired rather well with their traditional skill in relieving other tribes of their property through cattle raiding—just a change of scale!

As I discuss later, the view of several of Africa's nomadic tribes, including the Somali and the Maasai, was that originally God had sent down all the cattle in the world to their tribe so any cattle that were in the hands of others must, at some point, have been stolen from them, giving them the right of recovery.

One captured Somali pirate, during interrogation, apparently expressed a similar view about ships—that Somali pirates had the same right to take ships as to take cattle. Worth a shot I suppose, but there can't be many objects with less in common than a cow and a ship!

On one trip in Somalia, I was driving through the semi-arid rangeland areas with a Somali official and our driver. We were traveling from an inland area back to the coast at *Brava* (Baraawe). We were running late and hoping to find a bed for what little would remain of the night.

On a remote sandy track, we were flagged down by a scruffily dressed policeman. He asked the Somali official sitting in the front seat if we could give him a lift to Brava. We agreed. But then he ducked behind a thorn bush and came out pushing in front of him a rough-looking character in handcuffs. He had neglected to tell us that he had a prisoner. They both squeezed into the back seat of the Land Rover beside me, the prisoner in the middle pushed up against me.

As we drove on, I nodded to him warily. He was sullen and pale. After some miles, I realized that what I had thought was his sweat wetting my upper arm was blood seeping from his shoulder through my shirt. I mentioned this to the policeman and he roughly jabbed his charge in the ribs and ordered him to slide away from me. The man wriggled far enough over to allow my blood-stained shirt to start to dry. The policeman then divulged that his captive had been in a knife fight. He had been the attacker and had killed the other man!

He had been cut on the shoulder during the struggle and was being taken to the police station to be charged with murder. "Great!" I thought to myself, "This man has nothing to lose. His prospects are not good. If found guilty, he will be hung. With an armed policeman on his other side, his last shot at freedom is past me!" I saw that, like many Somalis, he had rather thin wrists and narrow hands and the handcuffs looked alarmingly loose, American size.

The policeman assured me, "No problem. This man will not run away." He waved an ancient weapon at him. I gave the man the fiercest glare I could muster, which I immediately regretted because I could now see that what I had taken for sullenness, perhaps even aggression, was really fear. We drove on in silence through the scrub, the wheels drumming on the corrugated dirt track. The desert air, along with the swirling dust being pushed through the open windows, added a patina of fine sand to the blood. It was not the most relaxing drive, but we reached Brava with no attempt at escape.

After dropping off our hitchhikers at the police lockup, we went to a guest house; a large, old, colonial-type house. It was late in the evening, and they were already full. All three of us, the driver, the official and I, ended up sleeping on hastily-assembled camp beds in a large, high-ceilinged communal room with four others. Judging by the intermittent smells, one of them had been drinking camels' milk. As I had discovered myself, camel's milk can wreak havoc with the gut flora unless you consume it regularly enough to reach some degree of negotiated peace between the warring bacterial factions.

It was on that same desert track a few years later that I encountered the final skirmishes in the global war on smallpox. Somalia had the last smallpox case in the world in 1977. It was the finishing sprint in the cleanup. It seemed that every few miles, there was a large bush hiding a canvas tent. In the middle of nowhere, government Health Assistants would leap out at approaching vehicles brandishing vaccination packs. They would stop you to check everyone's smallpox certificates. Anyone who didn't have one, regardless of evidence of arm scars from an earlier vaccination, even recent, would earn another puncturing. They were relentless and well organized. It was a fine World Health Organization effort, with excellent Somali participation. It finally eliminated the scourge of smallpox from the world forever—an extraordinary achievement in the reduction of human suffering.

Travelling in tsetse fly areas in Somalia, or for that matter any tsetse zone in Africa, presents an unusual test of bush skills and manual dexterity. The tsetse fly is a type of large horse fly that can only survive in quite dense bush areas that offer enough shade. When they suck blood from cattle, they can transmit a cattle disease, *trypanosomiasis,* a wasting disease. In some areas, they can transmit a human version, sleeping sickness. To find cattle or humans to feed upon, tsetse instinctively fly towards darkish moving objects.

You will sometimes see swarms of them following your vehicle. Getting out for a pee calls for coordination; you need to work as a team and pee as a squad. Good drivers have it down to a fine art: First, if possible, you try to choose a more open location with less bush and fewer flies, then you all make your moves with precision. You get out quickly, slam the door and, if the flies have been following the vehicle, you quickly move away from it. You do a lightning unzip if you have not already done so in advance and you pee like a fire hose, damn the farts! You keep one hand free for swatting. Then you all dive back into the vehicle together, chasing off gate-crashers that try to sneak in.

Once back inside, you do a search for any that got in, especially under the seats. As you drive away, you need to be careful about the way you swat any in the vehicle. I once slapped an engorged fly on my neck, splattering my own blood and the fly's—all over a colleague's face and glasses.

On breaks to Mogadishu, the capital, after field trips, I would stroll north through the town and up the beach to the small U.N. Club, little more than a large shack in those days. It was a pleasant spot for swimming and body surfing. I looked forward to this because you couldn't body surf along most of the Kenya coast, due to the reefs. For several years, this routine had worked well for me. Then on one mission, back in town for a day, I headed up to the club, dropped my towel, and waded in.

The beach was surprisingly empty. A servant at the club came running after me and told me it was not a good idea to go into the surf. He pointed to a sign. Apparently, somebody had been taken by a shark the previous week and they had figured out the reason. It turned out that a slaughterhouse had just opened a couple of miles up the coast, and the washings of blood and bits of meat from the slaughterhouse floors were being hosed out into a drain running to the sea. The prevailing current swept these bits and pieces south toward the club beach. It hadn't taken the sharks long to figure out this new dining arrangement. No doubt the occasional surfer was a welcome addition to a menu of small beef scraps. That was the end of my Mog surfing.

SUDAN AND A COUP

In April 1985, while he was out of the country, President Nimeiry was overthrown in a coup led by his defense minister. I was holed up in the Khartoum Hilton for about eight days with some colleagues. By that time, Sudan had gone dry, so there was no alcohol to relieve the boredom of our incarceration. We were stuck with the local hibiscus flower infusion *karkadeh,* refreshing and thirst-quenching on a hot day, but short of staying power.

The evening before the coup, our small three-person team had driven back into the city after three days of field visits to the southwest. As we came into the city, we had seen rocks strewn all over the roads and realized that the long-anticipated coup must have finally generated some lift. We detoured cautiously by side roads through the town. The next morning, there were tens of thousands of people marching along the road where the White Nile and the Blue Nile meet. We heard reports of rioting in the center of town. Many of the international journalists and television reporters who'd assembled days earlier in anticipation were holed up in our hotel. No taxi drivers were prepared to risk the trip into the center of town until one of the more intrepid correspondents, I think from the BBC, persuaded one of them by offering a fare the driver couldn't refuse.

After several days in the hotel, and with the airport still closed, we ventured out to see if we could meet a senior official at a government ministry we had been dealing with. We'd heard that someone new from the winning side had replaced the previous man. We met the new man and congratulated him on his appointment.

With a stream of officials passing through to congratulate him, we made no headway with our business and agreed to meet again when things had quieted down. Two days later, with the city more settled, we returned. We were surprised to find the original man back in. Apparently, there had been some further trading of positions.

We sat in his office as he held forth in front of his staff watching a procession of functionaries passing through to congratulate him on his reappointment—the very same people we'd seen congratulating his replacement only a couple of days earlier! It was a reminder that, regardless of one's political inclinations, it is sensible to stay on the winning side when jobs are up for grabs, particularly where the government is one of the main players in the job market.

On missions in Sudan, I generally traveled southeast from Khartoum towards Gedaref, in the direction of Gallabat on the Ethiopian border. Sometimes I visited the Gezira Cotton Scheme, one of the largest in the world, first developed around 1914 in the days of the Anglo-Egyptian Sudan Condominium (1899–1956), the arrangement then for the governing of Sudan.

On one trip, I was traveling with a driver and a consultant. We were northwest of Gedaref, heading back towards Khartoum, when we were stopped by a soldier who emerged from a tattered tent at a crude roadblock of heaped thornbush branches.

The soldier demanded to see "our letter," claiming that, due to the conflict with the South, we were supposed to have an official letter of transit. I summoned up my humility response, profusely apologizing for not knowing about the important letter. Here was a case of a low-level soldier bearing a burden of responsibility. If he let someone undesirable through, he could be in grave trouble. One had to be sympathetic.

He told us this was a serious matter and ordered us to return to Gedaref to get the required document. I could see this taking us several days, being bumped from office to office, and, based on past experience, eventually being told that you didn't even need one. After further apologies, and without paying any bribe which, beyond the odd lubricating bottle of beer, I never did in all my years in Africa, he relented. He announced that he would allow us to continue but that, immediately on reaching Khartoum, we should report to a certain office. He said he would send a radio message that we were to be expected.

He opened one of my passports—I had three at that time—and I saw him copying in the margins of a local Arabic magazine what I thought was my name and passport number. I moved a little to the side and saw he had written shakily, "D a r k B r o w n 612 184." This was the color of my hair, my height in feet and inches, and the equivalent in meters. After a further stern admonishment, and strict instructions to report to the office in Khartoum, we drove off. We never went to the office; the address was indecipherable anyway. Perhaps a Mr. Dark Brown is still listed in some yellowed file in a government ministry as a long-lost missing person.

RETURNING THE EMPTIES

As most travelers quickly become aware, Coca-Cola long ago barged its way into the most remote corners of the globe. In this respect, the South African movie *The Gods Must Be Crazy*, with a storyline built around a Coca-Cola bottle falling from the sky, was considerable poetic license.

From way back, such artifacts of Western civilization were well-known in Africa to anyone of any tribe in even the remotest parts. However, there was a bottle supply problem across much of Africa in the 1970s. Coca-Cola bottles could be refilled with the real thing only when there were bottles to refill. Bottles—*any* type of bottle—were in short supply. Shops and village kiosks husbanded them vigilantly. There were interesting consequences that came out of this shortage, as I discovered in Sudan one evening driving south on that same road towards Gedaref.

It was dusk, and we were late for our night stop, having had a hot day of discussions with farmers. This was an area dotted with gum arabic trees (*Acacia senegal*) that produce an edible, soluble gum. It is used, in fact, in Coca-Cola. Osama bin Laden was said to have had his fingers in this trade. The dry scrub was interspersed with patches of sorghum crop and we passed through small villages of thatched, mud-walled houses. The temperature was dropping rapidly, as it does in continental desert regions at night. After about an hour, we pulled off to get a drink at a roadside shack, a truckers' stop by a small settlement.

We all knew the drill. You could get your bottle of Coke, but you had to drink it there and leave the bottle on the counter. If you strolled towards your vehicle with your half-consumed bottle, the kiosk owner would get fidgety thinking you might be a flight risk. From multiple re-use, the bottles were chipped and sandblasted. But those old Coca-Cola bottles were nothing if not tough; they could have endured space flight re-entry with only minor pitting.

As we stood around the kiosk finishing our Cokes, a well-dressed professional man walked up the street from an area of new houses. He ordered six Coca-Colas. The stall owner opened six bottles. Then, from below the counter, he pulled out two plastic bags. After shaking some sand out, he stuffed one inside the other.

With a serving boy helping to hold them open at the top, he proceeded to fill the double bag with the contents of the six bottles of Coca-Cola. Each bottle frothed and subsided as it went in. The stall owner then neatly tied a knot in the top and took the cash. The buyer nodded politely to us as he turned back down the road with his bag of Coke. I presumed there were children expecting it for dinner, perhaps a birthday party. But with Sudan by then dry, many adult Sudanese had been forced to switch from Scotch or Vodka to Coca-Cola. Expatriate parties in Khartoum, where alcohol was still permitted, had become extremely popular with government officials. Rarely was an invitation declined!

The widespread shortage of bottles was also a problem with beer. I once met a Maasai herdsman at a border post between Kenya and Tanzania. He was late middle-aged, tough as old boots, wearing his *shuka*, his red shawl, and carrying his *orinka*, his club.[24] Talking to him, I discovered he had spent much of his life moving cattle from Kenya to Tanzania, less often in the other direction, but depending on price gradients. He was a drover and a trader. But he was not simply moving them a short distance across the border. He told me that often he was taking them far to the south towards the grazing plains near a place called Iringa. He was not as tall as most Maasai and I thought perhaps had a non-Maasai mother. He had an infectious grin displaying a missing tooth. He was brim full of memories and unusually open in sharing them with a stranger.

This openness, I thought, was probably because he had become accustomed to meeting new people from other tribes in his extensive travels. I asked him if he paid the government transit fees, taxes and duties and followed the required veterinary inspection formalities when he moved his cattle across the border. He cackled with embarrassment.

He explained that he simply left a crate of Kenya Tusker beer for the border guards. He was a regular. He had a deal with them. Then he added in passing that, when he returned some weeks later heading back into Kenya, he would collect the empties! He assured me he was strict. He made sure there were none missing or cracked. Both parties knew the drill. The border guards had been conscientious in keeping to their side of the deal. I guessed out loud that he occasionally threw in a goat. He smiled.

DRIVERS

Drivers in Africa are often a rich source of information about how their country functions—the flywheels of power and possession. Drivers get around a lot and interact with many different people. (For similar reasons, prostitutes at bars can be useful, if they don't mind wasting their precious time, but I will pass on that one!) Some drivers are quiet and discrete, others garrulous and opinionated. Both can have value.

In Ethiopia, in the mid-1980s, when I was trying to understand the impact of the villagization program, officials, even in private, had clung to the official line that it was a promising program, that there was no compulsion, that the people supported it, and that it would transform the rural economy. The emerging evidence was pointing in other directions.

The straightest shooting I got was from a remarkably astute driver. While my official guide went off to find a local village head, he leaned over the back of his seat and gave a brilliant fifteen-minute assessment. Turned out, he was a part-time farmer himself, so he saw things from the farmer's side.

In Tanzania, in the days of economic decline in the 1970s, drivers, with their access to transport, had the means to benefit from commodity price differences between rural villages and towns. Sometimes, we would find our Land Rover groaning under sacks of bananas and bags of maize or cassava chips with a bouquet of disconsolate chickens tied by the legs bouncing around behind the rear seat. But as a ridiculously well-paid expatriate, I could never begrudge them this sideline in trading. Indeed, most drivers were conscientious in their duties far beyond reasonable expectation given their stagnating wages against inflation.

My attitude towards safety on the roads in Africa was fatalistic. There wasn't much choice. On one trip, I was riding in a Land Rover carrying a large drum of fuel behind the rear seats, an insurance against fuel shortages out in the remoter districts. Carrying gasoline in a vehicle in an old, dented drum would have been of only mild concern had it been sealed with a screw-top cap.

But the cap had long ago been lost, so it was sealed with a piece of old rag stuffed tightly in as a makeshift bung. With the gasoline slopping around in the drum and the Land Rover careering along potholed roads, the cloth acted nicely as a wick. It was not long before the floor in the back had about a half-inch of fuel, even after we had tried several alternative stoppers using bits of plastic bag and string.

As I remarked, perhaps a little unkindly, to a nervous American companion on his first visit to Africa, "Par for the course, Bill, we're in a mobile Molotov cocktail. But I've never seen one blow up...Yet!" However, I did draw the line on this occasion, when our government official casually leaned over from the front seat and offered us a cigarette! Bill nearly leapt out. We kept the windows open, of course, but for all I knew this was ensuring the optimum oxygen to gasoline mixture for ignition.

While I never witnessed a person injured or killed by a government vehicle in Tanzania, on a couple of occasions it was a close call. Once, traveling as a passenger on a remote dirt road, I saw a local farmer walking ahead of us going in the same direction on the same side of the road.

He was carrying on his head a bundle of sisal poles each about two inches in diameter and ten feet long, probably for some small roofing job on his house. Hearing us coming up fast behind, he made the mistake of turning his head to look back. The poles, resting on his makeshift turban, followed his head. As they swung across the road in front of us, they caught the top of the windscreen of our Land Rover near the frame. There was a report inside like a gun going off. Surprisingly, the windscreen didn't shatter.

Looking back, I saw the poor man pirouetting down the road like a drunken ballet dancer. His head was attempting to keep up with the rotating bundle of poles, his neck was trying to keep up with his head, and his body and feet were trying to keep up with his neck. Finally, like a spent top, he fell over onto the road. We stopped to make sure we had not spun his head off. The man picked himself up off the road and was very apologetic. We checked him over and he had only a grazed arm. I told him he need not apologize at all and that it was us who should be apologizing.

Here was a man from a rural society, grown up in a system that had demonstrated that officials, especially those with government vehicles, could cause you problems. Deference was the safest response, although *we* were the intruders charging through his district. We offered him a lift, but he declined because he was near the pathway across a cassava patch to his house. We gave him one of our melons that we had bought in a local market, helped him reload his poles, and went on our way.

Everywhere in the world, I have found drivers are a special breed. I owe them a debt of gratitude and—despite a few close shaves and one or two questionable detours—my life.

A BED FOR THE NIGHT

In Africa of the 1970s, accommodation in remote areas was always something of a lottery. But it was always an opportunity to learn more about how a district functioned, especially if there was a local bar.

In the small town of Kibondo, in the northwest of Tanzania, there was a small, four-roomed hotel where I sometimes stayed. The mud-walled rooms had cracked wooden shutters barely holding onto twisted hinges. The mosquito screens and mosquito nets on the beds were torn and almost worthless. Socks, or loosely balled toilet paper if you had any, were handy to stuff mosquito net holes. The beds were army type, metal frame, diamond wire-mesh sprung, stretched into a deep sag. The mattresses had been a source of nesting material for mice. There was an old threadbare blanket and no sheets.

I used to take a sheet sleep-bag of my own. At night, squadrons of mosquitos poured in through the shutters and the gaps under the thatch. The toilet was a mud-walled long-drop outside. An old, torn maize sack hung loosely for a door. But there was a crazy bar up the road with a good supply of Primus beer from Burundi. You could learn a great deal in a bar like that if you knew how to listen and interpret selectively and how to allow for the escalating hyperbole of inebriation, especially one's own.

Sometimes I would stay with the White Fathers. At the typical mission station, there were one or two spare rooms; spartan but functional. Sometimes the floors of the rooms were well-worn stone, sometimes cracked concrete, sometimes tiles shiny with the familiar African red wax floor polish, along with its distinctive odor. The bedroom would have a simple crucifix on the wall above a neat, metal-framed bed. There would be a small window, a rush mat, a single, bare light bulb hanging from the ceiling, a couple of geckos, and an old wooden wardrobe, the doors of which were inclined to swing open mysteriously during the night. The bathroom would be down a corridor. As a visitor, it was customary to bring an offering of beer, spirits or wine.

On one occasion, staying with them during the sparser days of economic decline, I had been unable to find any alcohol in the shops that I had tried along the route, so I arrived empty-handed and embarrassed. Before we sat for dinner, I apologized for my failure, reminding the old father about the state of the economy and the difficulty of finding beer.

He patted me on the shoulder and said, "Oh, my boy, I quite understand, quite unnecessary to bring us anything." He went to a tall cupboard in the dining room, opened the door and waved at three full shelves stocked with all sorts of spirits and wine. "Don't drink myself," he said, "But some of the others do. What would you like?"

"A gin, thank you…A dash of water would be fine," I added quickly, knowing they would not have tonic.

"Please," he waved, "Help yourself. Was never a barman myself, other than sacrament wine. Not one of my skills!"

Some of the orders of the White Fathers had a practice of eating in silence, so most of them would bring a book to dinner; sometimes a bible, but often not. They would prop their books up on hinged wooden book-stands and quietly read through the meal. If someone needed to be passed the salt or the water jug, a low grunt with some indication of the item was all that was needed. But the moment the meal was over, like small boys released from class, talk bubbled over and they joked and laughed with gusto. I admired them for their sly, unexpected humor.

Further north, in Somalia, at the level of a two or three-star hotel, but posing, I think, at the time as a four-star, the Al Uruba Hotel in Mogadishu was, shall we say, memorable. I am unaware of its condition today, but in 2013, it had been heavily mortared and was in ruins.

In its heyday, the Al Uruba was a quite impressive Italianate Arab design fallen well short of its promise by being assembled, apparently, without reference to the plans. You could see that many of the doors had once been hung the wrong way. Those who stayed there had endless tales of inexplicable quirks.

My own theory about the gurgling sounds in the plumbing, the sewer smells, and the unexpected jets and leaks from the taps and drains was that all the pipes in the hotel, both supply and drainage, somehow came together in a great underground cavern of Hades.

On one occasion, immediately after I had flushed the toilet in my bathroom, I heard an anguished cry from the room below and a stream of British invective. It seemed that my act of flushing had triggered some unspeakable event down below. I didn't dare venture downstairs to offer apologies for my thoughtless act.

BEDOUIN HOSPITALITY

In many societies outside the West, especially Islamic societies, hospitality to a stranger or traveler is demanded by culture and religion, and hospitality really means *hospitality*. This tradition exists, but to a lesser extent, in rural societies in America or Europe and in the Australian outback as well, where helping travelers may be quite critical in hot remote areas. It is largely absent in Western cities.

In some Islamic societies, it is demanded, at least temporarily—typically for three days—even if you are planning to later do your guest in over some family feud. In Afghanistan and Pakistan, it is a part of the Pashtunwali honor code. The Koran instructs that a man who withholds water from a wayfarer will not enter God's kingdom.

Hospitality is particularly evident among the Bedouin in Egypt, where water is precious and human settlements are often located near water. A traveler will not survive without access to your water; you are killing him if you deny him.

On one occasion in the northern part of the Western Desert of Egypt, inland from Marsa Matrouh, I was interviewing Bedouin households ("tents" as they call them), if I remember correctly mostly of the Awlad Ali tribe. I was assessing the performance of a project that had helped them improve the management of their rangelands and their ancient underground water storage cisterns.

I was scheduling four visits a day. This meant long drives on seldom-used desert tracks across patches of stony desert and scrub, past slow-chewing camels and quick-nibbling sheep, often cutting along dry *wadi* beds. This was the area that Montgomery, with his British Eighth Army and Rommel, with his Afrika Korps, had been contesting in the North Africa campaign. There were still relics of war visible in the early 2000s.

One family I interviewed was using a British soldier's helmet with a small square pickax hole punched in the middle of the crown as a funnel to fill plastic water containers from their underground water cistern. These ancient cisterns filled only a few times a year with channeled storm floodwater. Around many of them there were hundreds of broken shards of Roman occupation pottery from Cleopatra's time, in some cases six inches deep. She had cavorted, and it seems rather more, with the Roman General Mark Antony in a sea cave at the coast some miles to the north. In 40 B.C., she had twins by him.

At every meeting with Bedouin we sat cross-legged in a circle in a concrete hut or a large traditional tent on a large carpet—men only. I never got within three hundred yards of a Bedouin woman. It is impossible at such meetings to avoid a banquet. Eating is done with the right hand, the left being reserved for, well, another bodily task. Out of sight, the women would be preparing the food. We would sit around the edges of a large rug on which the dishes were laid out; an array of rice, goat, fat-tailed sheep, other meat stews, meatballs with vegetables, and baskets of unleavened bread. I never had the full traditional dish with a sheep head sticking out of the rice and vegetables. After the main dishes, local desert fruits, nuts, and coffee would be brought in before a quick wrapping up of our business and departure.

One day, running hopelessly late for my fourth meeting, I apologized to our third sub-clan head that we really could not stay to eat after a somewhat rushed pre-meal meeting because we were already an hour behind schedule for the next group. I knew it was a long shot, and quite rude, but it was worth a try because it seemed that, either way, I was going to upset one party or the other.

The host drew himself up and his eyes narrowed. In his traditional Bedouin robes he was an imposing figure. He spoke to three men standing near him. One turned out to be his oldest son. He smiled and nodded. I thought for a moment I was home and dry. But then he said, "You will go on to the next group. But I will send my son here to travel with you. He will bring you back to eat afterwards. You must eat with us."

I glanced at his son; he carried a rifle. I bowed my head. With the trusted son following in a pick-up, we drove on to meet our final group of the day, who were equally insistent that I eat with them. On arrival, the son accompanying us parked some distance away and watched. I got the impression that there was a strained relationship between these two groups, probably some grazing dispute or ancient feud.

With my translator, I interviewed the men and ate at the same time. Since I could not talk to women, I had contracted a local woman to interview women as a separate part of our study. When the meal was over, I thanked them and took my leave. Then, as it was getting dark, we followed our shadow in his pick-up back along the desert track from where we had come to tuck into the fourth banquet of the day with his father back at our prior group.

Traveling in Bedouin areas, one soon learned to skip breakfast and to fake eating ravenously. The hospitality is extraordinary, delightful, and leisurely, the Islamic way, thumbing its nose at the passing of the hours, but a little challenging for a Western professional on an unforgiving work program.

FLYING IN EAST AFRICA

Flying in East Africa in the '70s could deliver the unexpected, but it was a wonderful opportunity to look down on country inaccessible by vehicle and to puzzle about reasons for patterns; for example, bare patches, perhaps a recently abandoned cattle yard, or a patch of soil salinity.

About 1977, I was flying from Mwanza, in Tanzania, back to Nairobi in Kenya, via Kisumu on Lake Victoria, where we had to pick up two more passengers. It was a small aircraft charter flight that had been given special clearance to fly once a week across the closed border between the two countries. The border had been closed due to a spat between Kenya and Tanzania over the East African Community and other things. It was a twin-engine, eight-passenger Cessna into which they stuffed ten people by putting me in the co-pilot's seat and a woman at the back on a folding seat.

We left Mwanza far too late to make Wilson Airport in Nairobi by dusk and we were delayed at our stopover in Kisumu waiting for a passenger. I am not sure if Wilson Airport even had landing lights at that time but if it did, they were turned off at dark and the airport was shut down.

As we flew through the gathering dusk, I heard behind my seat a very faint rhythmic clicking sound. I thought there might be an avionics fault and wondered if I should alert the pilot. But then I realized that the clicking was the prayer beads of an elderly Arab gentleman in white robes in the front seat just behind. I later realized that the clicking frequency was an indicator of passenger nervousness, since it sped up with every bout of turbulence. By the time we got to Nairobi, darkness had fallen fully. There was no moon and a building fog.

As our young Australian pilot felt his way in over the Ngong Hills, a knuckle-like ridge west of the city, we could barely pick them out. We descended slowly. From my second pilot's seat, I spotted momentary smudges of street lights in the suburbs through the mottle of fog. As we descended, searching for landmarks, he was flying so slowly that the stall warning was beeping urgently.

Suddenly he reached under his seat, pulled out a flashlight, and handed it to me saying, "Keep this on the altimeter, mate, we've got no panel lights." I noted that he had said "we" and not "I." Somehow this seemed to implicate me in the endeavor to get us down on the ground. Ye Gods! I thought, *here he is trying to land at a closed airfield with no runway lights and he can't even see his instrument panel!* As I held the flashlight, he continued to feel his way in, the altimeter winding down. The prayer bead click rate behind me was rising.

The pilot and I were both straining to spot something recognizable. He seemed not to be using any instrument guidance, but I preferred not to confirm with him that that part of the system was also out of commission. Every now and again, he would mutter something under his breath. I was not sure whether to hope it was not a prayer or to hope that it was, but he didn't seem the praying type. Perhaps he was cursing our late passenger from Kisumu.

As we dropped lower, I thought I saw the Nairobi Game Park headquarters on my side and ahead of the aircraft and I pointed it out to him, suggesting that Wilson Airport should be about another mile further on and, I thought, a bit to the left. Sure enough, in a break in the fog, we started to be able to pick out the faint outline of a runway.

At that moment, his hand shot down and he slammed on full power. The engines screamed, and we banked steeply. I thought perhaps we had just missed another aircraft. He turned to me and murmured, "Always best to come in too high the first time." I gulped and nodded, still trying to concentrate on my job of holding the fading flashlight on the altimeter.

The old RAF Spitfire pilot's bragging line at the bar came briefly to mind, "...there I was upside down, nothing on the clock but the maker's name!" Recalling a gliding course in my youth, coming around again for a second shot was never an option; in a glider you had to get the approach right the first time or make the best of it with air-brakes and tricks like side-slipping. I thanked God for engines.

He lined up again and felt his way in on the same bearing, but at lower altitude. To my great relief, the runway again came briefly into fuzzy sight and then, shortly after, more clearly. Our pilot put us down a little off center for a fair landing. There was a collective exhaling as we taxied up to the unlit buildings. The place was deserted and in total darkness.

When I saw how much baggage came out of the inside of the aircraft and the wing lockers, I was surprised we had defied gravity for so long at such a hesitant speed. But I recalled his remark from a previous trip: "No worries, mate! In these aircraft, if you can close the doors and lockers, you're okay!"

I suspected that the aircraft manual was less gung-ho about that.

With an aviator father who flew open cockpit biplanes and operated off the first aircraft carriers, I have always had an admiration for those who venture aloft in heavier-than-air machines. Kenya produced several famous early bush pilots, including the crazy Beryl Markham, the first woman to fly the Atlantic solo, non-stop, East to West. (See her book *West with the Night*.)

Also living in Kenya was a well-known aviator of two World Wars, Air Commodore "Daddy" Probyn who, of course, knew Beryl well. The bar in the Aero Club at Nairobi's Wilson Airport is now named the Daddy Probyn Bar. His single-engine Jodel D9 is on display; my son Sinclair, on a recent visit to Kenya, saw it under renovation.

My father had served under Probyn at Number 11 Fighter Group at RAF Uxbridge at the start of the Second World War. During the First World War, Probyn had flown with No. 34 Squadron in the Royal Flying Corps in B.E.2 biplanes, doing many reconnaissance missions over enemy lines in the areas of Ypres and the Somme, often under heavy fire.

Interestingly, these aircraft were not designed to carry armament because the designers had not anticipated the need for aircraft to have to defend themselves; how war changes! In 1917, Probyn was awarded the Distinguished Service Order for conspicuous gallantry. Later, in 1943, as Commandant of the Royal Air Force College at Cranwell, a post my father later held, he was closely involved in supporting Frank Whittle in the early testing of the first British prototype jet aircraft.

My father recalled before the war being flown by him as a passenger in a Miles Magister two-seater single engine monoplane training aircraft through thick fog over London's docklands. To his alarm, my father glimpsed from the rear cockpit a dockland crane flit past and quickly reported to Probyn.

"Sir, I think we're a bit low. I just saw a dock crane above us on the starboard wing."

Probyn shouted back, "Don't worry, old boy, don't worry, I know this area well, we're alright through this gap here."

And indeed, they did make it safely back to base. The flight is recorded in my father's flying log.

During the late 1970s in Kenya, Probyn was said to be the oldest flying pilot in the world. I believe he continued flying until he was nearly ninety. We used to go to visit him at his house on the edge of a coffee plantation outside Nyeri, a town north of Nairobi. He had built his Jodel D9 himself from a kit, a French-designed single seater with a modified VW engine, two plugs per cylinder.

He was an ebullient character, always full of plans. During one of our visits with my father, Probyn was showing us a crumpled map of Kenya. He was jabbing his finger at a spot up in the Northern Frontier District, a place he had flown to the previous week. I peered at the map to spot a familiar name. I knew much of Kenya through my work and game viewing and had been through parts of that area. I said to him, "I didn't know there was an airstrip there!" He replied with a twinkle in his eye, "*They* don't know there's an airstrip there, but *I* know there's one!"

Once, his Jodel 9 was parked on the lawn for maintenance, which he mostly did himself. He got it there in sections. After my children, Jaime, Antonia, and Sinclair, had all taken a turn sitting in the cockpit, he offered to start it up. His cook stopped peeling potatoes and came out wiping his hands, wearing a white apron. With the aircraft well chocked and pegged to the lawn, he leaned into the empty cockpit and turned on the fuel tap and ignition switch. On the shouted command, his cook swung the prop. His apron flew up as the engine burst into life. It seemed to me to be quite dangerous for the person swinging the prop to be dressed in a chef's apron, but they seemed a well-practiced team.

Daddy Probyn was a memorable character and a great early aviator. And lucky. Many pilots did not survive the First World War. I knew a British lady who had ended up in Zimbabwe whose husband, just a few days after they were married, was shot down and killed on his very first combat mission over France in 1916. He had flown in action for about thirty minutes. Reconnaissance pilots had a somewhat better survival rate than combat pilots, but the worst month for British reconnaissance pilots was April 1917 when they had an average survival rate of 69 flying hours. And these were the ones that had lived through the hazardous flying training. For most of the war, casualties in training were even higher than casualties in combat.

CAMPFIRE YARNS
OF AFRICA

You know you are truly alive when you're living among lions.

– Karen Blixen[25]

Wildlife were a source of food and clothing for our hunter ancestors, an earlier species of which took its first bipedal steps on this continent. Our relationship with wildlife, while altered today by population density and the technologies of a super-charged brain, is still hard-wired into us.

Our behavior evolved partly in response to the behavior of wildlife, and wildlife behavior evolved partly in response to ours. We can learn from understanding them, as they have learned, less benignly, from trying to understand us. But that is the more serious side of the wildlife scene.

Campfire yarns are the lighter side, generally, and no doubt have been part of the African bush scene since those earliest humans, squatting outside their cave around the campfire, replayed the hunting of the day, especially the close encounters. These stories are organized by species and selected purely for interest. Grab a whisky and pull up a chair.

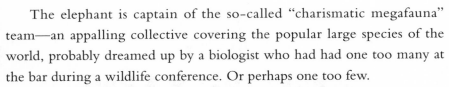

The elephant is captain of the so-called "charismatic megafauna" team—an appalling collective covering the popular large species of the world, probably dreamed up by a biologist who had had one too many at the bar during a wildlife conference. Or perhaps one too few.

Elephants, in certain respects, mirror our human social relationships within and between groups. They live in matriarch-led herds, sort of sub-clans, that have tight relationships internally and looser relationships with sub-clans sharing blood lines. The males we can largely ignore in looking at social bonding relationships, since most of the time they operate separately, either as loners or in loose male groups who compete to service females at breeding times.

Elephants are curious and playful. Douglas Chadwick, in his book *The Fate of the Elephant*,[26] reports an encounter by elephant researcher Joyce Poole who worked in Amboseli Park in Kenya. She told him how she was using string to mark out a vegetation sampling plot and described the elephants' reaction to discovering the squares of string pegged out on the ground as, "Omigod! There's a *string* in the environment!" The string became the happening of the day. There was a lot of trumpeting and fuss. Elephants do indeed show curiosity as well as other seemingly human traits.

Elephants have given campers many sleepless nights, but I have never heard of an elephant attacking a tent or walking through one by mistake. On one occasion, when camping in Tanzania at Lake Manyara, a large tusker was standing within a foot of a neighbor's tent. It was treating it as a solid barrier. The campers, who were familiar with African wildlife and were outside the tent at the time, were sensibly wary, standing back about a hundred yards.

After about ten minutes, the elephant picked up the foot nearest to the tent, turned slowly to the side, deftly missed clipping a thin guy rope, and ambled off. Left alone, and with no young to protect, elephants will generally go about their business without bothering you. But no large wildlife are reliably and completely safe, and a lone male elephant in *musth,* with testosterone raging, or a female with a calf, should always be assumed to be potentially dangerous.

One elephant story passed on to me was about an English woman who I had known briefly many years earlier. She was working in Uganda in the 1970s. As I heard it, she was camping with her boyfriend in Queen Elizabeth National Park.

During the night, she woke up and found she couldn't sit up because there was something heavy on her hair. She had a pony tail, I think, and it had been lying straight out on the tent floor behind her pillow. She nudged her companion awake. He unzipped the tent, peered outside, and saw a large bull elephant standing up against the back of the tent.

A fold of the tent canvas had gone over her hair and the elephant's foot was planted firmly on it with her hair trapped in the fold. There was a frenzied but whispered discussion. They were not sure whether to tug it out, make a noise, or stay completely still and quiet. Which way would it move when it lifted its foot? They decided to make a timid, not-too-aggressive noise to confirm that they were there. The elephant, no doubt familiar with campers, calmly lifted its foot, reversed backward, and ambled off, leaving her shaken, but with an unbeatable story that has been doing the rounds for years.

Speaking of elephant feet, a trivia digression: There is a well-known formula for Asian elephants—well-known, that is, to the *mahouts,* the elephant riders/trainers, of India, but less well-known in Africa. The height of an elephant at the top of the shoulder blade is exactly twice the circumference of one of its front feet. In other words, feet are proportional to height or vice versa. It makes sense. I have measured this myself on a trained Asian elephant, but not on an African elephant, since few have been trained—and I value my longevity. There may be a small relative difference between the African and Asian in this ratio, but I doubt it is much.

I once met a young woman who tragically, a few days earlier, had seen her boyfriend killed in front of her by an elephant. They had been filming elephants in a Uganda national park in the mid-1970s. If I recall the story correctly, he had set up a movie camera on a tripod some distance in front of their Land Rover.

A herd of elephants with young had become agitated. The matriarch made a mock charge towards them several times, but stopped short. They both retreated to their vehicle to let them settle down. After about half an hour, he decided they had moved away and calmed down sufficiently for him to retrieve his camera. He went forward on foot. The matriarch spotted him, charged, caught him, threw him to the ground and trampled him. He had underestimated how fast an elephant can react and move.

Elephants have been shown, sometimes, to have protective feelings towards humans. One of the classic stories, which I first heard in the New Stanley Hotel bar in Nairobi, was about a herder on Kuki Gallmann's ranch in Laikipia, in Kenya. It is told also in Joyce Poole's book *Coming of Age with Elephants*.[27]

As I heard it, a camel herder was charged and knocked down by an angry matriarch elephant who broke his leg. When the camels came back to the ranch yards for the night on their own without their herder, the staff knew something had happened. A night search failed to find him. At first light, they headed out and eventually found him sitting by a tree with a female elephant protecting him. They had difficulty approaching.

She was guarding him and charging to keep them away. They thought they were going to have to shoot her to get close enough to him to pick him up, but the injured herdsman signaled for them not to. The manager shot over her head, which scared her away enough for them to drive in and get him.

Later, the herder described how, after he had been injured and the matriarch and family had moved off, his protector who stayed had, with her trunk and foot, gently moved him under the shade of the tree. She had stayed to protect him through the afternoon and night and into the morning. At one point, she had even chased away some threatening buffalo.

One can deduce that this female would have been related to the matriarch, but lower in the hierarchy, and would have had no calf to care for. Remarkably, she had been prepared to separate herself from her herd when they moved on and had remained to protect him.

You will have heard that an elephant never forgets. This seems to be true. An escaped, trained working elephant in India many years ago was seen fifteen years later running with the wild elephants in the forest. He was recognized by one of the mahouts while he and a fellow mahout were out on their elephants in the forest. The mahout got off his elephant, went up to the escaped elephant and ordered it to kneel for him to the mounting position.

It did so, and he climbed up and rode it back to camp. It recalled all the commands it had learned so long ago. Perhaps it was not smart to obey the orders and lose its freedom or perhaps it was not so averse to a working life. But it certainly had remarkable recall of the commands.

So what about facing elephants and other wild animals? Well, get local advice. In all animal confrontations, not showing fear is important. But when I once commented to an Indian elephant specialist that, in confronting a threatening animal, one should show no fear, he corrected me. He said, "It is not just that you must *show* no fear, you must *have* no fear. And *that* is a very different thing. Wild animals can tell when you are acting." I immediately acknowledged that he was right, even though actually having no fear is a tall order. Animals have an uncanny ability to spot the expedient thespian.

But what should you do when faced with an aggressive elephant? Well, again, ask local experts because, with elephants especially, the history of past human interaction in that area will be much more important than the typical behavior of the species.

If you are in a vehicle, you should stay inside and plan an escape route for the vehicle where you will not get stuck or blocked by an obstruction. A steady revving build-up of the engine sometimes works as a deterrent, but some guides warn against foot-pumping revving, which may sound too aggressive.

But what if somehow you ended up facing an elephant on foot? If it seems threatening, initially stand your ground—and then walk away backward. If it mock charges with ears out, head held high, and trunk raised, it will stop short. You can encourage it to do so by standing your ground and repeating, "Steady, steady, steady," or some other soothing words.

If the elephant is trying to make itself look bigger, it's a mock display. If it is coming at you with intent to do harm it will have given up trying to look big; it will have its ears back, head down, and trunk lowered or curled backward—the efficient charging conformation. You will not outrun it. A real charge has very rarely been downgraded to a mock charge. Once the fury button has been pressed, it seems it is very hard for an elephant to reset it. Unless there is an easy large tree to climb up, or a large obstacle like a building or truck to get into or behind, you should stand and face it and yell and scream. Make yourself big and aggressive with the help of a tree branch or backpack. Try throwing things.

I know of one rare case where a camera thrown at an elephant's forehead turned it away from an injured woman tourist. If an elephant gets you, your chances are small, but playing dead until it loses interest has, I believe, sometimes worked.

But let me now confess. Despite, or rather *because of*, a lifetime's interest in elephants, I am a believer in shooting them—at least under certain circumstances. Briefly, the elephant population problem in Africa is that in the few countries (about five) that can adequately protect their elephants, there are too many elephants in many of their parks. The weight of the evidence shows that an increasing elephant population does not start to level off and decline due to loss of nutrition from over-population until after vegetation and soils have been seriously damaged—in most cases irreversibly.

For example, Kruger Park in South Africa is carrying about three times the number of elephants it should carry. Consequently, in some parts, the large canopy trees are down by over 90% of their density from fifty years ago. This tree loss takes with it a great deal of biodiversity, the loss of other animals and plants. Elephant populations at this level are unsustainable; a collapse of the ecosystem is inevitable.

The problem is that elephants rarely now live in unconstrained range; the option of long-distance migration to avoid over-stressing rangelands has long ago been closed off by human settlement that cannot now be undone. The elephant population problem in these high-density parks is already being compounded by the climate change drying trend in Southern Africa which is expected to create even more stress in the coming years.

Due to their social structure, the least socially disruptive way to control elephant numbers is to wipe out a whole herd in a single operation—adults, teenagers, and babies, because moving them together, on a large scale, has so far proved too expensive. It's a nasty business and, however well done, causes horrible (although brief) trauma, usually a minute or two.

This suffering must be weighed against the alternative of taking the do-nothing approach; watching nature take its unforgiving course. The natural destruction of a herd is a slow and painful movie of collapsed calves finally abandoned by desperate mothers, weakened individuals dropping back one by one, and the last surviving herd member standing under a tree alone in a drought-devastated landscape, her calf and all her family gone, getting weaker by the day until the legs finally crumple.

In the end, hard-headed realism, drawing from the weight of the eco-system evidence and looking at the impact on all species, could save the elephant and its associated fauna and flora. Soft-headed sentimentality, putting off population reduction measures to placate animal welfare pressures until it is too late, will lead to the elephants' demise, taking numerous other species down with them. I doubt that the right course will be taken. I think in another hundred years, elephants will be mainly zoo or boutique park animals. We will have loved them to death.

Apologies to *Lion King* enthusiasts, but the lion is *not* the king of the jungle—the tiger is. Lions rarely live in what is generally considered "jungle," although the Hindi word *jungli* can mean either a forested type of jungle or a more open savanna. Lions are adapted to hunt cooperatively in relatively open country. Tigers are adapted to hunt alone, in or near denser vegetation. Lion and tiger would never actually meet in their natural habitat today. There are no tigers in Africa and, in India, where there are tigers, the last population of the Asiatic lion is only found in the *Gir* Forest in Gujarat—where there are no tigers.

The lion as king over the tiger is also improbable in terms of strength. The Romans did put them against each other in combat for public entertainment. It was said to be one-sided, the tiger usually winning. But presumably, the lion sometimes prevailed—otherwise the Roman audiences would have asked for their *denarii* back. Perhaps they followed a boxing weight rule to even out the contest; tigers being generally heavier. In occasional accidental fights in zoos, tigers have usually been the victor. The tiger has a powerful front paw that can rip a jugular vein with one swipe. Nevertheless, the lion is a fascinating social animal and more interesting because of it.

I was once camping out in the bush in Kenya in the early 1970s on a bird-hunting trip with a friend, Hugh Sterling. I was the "beater," stirring up guinea fowl and yellow-necked francolin for him to shoot at.

We had reserved a hunting block on the plains below Mount Kilimanjaro. On the first morning, he was standing with his shotgun at the ready, about five hundred yards from me. The nineteen-thousand-foot-high, snow-capped mountain rose magnificently as a backdrop. I was advancing through the bush, slashing at thorn bushes with a long stick, trying to persuade guinea fowl to take to the air. They are not easy birds to beat into flight, preferring to scurry around on the ground unless really pushed.

I went up to a large overhanging acacia bush where I thought I had seen movement and gave the branches a slashing hit with my stick. A lion shot out, running away from me and towards Hugh, who was scanning the sky for birds so at first didn't even spot the animal heading straight towards him.

When he saw it, his eyes turned to saucers, but he kept his cool. He quickly broke his shotgun to unload his bird shot and stuff in a couple of "heavies" from his cartridge belt for defense. But by the time he had the gun reloaded, the lion had raced past him and was gone in the direction of the mountain. We sat down in the dirt, broke into nervous laughter and had a long swig of whisky from his flask.

That evening, with only one bird to show for our effort, we were having our evening drink by the campfire. Just before dusk, a lone Maasai man walked up and, after a mumbled greeting, stood leaning on his staff about twenty yards away. He watched us for about half an hour, as locals in Africa often do; not rudeness, just an unblinking, nothing-better-to-do, curiosity.

Eventually, we asked him, partly as a hint, whether he was going to stand there all night. He replied as he turned to leave that he was going home because "the simba is walking tonight." And, indeed, we did hear the simba most of the night roaring in our area, once very close to our tents.

Africans say that the lion is roaring in Swahili "Nchi ya nani? Yangu! Yangu! Yangu!" Whose land is this? Mine! Mine! Mine! Whether this was the same lion we had disturbed earlier in the day there was no way of telling.

A lion's roar at night can be deceptive. My rule has always been, if you only *think* that the lion might be close, it is almost certainly still quite far off, say a mile or two. When it is truly close, you will not just *think* it is close, you will *know* it is. In fact, you will *feel* it. (By the way, a good way to try to scare away a lion at night is by the quick flashing of a flashlight.)

I have been in tents and thatched huts on several occasions with lions very close—once, just outside the tent canvas—but I have never met anyone who reported a lion ripping open a tent and attacking someone inside. While it may be hard to sleep when you can hear a nearby lion patrolling his territory, you are very safe, provided there are no known habituated man-eaters in the area.

I have a photo that I took of a foam camping mattress sticking out of a collapsed tent with a lion claw rip in the foam. But this tent had been trashed by lions *after* the campers had left. It happened at an unfenced camping spot above the Chania Falls in the Aberdare National Park in Kenya in about 1976.

On signing in at the park gate that day to go trout fishing, the ranger had told me to be careful. I thought this was odd, since he knew me as a regular. He said there had been a bit of a problem the previous night with some lions, but he was reticent to discuss what had happened. Reaching the falls, on an open grassy patch by the river, I spotted a mangled tent with twisted tent poles and shredded canvas. The foam mattress was sticking out with a perfect claw mark in it. Later, I heard the full story:

An expatriate family had been camping there and during the night, some lions had come close to the tent; unusually bold. The family was scared, so when the lions moved away a little, they made a dash for their car. They drove up to the park gate and spent the rest of the night in one of the empty staff quarters. At some point during the night, the lions must have jumped on the tent and destroyed it. They would never have jumped on it if the family had still been inside. But once they had vacated, the lions considered it fair game for some fun. They were probably young males, familiar with people and perhaps recently relocated for having caused problems in a populated area.

I was a little more wary that day when I was trout fishing, especially upstream from that spot where there were bands of dense streamside bushes. But I did not come across them.

The leopard is the most skilled hunter in Africa, hunting alone with remarkable agility, using stealth to creep up on its prey before the final leap. They have even been known to take a medium-sized crocodile in the water. But, as we witnessed one evening in Botswana, they can miss a kill like any other carnivore.

In this case, the leopard failed in an attempt on a big male impala, failing to get a good enough grip on his neck. She slid off and walked away, resigned to her failure. The male impala, emboldened in his victory, stood his ground, turned, faced the retreating leopard, and snorted fiercely. Probably, the leopard had failed because our sudden arrival had broken her focus for a moment.

All hunting cats have a high failure rate. Leopards are generally the most successful large cat, with a success rate between about fifteen and forty percent; an average of about one in four attempts. Evolution has closely matched hunter and prey by giving them countervailing skills. An impala's horns can be lethal, and its speed and turn are a good defense. Every kill by a leopard entails risk. She reduces that risk by also eating easier smaller prey like young warthogs, mice and dung beetles.

Peter Jenkins, the Game Warden at Meru National Park in Kenya in the 1970s, told me a story about an expatriate family's encounter with a leopard at Ngulia Lodge in Tsavo West National Park, on the edge of the steep Ndewe escarpment. In those days, there were just three or four quite basic thatched *bandas* at this low-budget lodge, not the large safari lodge that is near there today. It was a perfect site for a view over the plains, with the bandas clinging to the side of the escarpment.

On the first night of the family's stay, a leopard started to make aggressive efforts to get in. It first tried windows and doors. Then it leaped onto the roof and started ripping at the roof. The family was terrified, but the leopard never got in. They left the next morning, heading for a less exciting night at one of the larger lodges.

Later that morning, the two lodge servants were sitting and talking on the verandah of one of the bandas. Without warning, the leopard sprung from some bushes below. In one movement, it took the nearest man by the head and dragged him off through the brush down the rocky hillside. It happened so fast that, as the other man later described it, he just saw a flash of yellow.

But he acted quickly to help his friend. He grabbed an old piece of iron water pipe that lay against a wall and ran down the hill after the leopard. He caught up with it about a hundred yards down the hill, still dragging his friend by the head. He gave it a whack across its back with the pipe. It let out a snarl, dropped the man, and ran off into the bush. Surprisingly, the man survived, although his face was badly chewed up.

This leopard had been one that had caused trouble in some villages up near Lake Victoria in the west of Kenya and had been relocated. Reportedly, during the relocation trip, it had been taunted in its cage on the truck by some men who had hitched a ride. So perhaps it had a grudge against humans. But it's more likely that the main reason for its aggression was that it was struggling to make a living in its new, more arid, environment, having grown up on Easy Street, snatching goats and dogs from farms.

In this case of relocation, the leopard seemed to have remained in its new location. Frequently, they find their way back home. Peter Jenkins was once sent a problem leopard in Meru Game Park that found its way back to Western Kenya, about two hundred miles away, within a few weeks. They are skilled navigators.

Here, I indulge in a brief detour to England. Other than perhaps the plump Cheshire cat of *Alice in Wonderland*, England has had no indigenous large cats in recent millennia. But in the 1960s, there were rumors of a puma roaming the rural areas of the county of Surrey, southwest of London. These reports had always seemed to me to be implausible. Like so many strange beast and Bigfoot reports, nobody ever seemed to be able to produce a photograph, a spoor print, or fur.

In 1964, I was living with my grandmother in the village of Lynchmere, near Haslemere, in Surrey, close to the commercial company I worked for at the time. One winter morning, with snow on the ground, she woke me up quite flustered and told me to come quickly.

I threw on a dressing gown and went to her room. She showed me a large footprint in the snow on the brick wall of her bedroom balcony. It was an upstairs balcony, only accessible from her room through double glass doors. There was no snow on the floor of the balcony because it had a roof over it and what little may have blown in must have melted the day before.

The single, clear, cat-type footprint on the balcony wall faced outwards, away from the house. It was not a large dog; it was not the right shape for a dog. In any case, no dog could have leaped onto a balcony that was sixteen feet from ground level. The only alternative hypothesis to a large cat-type animal that I could come up with was that a sparrow had replicated a paw-shaped pattern by sitting in several adjacent positions. It seemed highly unlikely. Even the ridges between the pads were perfectly formed.

The obvious test to eliminate the fidgety sparrow hypothesis was to see if the same footprints were in the snow on the lawn below. I hurried downstairs and there they were, huge, cat-type spoor with no claws evident as would have been the case if it was a dog. And immediately below the balcony, I found four deep imprints close together surrounded by disturbed snow. This must have been where it had landed, heavily.

It was clearly the Surrey puma. There was no other animal that could make such huge prints or leap clear up to a balcony without touching the balcony wall on the way in. It must have checked the place out as a potential lair, rejected it, and then put one foot on the balcony wall as it jumped down. I followed the large tracks across the lawn and along the side of the road for about a mile. I called a friend as a witness.

A few days after a letter I wrote to a UK newspaper about this incident had been published, I received a letter from a woman living in the north of England in the Lake District, an area renowned, at the time, for witches and weirdos. In spidery handwriting, she warned me that a spirit was after my grandmother and that I should, "Lock her up and keep her very safe because this spirit has assumed animal form and needs to drink human blood to stay in matter for a time."

We never saw evidence of the puma again, although if it had returned without snow and curled up there for the night it would have left no trace. Perhaps it was a regular visitor. Despite the vampire spirits I had been warned of, my grandmother lived to a ripe old age and as far as I know never involuntarily gave blood!

There is no reliable data on the number of people killed in Africa by different animal species. You will hear from guides almost every animal with teeth, tusks, or horns touted as the most successful predator of Homo sapiens. Of course, if we count humans killed by anything from the animal kingdom, then the *mosquito*, along with its parasitic malarial organism, takes the prize. But for what we usually refer to as wildlife, crocodiles certainly have a claim to be the winner, although deaths have undoubtedly declined with the improvement in village water supply and less need to collect water from, or do laundry in, rivers.

Crocodiles have been widely hunted in Africa for their skins, although today a lot come from farms. I once knew a European colonial character in Zambia who, some years earlier, had been a professional crocodile hunter on the Zambezi River. He had an African employee and they hunted from a small aluminum boat with a small outboard. I forget the type and caliber of the rifle he used, but he carried a flashlight to spot with.

Many crocodile hunters liked to have a light mounted on a headband, leaving two hands free to fire. But this man preferred to hold the flashlight in his left hand and shoot the rifle using only his right hand. It allowed him to swing the light back and forth while holding his aim. He must have had a steady right arm and strong wrist.

He would start hunting around eleven at night and would work his way down the river, shooting any that were big enough. Once a croc was shot, he and his helper would grab it and rope it to the side of the boat before it sank or was carried away in the current. They would bring it to the bank, pull it up, and leave it hidden under bushes, out of sight of predators, and with some chance of morning shade.

They would carry on down the river, shooting, until dawn, then head back up the river, skinning each one in turn and putting the skins into the boat. The skinning of the last of them had to be completed before the temperature became too high, otherwise the carcasses would quickly rot, leaving the skin spoiled and worthless.

One night when he was hunting, he heard a bloodcurdling howl about half a mile down the river. He had never heard a sound quite like it before. He carried on down the river, shooting several big ones. On the way back, while skinning a large one in the general area where he had heard the earlier howl, he found an undigested adult lion's foreleg in the croc's stomach. This was clearly the source of the howl. The lion must have come down to the river to drink and the crocodile must have slid quietly through the water, launched itself at the lion, and taken off one of its front legs. A lion with a missing leg would find it difficult to hold a place in a pride or to defend itself against hyenas, the lion's arch-enemy.

I did once see a three-legged lion cub about three months old in Ngorongoro Crater in Tanzania which had probably lost its leg to a hyena. It looked healthy and was being well-tended by its mother and the pride, but I never heard how it fared into adulthood. Generally, nature is unforgiving to the maimed, though I have heard of one or two cases of fully-grown, three-legged male lions that have managed quite well.

In the mid-1970s, an expatriate family in Kenya had a nasty encounter with a crocodile. They were in Samburu Game Park, a dry area of riverside acacias, bush and grasses bounded on one side by the Ewaso Ng'iro River and, in the distance, a ridge of hills. They were doing what many visitors there did on a hot day, taking a dip in a shaded, natural, spring-fed pool about thirty feet in diameter about half a mile from the river.

As I heard the story—and having received it second-hand, I may have some of the detail wrong—their eight-year-old son was swimming in the pool alone while the others were getting ready to join him. As the boy was swimming across the pool, a crocodile that had come up from the river slid out from among the boulders, grabbed him by the leg and started to drag him under. It was not a big crocodile, though quite big enough.

The boy's mother was standing nearby when he screamed. She managed to immediately grab one of his arms. Hanging on, she shouted to another woman who ran quickly to the car, grabbed a *panga* (machete), ran back and started desperately slashing at the side of the crocodile's head. I believe someone else ran up and hung onto her waist to stop her from being pulled in. As the woman slashed at it, the crocodile let go, but it grabbed him again across his middle. She kept slashing and finally the crocodile let go and sank below the water.

I believe one of the women was a nurse. She was able to clean him up and patch his wounds. He was in hospital for many weeks. The wounds went septic due to the bacteria on the teeth of the crocodile. But gradually, the various antibiotics that they administered gained on the infection.

About six months later, I saw the young man splashing around at the edge of Lake Naivasha, at the sailing club. I would have expected him to be nervous about water after his ordeal, although there were no crocodiles in the crater lake at Naivasha. He was a brave young man with a determined mother. And very lucky.

The Cape Buffalo is no mean foe for a hunter. This is not your placid Indian water buffalo that wallows at the edges of flooded rice paddies. As novelist Robert Ruark described them, "A buffalo looks at you like you owe him money."

For some hunters, that glare has been their last. Ruark also wrote that you could kill a buffalo with one shot—but if you didn't, the next fourteen would serve mostly as a minor irritant. Hyperbole perhaps, but when wounded, they are known to be doggedly determined to stay on their feet long enough to take revenge.

Some hunters have feared the buffalo more than lion or elephant. Others say that their danger has been somewhat overstated. I have never shot African wildlife, other than helping my bird-shooting friend once. (I just don't feel comfortable shooting wild animals just for the challenge or brag-ging rights. You can get an adrenalin rush just walking unarmed near them when game observing or trout fishing.) However, I do place buffalo high on my list of animals to keep an eye on, particularly for a shift of mood.

I had an encounter with a buffalo on the slopes of Mount Kenya that quickened the pulse. I was fly fishing for trout on a small forest stream, casting from an outcrop of rock about fifteen feet above the river. I was alone. I hadn't noticed that I had been standing on a nest of safari ants. They bite fiercely. In an uncanny way they seem to coordinate. They crawl up stealthily inside and outside your clothing and then it seems as though a leader somehow gives a signal and they all bite at the same moment.

Suddenly, I felt the stinging bites all over my body. I flung my rod on the ground, ripped off my trousers, and opened my shirt. I was leaping around trying to pick the ants off when I spotted a buffalo glaring at me about thirty yards away, in a clearing.

Since my escape route was blocked on three sides by rocks, dense bushes and a cutaway river bank, to get away meant initially moving towards the buffalo before turning away onto the track upstream. Grabbing my fishing rod and my ant-covered trousers, and wearing only my unbuttoned shirt and underpants, I cautiously walked towards it and then crabbed sideways, keeping my eyes on it all the way.

It lowered its head at one point and snorted. I paused for a minute and murmured something soothing like, "Piss off, mate." Then I sidled around, watching it the entire time as I retreated up the track. It watched warily but did not come after me.

Safely back on the dirt road at my car, it took me half an hour to pick the ants out. They were latched deep in my beard, inside my underpants and under my shirt. While I was performing this delicate operation, a local farmer came walking past with his *jembe*, his hoe, on his shoulder. I thought he would find the sight of a *mzungu*—a white man—leaping around on the road in nothing but his underpants amusing. But he politely greeted me with a *jambo* as though he witnessed such scenes every day.

This was the wonderful African politeness for you. But perhaps he doubled up with laughter when he got around the bend out of sight! No doubt it became a story back at the village that night.

On a similar riverside track on the slopes of Mt. Kenya, again while trout fishing, I had a more frightening encounter; in this case with Homo sapiens. Five young men, about seventeen years old, all carrying *pangas*, suddenly emerged from the forest along the river. Their leader came up to me quite aggressively and asked me what time it was. This was not good because most rural Africans in Kenya know perfectly well what time of day it is since they are close to the equator and the sun gives accurate enough time.

He clearly wanted a better look at my watch. I looked at it and told him in Swahili what time it was. He remarked that I had a nice watch, very pointedly touching it on the glass face with the flat of his *panga*. He rejoined his group and they hung around about thirty yards away, talking to each other in low tones.

I pretended to change a trout fly, keeping one eye on them. I generally give people the benefit of the doubt, but I am not foolhardy, and it seemed they were trying to decide whether to chop me for my watch and my money and whatever else I might be carrying. I decided it was time to get back up the track to my car.

I chose a route that I thought would avoid having them walking behind me, but they took a detour through the forest and ended up following me anyway. It was a twenty-minute walk. I ran through several options. As I walked, I kept an eye on the ground for suitable fallen branches as defense, but I realized there was little I could do against five *pangas*.

This was long before cell phones, and there was no help within many miles. A body could easily have been hidden in the forest for leopards to clean up. I considered what downsides they might face if they killed me. Very few. Their chances of getting away with it were good. One option was to throw my watch, my cash, and my bits of fishing gear widely scattered across the forest floor, so they had to scramble for them—and then make a run for it.

But their leader knew I had got a very close look at his face, and if given the opportunity, I would surely talk. I walked with my eight-foot fly rod pointing straight back towards them to make it more difficult for them to jump me from behind without warning. I kept my other hand deep in my safari jacket pocket, clutching my old, leather-sheathed Norwegian fish filleting knife which I had been able to work free from its sheath inside my pocket. I hoped that my hand in my bulging pocket might make them think I was carrying a revolver and I tried to make it look big with my fist. But they would almost certainly have known that no one like me would carry a gun. This was a national park and carrying a weapon was illegal.

It seemed an interminable walk to the car, but I reached it without incident. I had rehearsed in my mind every move as I approached it and very quickly opened the door, threw my rod in, climbed in, locked the doors, and started the engine with a roar. As I drove away they stood watching me. Either they had concluded that I was not worth the risk, or my fears were entirely unfounded. They may have realized that I would likely be carrying little of value other than my quite ordinary watch. Fishing gear would have been of little interest to them. If they poached for trout it would have been with a plant poison or a short stick with a few feet of nylon, a hook, and a live grub; gear easily obtained and cheap. And actual car theft was out of their league.

But for all I knew they may have been just good, honest boys—well, *somewhat* honest—heading home from an illegal forest plot of chewing *khat* (a stimulant shrub more commonly grown further round the mountain), or from the site of an illegally-felled hardwood tree lying over a dug pit for operating a two-man pit-saw. I had come across tree-felling sites before in that area when taking a short cut over a ridge.

Like the buffalo, the hippo is not to be trifled with. Three people were killed by a hippo very recently in Kenya at Lake Naivasha. Some people claim that they kill more people than any other animal. I doubt that, but they can certainly be very aggressive. They may look like they have an obesity problem but, as I once witnessed in Northern Zambia, leaving my banda for an evening pee, they are deceptively fast.

This one, which fortunately I surprised more than it surprised me, did the hundred yards to the lake much faster than I ever could have run. They can hit about twenty-five miles per hour; humans can run up to twenty-seven. Usain Bolt might outrun an old one for a short burst—but even he would be foolish to take the risk of having to.

Once, racing a sailing dinghy on Lake Victoria, leading the race by one boat length, with my wife at the time, Anne, crewing, we saw hippos ahead. If you sailed near them regularly you knew your own "rafts" of hippos and learned which had calves. So, our opponent from the home club who was close on our tail had the home field advantage. I knew if I gave them a wide berth, and if he cut them very close, he would win the race. I kept an eye on him behind me, but mostly I kept an eye on the hippos.

We were sailing fast in a good wind and when we were twenty yards short, we pulled the center board up and slid around the hippos, crabbing sideways a little. There was nothing I could do about the rudder sticking down two feet; I had to be able to steer. Looking behind me, I was happy to see that our opponent was giving them about the same margin, so we crossed the finish line a couple of yards ahead of him.

At our Lake Naivasha club, the hippos sometimes damaged our boat jetties, treading on them or, more often, scratching against them. It takes a tough jetty to stand up to a hippo; a big male can weigh as much as nine thousand pounds. Surprisingly, giraffes can also damage sailing dinghies.

In our worst giraffe altercation, a big giraffe had started "necking" with the mast of a sailing dinghy on a parked trailer. ("Necking" is the male giraffes' ritual contest when they cross necks with an opponent repeatedly to establish dominance.) This one got its head caught under the shrouds—

the cables supporting the mast. Feeling the wire restraining its neck, it panicked and pulled back, dragging one of our boats off its trailer and across several other boats, smashing them quite badly. The giraffe was able to get its head free and was not hurt at all. It must have learned a lesson that sailing dinghies were unsuitable necking contest partners because it never came back to try it again.

PROFILES OF POVERTY

We think sometimes that poverty is only being hungry, naked, and homeless. The poverty of being unwanted, unloved, and uncared for is the greatest poverty.

– Mother Teresa

I cannot claim any greater understanding of poverty than many others in my field, but I suppose that we speak to more poor people than most casual travelers. I have learned that you generally know poverty when you see it but that you may not easily see it if you are unfamiliar with the signs.

Poverty hides well—especially if we help it to. This is particularly so when the poverty arises from lack of rights to assets like land, which is not always obvious at first encounter, or when it arises from lack of time to perform necessary tasks, like women's time to collect water, cultivate, gather fuel or prepare food. If you should choose to delve deeper, Robert Chambers,[28] one of our gurus, has written better than anyone about reading poverty in the field.

One of the most telling anecdotes about poverty came from Mother Teresa. If I remember correctly, she came across a young girl on a Calcutta (now Kolkata) street who was destitute and very hungry. She handed her a chunk of bread. The girl ate some of it, but then stood there holding it, not eating any more. Mother Teresa encouraged her and asked, "Why are you not eating?" The girl replied, "I'm not sure if I will get any more tomorrow. I want to save some. I want something to look forward to tomorrow."

This is the type of wrenching dilemma of destitution.

In India, in the 1990s, I sometimes travelled by train from Delhi to the East or the South. Join me at one pre-dawn departure. I am sitting, waiting, my train delayed, in the end, for nearly three hours. Across the next track, three boys of about twelve, ten and eight years old, are waking up. They have spent the night sleeping on a concrete slab between the tracks. Perhaps they are brothers.

I am surprised that they have been sleeping on the ground; many prefer to go higher to stay away from toe-nibbling rats. As they awaken, they stretch like cats, one limb at a time. They shuffle over to a water jar hanging on a signal post and drink. The older one heads off, walking along the track, then probably, out of my sight, skipping across the tracks between trains. Perhaps he has gone to a street food kiosk.

The kiosk owners often cut deals with street children, looking after their money, for a cut of course, giving them protection from gangs and police, and using them for cleaning jobs or errands. Soon, the boy is back with an old rice bag. He takes out some wrapped food that looks like last night's rice, dry and crumbly; not much for three. They eat hungrily with right hands, there is banter and laughter, the older two poking at the youngest, one of them giving him a cuff on the head.

Just before the morning crowds build, the older two cross over to my platform and disappear. I read for a while as the younger boy sits waiting. Soon, they return with a plastic bag and three head-baskets They open a newspaper, just one double spread, and the older boy tears it skillfully into rectangles with a piece of straight-edge board. They pull out a large bag of peanuts, spread them on paper, pick out some debris, and roll neat cones, filling each with peanuts.

They close each one with a push and a twist of the wrist. They stack their head-baskets with the peanut cones, raise them carefully onto their heads, and cross to the platform to start their long day of working the trains. Someone near me in the carriage buys one from the youngest boy through a window. Ten rupees. I figure they probably gross about 300 rupees a day, but net much less after costs, bribes and protection payments. Enough to survive, but little more.

Competition is fierce. Seven or eight sellers jostle at the window, survival of the fittest. An argument erupts about the poaching of territory. The younger boys are at a disadvantage on strength but gain on agility, ducking under outstretched arms and offering beaming white smiles to lure customers, especially women and tourists.

So here, playing out on this concrete slab, is a life of sorts. There are reportedly about fifty thousand street children in Delhi today. If they are not orphans, there will be parents back in the home village or in a Delhi slum; a family decision made that these children must fend for themselves and send home savings. Schooling is impossible; that would mean lost earnings. There may be sisters back at home helping out. They will soon need dowry money to marry. Hopefully they are not also on the streets in Delhi plying a sex trade.

On cold winter nights, these boys will make a meagre fire of twigs, trash, and dry dung outside the station in the corner of an abandoned walled building yard, a local toilet enclosure, a squatting area. In monsoon and summer, even into the night, there will be a stifling heat along with untreated sores that come with humidity.

Hunger is not always the main problem; Sikh temples, *gurdwara*, offer free food to the poor and homeless. But there are other problems than hunger. They face the risk of getting hooked on sniffing glue, although these three boys seem to have avoided it so far. You can generally spot the sniffers; lethargic, skinny, coughing, nose bleeds. There are also railway station pimps and touts ready to offer alternative lines of work. Whatever the occupation, there is always a trust problem. To make it, you need street-smarts and wariness.

But paradoxically, there can be a heady freedom in this life, too. Some street children, enticed off the streets by NGOs and offered shelter, food, and education, miss the freedom and camaraderie of their street community and return to their old life.

But shift focus, now, to poverty in Africa. One of the great myths about poverty is that most poor people live in permanent abject misery. Those who really know poor villages in Africa generally find that the poor, even the destitute, often can be found smiling and laughing despite what to us in the "rich" world would be unthinkable deprivation.

As my good friend Stephen Carr, who wrote a wonderful book, *Surprised by Laughter,*[29] has observed, even in desperately poor villages in Malawi with high AIDS fatalities, where he and his wife Anne live and work to help the rural poor, there is often drumming, dancing, and laughing. And always there are the inevitable village soccer games.

Those who have been surprised by such signs of merriment alongside the sadness and worry are not saying that people in poverty have no wish, even desperation, to live more easily. The "hungry gap"—that period after the last grains of maize have been cooked and eaten and before the next crop is harvested—is a time of hardship and uncertainty, a time for harvesting wild foods, and a time for tapping into a fragile network of reciprocal obligations among friends and relatives. Such times are no light matter. But still, they can include times of contentment, acceptance and laughter, given some extended family support and the right state of mind.

And for some families, poverty is *not* a permanent condition. It is something they fall into and out of as fortunes change, perhaps through human disease, livestock disease, drought, conflict, or just a government messing up.

There is also a different form of hunger; a hunger for self-esteem. This was Mother Teresa's point. I recall, some years ago, speaking with a farming family in Bangladesh who farmed on the far side from the capital of a recently-built bridge over the Jumuna River.

They explained how a combination of the bridge, better roads, and an agricultural and marketing support project had given them easier access to the lucrative vegetable market in Dhaka city and the capacity to supply it from their increasingly intensive one-acre plot. They had been very poor, but now they sent vegetables to market twice a week through a community trucking arrangement. Their active cooperative group had gained bargaining power against the wholesale sharks. It had transformed their lives. They described the changes as much in terms of social status as in terms of income or food.

Showing me their well-tended vegetable crops, they summed it up by saying, "Before the bridge and the project, we worried about how we were going to marry off our three daughters, we were so poor. We were nobody people. Nobody respected us. Now good families are lining up at our door for their sons to marry our daughters. We can even pick and choose."

As I write of later about India, women are the key to winning the battle against rural poverty. They provide much of the labor on farms. They nurture the rising generation. They collect water and firewood, often from many miles away. They prepare the meals. They decide what morsel of green relish they can afford to add to the carbohydrate dish to add a dash of variety, meat usually being out of the question. They husband the shrinking grain supply.

Poor communities have many different types of individuals, they are never homogenous. I once visited a community in Africa that was being provided donor support to improve the management of an area of communally-owned, semi-arid woodland, including some dryland farming plots.

Meeting under a thorn tree, it became apparent that there were wide differences of view about how the common land should be managed. There were farmers who saw the woodland as potential land for food crops if you cleared some of the trees and scrub. There were part-time hunters who saw it as a refuge for wildlife and who saw the farmers, at least too many of them, as a problem. They wanted to practice mosaic burning, burning patches to attract game to the green flush that comes after a burn. This would not be good for those who collected dry grass and herbs.

There were families who exploited the more remote forest for small timber and for charcoal burning; this was good for them but bad for the fruit and seed collectors and for those who lopped leafy branches for their goats to browse.

There were semi-nomadic livestock owners who came and went with the seasons, travelling far and therefore not getting a say in community decisions. One of them, who happened to be back in the village that day, spoke up defiantly from the back, "My people never get asked what we want. We travel far with our herds. People here make decisions while we are away." Faces turned to look at him, some hostile, seeming to suggest that he should not be given a hearing at all.

"This is our village, too," he continued. "*My* village. Our ancestors were here first," he said, stabbing a finger in the air. His group saw the woodland as forage for grazing or browsing and, again, for lopping bush and trees for their animals in dry times. But even among these livestock owners, there were different needs between mainly cattle owners and mainly goat owners, since their animals have different grazing habits.

An older woman spoke up at the back, diffidently. She wanted to carefully manage the portion of the forest closest to her own settlement so that they didn't have to walk too far for wood for their cooking fires. This was at odds with some of the other proposals.

There were, no doubt, many other conflicts that, as an outsider on a first visit, I didn't pick up on that day. In a community like this, there is never a right solution, a harmless one, or even an optimal one. So the questions become how the community comes to a decision without too much acrimony, who is going to be a winner and who a loser, and how to compensate the losers.

In recent years, there has been a welcome shift in development circles towards doing development *with* people rather than *for* people or *to* people. For development professionals, NGOs, donors or governments who are supporting them, it is more a feeling-the-way, iterative process, than a We-know-best imposition process.

The need to see community plans and actions as an interactive process was well described by Bruce Johnston and William Clark in a thoughtful book written back in 1982 entitled *Redesigning Rural Development*.[30] They believed that designing and implementing rural development programs with communities should be tackled more like an Inuit whittling a piece of bone:

"He carves a little not quite knowing what he is making, exploring the bone for its…potential. He pauses…carves a bit more…Finally, a smile of recognition: 'Hello seal, I wondered if it might be you.' Problem posed and resolved all in the same process…"

As you may have spotted, this metaphor has wider application to life, and I pick it up again in the final chapter.

THE AFRICAN FARMER
AS HEDGE FUND
MANAGER

**The rest of the world is fed because of
the use of good seed and inorganic fertilizer...
This technology has not been used in most of Africa.**

– Stephen Carr

I first got drawn into working on the challenges of African small-holder farmers in the early 1970s in Kenya, on a British overseas aid contract with the Ministry of Agriculture. Helping poor families who already have deep and ancestral knowledge of farming calls for humility and the suppression of professional arrogance. They typically have only one or two acres, little cash or credit, poor soils, erratic rainfall, use only hand labor, and face unpredictable government policies.

There are no fool-proof solutions and plenty of foolish ones. Of course, there are rules of thumb that experienced practitioners often agree on; but then there are rules of, shall we say, *toes and fingers*; in other words, the outlier, less predictable, solutions that in one situation may be sound but in another may be disastrous.

Avoiding the risk of crop failure is a big part of an African farmer's gamble on which crops to grow and how to manage them. The African farm family is a hedge fund manager in investment parlance, taking short and long positions (although, being poor, generally more short positions than long), spreading risk between crop types, and betting against drought or flood or both in one season. Farmers in rich countries in dryland areas face similar problems, but their decisions rarely affect what the family will put on the dinner table.

Few people in my field nowadays are aware that the late Louis Leakey, the renowned paleoanthropologist,[31] was one of the earliest Europeans to begin to really grasp the complexity, the system coherence, and the competition for resources playing out within traditional African farming systems.

A typed paper he wrote back in 1934, unpublished I believe, and edited by his son Colin,[32] passed to me many years ago, describes the typical traditional Kenyan Kikuyu tribe farming practices of that time. I greatly summarize what he said here, and I salute his skills in observation and interpretation. Many of these practices are still applied today.

A farm like this would have been in an intermediate rainfall area with two rainy seasons—the long rains starting about March, and the short rains about October. We begin the year at the onset of the long rains.

First, the household planted maize (corn) and pigeon peas, leaving gaps for later plantings. Once those seedlings appeared, they planted in the gaps two different types of beans; one early variety for eating fresh and one later multi-purpose variety, the kikuyu bean, mostly for dried beans. Once these plantings sprouted, they put in between them cuttings of sweet potato vine.

The first thing that was harvested was the leaves of the quick-growing beans along with sweet potatoes carried over from the previous rains. This could be eaten with the stored dried crops from the previous season. After this, the maize was coming into flower and the slow-growing pigeon pea was developing. Soon, the sweet potato vine was covering the ground, reducing loss of moisture and loss of soil and helping the slow-growing pigeon peas and kikuyu beans withstand the heat.

Once the long rains were over and the hot season arrived, the maize was harvested, leaving sweet potato, pigeon pea and kikuyu bean with full use of the soil and sunlight and no competition from maize. The kikuyu bean, by then, had fresh green pods, some dry pods, and still the green leaves for eating fresh. When the dry season was nearly over, the pigeon peas were harvested but only by picking and pruning so that they could flower again from new shoots after the boost from the second rains. The sweet potato started yielding after the first dry season but went on until after the second. With the second rains, a second plot would be planted in a similar manner, with staggered and mixed plantings, but in this case, the pigeon pea was replaced by millets that do well with little rainfall.

Confusing? Not surprising, this is far more complicated than most western farming systems and, whatever it is, it is certainly not primitive. In such systems, it is not easy for an outsider, even with strong professional skills, to suggest improvements. The problem is that if you change a crop, a variety, or a husbandry practice, or if you add livestock, then other things must change to release the land or the labor. A less complex system would miss using every bit of the available soil, water and sunlight and may put too many eggs in one basket. This type of farming is not like managing a roadside melon stand; it's like managing a thirty-player, mixed-age soccer team in a thunderstorm against a very wily opponent!

And it's tough, also, for research scientists who try to help. Pretend, for a moment, that you are a sorghum crop breeder in Africa trying to help dryland farmers. Sorghum is a grain for dry areas. You have done the final stages of your breeding crosses and selection to get your high-yielding variety, and you think you may have a winner.

What might have sunk your dreams along the way? Well, there are pale sorghums with low tannins and brown ones with high tannins—and everything in between. Pale ones are more palatable for humans but also for birds, so your pale variety may end up as bare stalks if a flock of birds descends on it. How bad the birds will be for a farmer will depend partly on what mix of tasty or nasty varieties the farmer's neighbors are growing. Birds have choices.

A pale, tasty variety that the birds prefer may still be alright if a farmer can hire boys with catapults and slings to sit on wooden platforms by the field and guard it from birds, but nowadays most are in school. And what happens to your variety if the rains start late? It will face too short a growing period to reach its full yield. If the rains look like being delayed, farmers may switch to a shorter growing period variety with less yield; this will at least give them something.

If your variety is quite brown with tannins, you could still grow it and the birds would mostly leave it alone and then, to make it taste better, you could run it through a milling machine to take off the bitter outer layer, but this adds cost. Also, if your sorghum is to be used for brewing beer, brewers are picky; special, slightly darker ones give the best malting and flavor.

And is your variety a hard or a soft-seeded variety? Soft is not good for storage; it will be attacked by insects and molds. And is your variety susceptible or resistant to the dreaded parasitic *striga* weed that can wipe out a crop and infest a field for years? And does it need a higher level of fertilizer to get the high yield? Can farmers afford that? And does it produce enough leaves and stems to chop or graze for cattle feed? Being dual purpose for grain *and* leaf can be useful, especially in a bad year when heads barely form. I could go on, but you get the picture: introducing anything new is complex; farmer preferences need to be read carefully.

Not surprisingly, mixed, or "companion planting" systems like the Kikuyu system evolved on other continents. The Mayan civilization in South America followed a maize, beans, and squash system known as "The Three Sisters." They followed it with reverence, literally; they had a maize god. As in Africa, their beans harvested nitrogen from the air with the aid of their root nodule companion bacteria and they climbed to intercept light on the maize stems. The squash spread sideways, protecting the soil, and keeping away insects with its hairy leaves. Same concepts as the Kikuyu system.

The attitude to risk of African farmers in dryland areas has some parallels with Western farmers. An Australian farmer named Tom Lane, who our team was working with near Wagga Wagga, once expressed skepticism about the idea of zero tillage (cropping without ploughing) that we were developing. After a long pause, he said, "In these dry areas, I reckon you can learn enough in one year to make a fool of yourself the next." He meant that you could cultivate and harrow in a certain way and on certain dates, sow a chosen variety of wheat at some ideal time, fertilize to an optimum level, handle weeds with the right timing, and get the best crop you had ever harvested. Eager to repeat your magic, the next year you could follow precisely the same formula...and get the worst crop you had ever had. Nature could blindside you; the rainfall might come out differently, a crop disease, whatever. It's the same risk for African farmers but, for them, the penalty for failure is much greater.

A question often asked by the casual visitor is: "Why in Africa would they not do what is done in the West and have large farms and tractors?" Well, there are some medium and large farms in Africa that have been efficient; in fact, the percentage of medium-sized farms in Africa has been growing recently. But look at it from the point of view of the cost of energy.[33]

With some oversimplifying, in America, the average cost of diesel fuel in recent years has been much lower than in Kenya while the cost of a day of labor in Kenya has been a fraction of what it has been in America. Without boring you with the math, in America, by my calculations, one day of human energy works out to be about the value of seventy liters of diesel fuel. In Kenya, one day's human energy costs only a couple of liters of diesel fuel. Labor in Africa is way cheaper than machinery or energy. And it is rare that using tractors will give higher crop yields than hand labor; hand labor can deliver plant-by-plant precision.

I recently listened to a man who had just visited South Sudan for the first time, telling his audience incredulously, "Farmers there don't even know how to plant crops in rows!"

The implication was that someone needed to *teach* them. I offered a different take. I told him, "In all my visits to small farms in Africa over many years, I have never come across a farmer who didn't know that he or she *could* plant in rows, in fact many do. But they are also aware that planting in rows has advantages and disadvantages depending on crop, soils, and other conditions."

He was skeptical, but ready to listen.

The main reason why in the West we plant in rows, I explained, is that most machinery cannot handle messy and mixed. In Africa, ox-drawn "weeders" will need crops in rows, and hand-tilled crops using a ridge system in lines will need to have rows. But hand labor is adaptable and doesn't need rows if they don't make sense. When you are dealing with a mix of crops, there will be different spacing needs for each. Not planting in rows—especially in the higher rainfall areas—allows for exploiting soil changes or patches of light. It allows for spacing plants closer around fertile anthills or increasing the number of plants in a depression with more moisture or leaving space for a spreading gourd or pumpkin or accommodating an existing banana or coffee plant or putting climbing plants near to tall, early maturing plants so they can climb the drying stalks.

It allows for three or four plants to be grouped in raised hills. It allows for building a small basin around a group of plants to retain rainwater or digging a small channel to drain a depression that can flood. Planting in rows must have advantages; sometimes it does, sometimes it doesn't.

Farmers' knowledge in Africa often surprises even the most experienced observers. In the 1970s, our team was trying to understand the soil potential of the north-west of Tanzania. All soils exhibit their history of formation. In that part of Tanzania, down the slopes below granite outcrops, the different-sized particles and clays have been eroded over millions of years.

Being eroded downhill, they have been sorted, leaving coarser, less easily moved, particles higher up and the finer, more easily moved particles, lower down. At the bottom, there are finer clays that have been sorted from above but also have been washed along valley bottoms from other locations. The result is that you get bands of different soils as you pass down the hillside.

The farmers had the same number of soil type names in their tribal language as modern soil scientists had; in fact they had one extra subdivision within one class. The *Sukuma* tribe's names were more succinct: *itongo*—brownish red loam, *luseni*—gray sand with red clay underneath, *ibambasi*—soil with a hardpan layer, *itogoro*—black sandy clay with calcareous material, and *mbuga*— heavy black clay. This was an entirely "modern" classification in its recognition of soil type and they knew very well which crops suited which soil.

If you find a lot of names for things, you can be sure they are important for survival. Professional jargon isn't dreamed up just to confuse those not in the club; it has purpose and, in Africa, often a cultural story to tell. More on this later.

It is a common misconception that smallholder farmers in Africa and Asia cannot produce high-quality agricultural products. It takes technical support, adequate roads, and efficient markets, but it has been done, and often.

For example, in Kenya, the best quality tea comes from the smallholders, typically with between about one and five acres of tea. They are lower-cost producers than the large commercial estates. In Kenya, tea production from the small farmers in 2014 was 37% greater than that from the commercial tea estates, although yield per acre was somewhat lower. Smallholder tea quality is better partly because smallholders adhere strictly to the picking rule—two-leaves-and-a-bud. Big estates have difficulty ensuring quality picking. A tea-buyer I knew admitted to me that he rarely bought smallholder tea. It was too good for him! Too expensive. He bought commercial estate tea in bulk for the lowly tea bags his company needed.

I have written here about farming families in Africa. What can we learn from them?

Well, everything in life begins with upbringing, so it is best to start there. Babies and children sleep close to their mother, often on the same mat or bed. They go to the fields on their mothers' backs while she cultivates or harvests. They are never alone. You hardly ever hear them cry. As they grow, the older children help. But once they reach the ages of eight or nine, the coddling phase shifts quite quickly to a responsibility phase.

Near universal schooling now has changed things, but traditionally a nine-year-old boy would have been herding goats with an older brother, or even alone, possibly even facing down predators. But there is still plenty of play, too; soccer games, handmade toys, ingenious model trucks of wire, dolls of clay and cloth. In the daytime, when not at school, a girl will help her mother collect firewood or water as well as helping with picking fruits, tea, or coffee; tasks best performed by the nimble fingers of a child. A teenage boy would have graduated to the warrior phase, calling for still greater responsibility, defense of the tribe and the cattle, courage against enemies and lions. So, compared to our Western societies, there is a swift transition from pampered dependency to serious livelihood-driven maturity.

Beyond upbringing, we learn about the importance of women in farming—but also about their limited legal rights. The husband usually owns or has traditional rights to the land. We learn about the benefits of being involved with a community, but also about the costs in time commitment and the pressures to conform. We find an acceptance of circumstance, but rarely a passive acceptance, a considered acceptance calling for action where feasible.

We learn about the importance of, and the perfidiousness of, national governments in the support they bring—or fail to bring. We learn the importance of an accountable local government. We learn the need for good seed and artificial fertilizer—organic farming alone cannot feed

Africa; it barely did with 140 million mouths in the year 1900. The population will be seventeen times that by 2050!

We learn from farmers, men and women, the value of minute and meticulous observation, spotting slight variations in soil, a hint of pest damage, barely perceptible water flow, the subtlest signs of sickness in a cow. We learn the benefits and risks of innovation. When you are living at a subsistence level, failures are costly. We learn the importance of keeping hand tools sharp to reduce effort, and the importance of keeping skills sharp, always learning, both traditional knowledge long practiced and new knowledge, but not accepted without measured skepticism. Farmers have been burned too often.

We learn about spreading risk, growing multiple crops for a better chance of one surviving when rains fail. Or, to spread risk, having a supplementary income outside agriculture to help at times of crop failure or to buy seed and fertilizer in time for the season. We learn the importance of good health and, so, of good medical services; the sick cannot work or learn. Above all, we learn the value of smiling in the face of adversity and believing there is light at the end of the tunnel. I salute them all for what they have taught us.

PASTORALISM AND THE MAASAI

A cow is as good as a man.

– Maasai Proverb

There are few cultures as far removed from our predominantly urban Western culture as pastoralists herding cattle and goats on the great African savanna. The pastoralist plays the role of the "herder" while we in the West seem to play the role of the "herded." But precisely because of this contrast, it is worth understanding pastoralist societies as a counterpoint to our own. We learn more from differences than from similarities.

Compared to African agriculturalists, pastoralists are haughty. They have good reason to be. They are more adventurous and independent. They travel further and face more risks even than farmers. To me, pastoralists always seem out of place in towns and cities, although one or two I worked with seemed to have made the adjustment. Socially, they are close-knit and suspicious of outsiders, especially if they seem to be threatening their communal land rights or their livestock.

The Maasai of Kenya and Tanzania, the Bedouin of Egypt, and the Berber Tuaregs of the Sahara are some of the better-known pastoralists in Africa. Their clever survival strategy is to manage herds against the ebb and flow of drought and flush times. Often, they clash with farmers who have been encroaching onto their grazing lands. Over millennia, they have learned to husband grass and shrubs and to keep sufficient cows alive to resume breeding quickly after drought losses so that herd numbers can bounce back.[34]

Cattle grow, produce, and multiply by eating plants. Their four-compartment digestive system—a large holding tank, a muscled regurgitation tank, a filtering tank, and a final digestive tank like our stomach—has evolved to play a complex biological trick. The design enables double chewing, often referred to as "chewing the cud," the regurgitation of a bolus of half-chewed forage back to the mouth for further chewing and the addition of some antacid saliva. This complex compartmentalized digestive system offers comfortable accommodation for bacteria to help with digestion; in return the bacteria get food.

The relationship between forage plants and grazing animals is extremely complex. Animals, both domestic and wild, are partly competitive with each other, each eating the same parts of the same plants, and partly complementary, each eating different parts or different plants. But all produce dung and urine, and, depending on their end, carcasses in some form, contributing to nutrient recycling.

The interactions between all the elements of the system generally help the mix of vegetation to stay somewhat balanced. But imbalance is always threatening. For a manager, whether an American rancher or an African pastoralist clan, managing livestock and forage is art as much as science. But science can contribute to explaining the complexity.

Drought can strike at any time. To appreciate the variability of production from dry rangelands, take the largest cattle station in Australia, a property called *Anna Creek*, north of Adelaide towards Lake Eyre. It is 9,141 square miles (nearly six million acres)—larger than Israel.

Over the eleven years from 2002 to 2012, it had a peak cattle population of 16,500 head. But it had a low population one year of just 1,500 head, and I believe even less at one point during that year. This is like owning a field that can feed sixteen horses in better times but only, in a pinch, three small ponies over bad times; highly unreliable as an annual grazing proposition.

Some readers may have come across the idea of the "Tragedy of the Commons." It draws from a 1968 paper by the ecologist Garrett Hardin.[35] It suggests that when grazing is on common land owned by a community, too many grazing animals may be stocked because there is little cost to an individual herder from adding one more mouth.

The cost of the extra fodder consumed and the damage from that one mouth too many is small for the individual owner of the animal because it is shared with everybody. The owner who is adding that extra mouth is a "free rider." With privately-owned land, any overgrazing damage, from grazing more mouths than the forage can support, will fall on the owner and hurt his own land.

In the years following Hardin's paper, many researchers challenged his idea, pointing out that pastoral tribes often have rather well-developed community grazing management practices. In other words, it is not really such a free-for-all as it might seem.

In some countries in Africa, partly to address the perceived "Hardin problem" of common property rights, unsuitable private ownership crept in. In some of the Bedouin areas in Egypt that I visited, some of the more influential individuals had been seizing ownership of land that had previously been communal property. Such land grabs invariably push out the poor.

"The Tragedy of the Commons" idea features in Joshua Greene's book, *Moral Tribes*.[36] He argues that human social evolution has made it beneficial for self-preservation by means of cooperation *within* tribes, like elder-managed tribal grazing rules, but has given an incentive for competition *between* tribes, like keeping intruders off of your rangelands. We can often get along with our own people, but we have not yet learned how to get along with our neighbors. Evolution has tended to make us territorial, like some wild animals.

It has often been assumed by Westerners that privately-owned land under commercial ranching would be more productive and profitable than traditional pastoral rangelands communally grazed, but the evidence has often pointed the other way.

Ranches are producing and selling only beef and hides, whereas an African pastoral system like that of the Maasai is taking off meat, milk, blood, hides, dung for fuel and house plaster, and supplying transportation, mainly donkeys and camels, while also using livestock as a savings bank, a medium for social ceremony, and payment for brides.[37] And pastoralists in wildlife areas today are increasingly making additional money off their rangelands from game-viewing tourism. On the other side of the profit and loss account, pastoralists have modest investment costs because there is no fencing cost, low labor cost, low veterinary cost due to traditional disease-resistant breeds, and modest water supply investment, since there are no fenced fields requiring individual water supply.

So the Maasai are fairly typical pastoralists in their survival practices, but what are they like as a people? Well, not surprisingly, the social is substantially driven by the environment.

"Life has seasons" is one of hundreds of *Maa* proverbs. Seasons affect forage and therefore the health and productivity of Maasai livestock. But their life passage has seasons too, marked by ceremonies from birth to moranship (warrior training), to marriage, and to elderhood. Beyond that, death is a more casual affair, attuned to nature, not as big a thing. Each Maasai ceremony has quite specific rules and protocols, such as who can eat what, in what place, cooked by whom, and in whose company. There is order in the customs.

The Maasai tribe has sixteen "sections," like large clans. They occupy parts of Kenya and Tanzania. Within each section, each rising generation of young men is grouped in an age set. Within each age set there is a left-hand and right-hand subset. Like regimental mottos, each of the age sets is given a name such as "The long-bladed spears" or "Who cannot be driven away" or "The unvanquished" or "Who fight by day." Some older Maasai can recite the names of each age set going back many generations, although I have found that they do less well at such genealogical feats of recall after a few drinks. Don't we all!

The boys in each age set are circumcised at section ceremonies held once there are enough for a sufficient batch, or in the event of some larger ceremony or necessity. So the age set may have boys of varying maturity across a span of about seven to twelve years. Usually circumcision is done at around the age of sixteen. But if a boy is to inherit his dead father's property, or if his sisters are old enough to marry and so need to be circumcised, then he must be circumcised first.[38] It is a family disgrace for the son to flinch at circumcision—but not for the daughters during female circumcision.

Leaders in the male warrior-trainee youth groups, the *moran,* are selected by their fellows for different roles. One would be expected to be a fearless leader in battle, one a wise counselor, one might be the acknowledged generous one, and, depending on section traditions, there will be other roles.

Traditionally, there was no single overall tribal chief; decisions were made by consensus, but the British in colonial times pushed African tribes that operated more by consensus into having a single paramount chief. It made them easier to manipulate.

Traditionally, the Maasai drink blood drawn from the jugular vein of a live cow. With the increase in maize consumption, this is now done mostly for ceremonies or for people who are sick. The puncture is performed with a miniature bow and a buffered arrow with a small collar on it to limit the depth of penetration. They take about two to three pints and bind the wound with a strap. If there is still some blood seeping, they will slap on a handful of mud and dung to seal it.

The blood taken is consumed undiluted or mixed with milk or sour milk; a well-balanced diet. It usually has a smoky flavor because the gourd, or calabash, in which it is kept has been sterilized with hot coals, but also from smoke inside the home and sometimes from charcoal soot of selected trees added for flavor and to aid fermentation.

The Maasai know their grasses, shrubs and trees intimately. They know the uses of each for forage through leaves, pods, or fruits and they know the uses of herbs for medicines for livestock and humans. They divide tree-types into those with thorns, known as the "warm-trees," and those without thorns, known as the "cold-trees."

Cold trees are considered holy. The without-thorn group is subdivided into those with milky sap and those without. Father Frans Mol, a great expert on the Maasai, who I met a couple of times many years ago, lists in his *Maa Dictionary*[39] some two hundred trees by name and their various uses. There are several bush fruits favored for human consumption, for example the ol-amuriaki (*Carissa edulis*) with very sweet, red fruit, a jasmine-like plant. In season, it can distract greedy herding boys from closely watching their animals—a lapse, by the way, that crafty lions can take advantage of.

Maasai medicinal plants are believed to be able to cure many ills, including stomach problems, pain, and sexually transmitted diseases. They can also be stimulants for ceremonial mood heightening. The *moran* warriors use *Acacia nilotica*, (babul, one type of gum arabic) milked also for its sap, to make a bark infusion to build their excitement or courage prior to a ceremony or before battle. At a *moran* ceremony, after consuming this concoction and after rounds of energetic leaping and dancing, some will go into spasms, trembling on the ground and frothing at the mouth. Potent stuff.

As with the Sukuma farmers' knowledge of soils and soil names, the Maasai have many words for different patterns of color on their animals—a different word for a solid color than a patchy color, different for splotchy brown than for splotchy black. They have at least thirty words for different colors and patterns of cattle, for example *naibor* (all-white), *arus* (spotted black and white), *mukyie* (dark brown), and *narasha* (mottled).[40] And then there are the many different words for horns pointing down or up, forward or back, and the mavericks with one horn heading north and one south.

In Maasai ceremonies, often involving the slaughter or gifting of cattle, goats or sheep,[41] there is an expectation of perfection reflecting their pride in their culture, their history, their age set and especially their livestock. When eighteen white heifers and one black bull are required for the graduation ceremony, all the cattle are expected to be "without blemish." They should be entirely white or, for the bull, entirely black, not splotchy. They should have no scars and should have evenly-balanced and pointed horns, good eyes, and no ripped ears or damaged tails. There is some parallel here with the cattle-breeding fraternity in the West, in Europe, America and Australia, where perfection of conformation in pedigree cattle is important for maintaining breed standards that are believed to be linked to meat or milk productivity.

For the Maasai, there is a similar demand for perfection in their warriors. The leading warrior chosen for the initiation of an age set must be physically and mentally without blemish. He must have no scars, not be left-handed, not be impotent, not be quick-tempered, not have committed murder, and be of pure Maasai parents.[42]

Through the middle of the 19th century, there was a series of devastating Maasai internecine wars. This conflict within the Maasai erupted over disputed grazing land and cattle recovery following droughts. It seriously weakened them. Some groups were entirely wiped out or absorbed by others. Tribal weakening also came with the rinderpest cattle disease epidemic of the late 1880s.

Following this period of conflict, there was the loss of about sixty percent of Maasai land to colonial settlement, initially for farms but later, also for game parks. Remember when you visit a game park in Africa that, wherever you are, you are likely on tribal land that once was taken from them with little or no compensation. This land was seized from people who, in many cases, did not kill wildlife and had lived alongside them peacefully for thousands of years, although back in those times at far lower human population levels.

Courage in battle and in facing wild animals is important. Traditionally, a Maasai *moran* was supposed to kill a lion single-handedly. It has been illegal now for many years and with fewer lions, it is more common for them to quietly go off and kill as a group. Or to not kill at all. But a justification can often be found that a lion raided their cattle. There are now voluntary "lion guardians" among the *moran* who commit to protecting lions and discourage their fellows from killing them. But tradition dies hard; not surprisingly there is still kudos in being a man who once killed a lion.

A young Maasai man I worked with many years ago who had recently graduated from his period of *moran*-ship, told me, "When we surround a lion in a circle and close in with our raised spears, the lion will scan the circle of eyes and will pick the man he thinks is most scared. That is where he will spring to escape."

He assured me that it was uncanny how the lion was invariably right. He went on, "We have lived as a group and tested each other's courage every day in hunting and in rough games. We know who among us is the most timid. The lion will always find him."

As I mentioned earlier, fear in the eyes of a human seems difficult to hide—from man or animal. The men who do the circumcision say they can tell beforehand whether a Maasai boy is going to flinch or lose control. They see it in the eyes.

Traditionally, the *moran* who inflicted the fatal wound on the lion got the greatest honor and the skin, but the one who grabbed its tail while it was still alive and hung on was a close second.

Girls' circumcision is usually carried out in a dimly-lit hut by an old woman who specializes in the procedure. It is not a large ceremony like it is with the boys, but it may be done simultaneously. Girls are also supposed to bite a cloth and bear it, but many scream in agony. It is done with a sharp knife or curved razor. Men do not attend.

Female genital mutilation, as it is called by researchers, is a highly dangerous procedure and can lead to health complications and even death. One argument by Maasai in favor of the procedure is that it reduces promiscuity, but the evidence seems to suggest the opposite.

Many outside organizations and governments have tried to end it, with some progress. For those who still hold to the tradition, "It has always been done. It must be done," is a common response. Their fear is that the man or woman who is not circumcised has not properly graduated into adulthood. They think that they could face mockery or not find a marriageable partner.

But an increasing number of families have given it up, usually made acceptable by some small symbolic procedure such as splashing milk over the thighs. The campaign to finally end it is a worthy campaign in principle, but sometimes has not been sufficiently sensitive to the culture. There have been negative impacts such as girls being circumcised very young so the mothers can avoid the pressures against it, or mothers being arrested and jailed, leaving children without a mother. While well-meaning, it has not always been helpful to have Western outsiders prying or supporting the rule of law to stop it. Not an easy challenge.

The Maasai have a godhead, *Enkai*. At creation time, when the earth was separating from the heavens, *Enkai,* so it is said, was in the process of sending all the cattle in the heavens down to earth on a rope—in some traditions on the aerial roots of a *ficus* tree—for the benefit of his chosen people. But a band of enemy forest hunters came along and cut the rope, or the root, before this heavenly download could be completed.

This suggests to the Maasai that all cattle in the world were supposed to belong to them, giving them the right of "recovery." The story is a little more complicated and is embedded in other background stories and there are some different traditions by section, but that is the gist of it.

There is the good *Enkai*, the black *Enkai*, *Enkai Narok,* perhaps better envisaged as one of the two manifestations of *Enkai*, and then there is the angry *Enkai*, the red one, *Enkai Nanyokie,* who is seen in lightning and thunder. *Enkai* is evident to the Maasai in the heavens, in the earth, in cattle, in mountains, and especially in grass.

When you walk around in Maasai country, you may come across knotted tufts of dry grass in sacred places that have been tied to honor *Enkai*. *Enkai* particularly resides on the top of the ten-thousand-foot volcanically active mountain, *Ol Doinyo Lengai*, the Mountain of God, just west of Mt. Kilimanjaro.

Some Maasai believe that after death, if you have been good, you go to a great productive grazing land with many cattle—but if you did not measure up, you are sent to a stony desert. But most seem to believe that there is nothingness after death. Many have converted to Christianity and some to Islam. The dead, traditionally, were placed in the forest or out on the plains with animal fat smeared on the body for the hyenas or other animals to eat up, but this is done less often now. It was a sign that you had not been a good person if you were not eaten up within a couple of days, a disgrace to your family.

Maasai herders sometimes find hairballs from the stomach of lions that have been regurgitated under shade bushes, as domestic cats sometimes do. They are believed to bring good luck. They are composed of densely matted hair from licking and from their kills. They are slightly oval, with a smooth, shiny, surface patina and have slight indentations from being tumbled for months in digestive juices. They are light and would float. Most are about egg sized or smaller and are dark in color. I have one given to me by a Maasai and I had a smaller one that I bought. Many years ago, my dog ate the smaller one…and as far as I know never regurgitated it reconstituted!

The Maasai have often been considered by outsiders to be tradition-bound and unaccepting of new ideas. This is far from the truth, although the core culture and ceremonies have stood up reasonably well to the modern world. As far back as the 1970s, I used to visit Maasai farmers in Kenya who cultivated blocks of wheat with tractors in the hills near Narok.

Whether individually-owned large farms in this area were the best or most equitable use of land that once had been common grazing land was questionable, but that is too big a story to take up here.

At one of these farms, I was walking into a field of wheat with the Maasai owner. Two of his wives were nearby, sewing up wheat bags. It was an area of rolling hills and good soil. You could see far away the yellow grass plains of the Rift Valley floor. They were harvesting with a modern combine harvester, a costly machine, hired for his own farm and several neighbors.

I gave the farmer a guess at the number of bags-per-acre on the crop. He smiled and nodded. I said that the wheat was very free of weeds and that he surely must have sprayed with herbicide. He nodded. I commented that I didn't see any wheel tracks from a sprayer. He banked his hand through the air to explain that he had sprayed by air. He pointed to an airstrip lower in the valley where I saw a limp windsock.

So here was a proud, grazing man whose father would never have stooped to the practice of agriculture; something practiced by lesser tribes. Yet this man's generation had readily made the transition. He stood like a statue. It was the typical Maasai look: polite but never deferential, barely concealing an air of superiority. But he was pleased to show a visitor what he had achieved.

Today, a Maasai cattle owner can be observed checking the cattle prices at markets around Kenya or Tanzania on his cell phone. If prices at some distant market look like a promising trade, he may instruct a trusted son to take cattle there to sell, or to go there to buy. To make an investment or a purchase, Maasai can also borrow money through their iPhones at the main local shops that are now linked to banks.

Maasai teenagers now mostly go to school and participate in traditional activities and ceremonies around the school calendar. Teenage Maasai can be seen using iPhones and listening to heavy metal music not unlike other teenagers around the world. Some have become almost entirely western-ized and urbanized; others keep their connections to their traditional lands and pastoralism, but all with adjustments. The Maasai have shown that they can take the technologies that benefit them and ignore the rest.

Sadly, British colonial administrations drew lines on maps all over the world to tell people where they should or shouldn't live and who owned what. I have stood at, or crossed, many of these lines, including the Durand

Line on the Afghanistan border that cut the Pashtuns in two, the still-disputed McMahon Line along the Himalayas, the Somalia/Kenya boundary that cut the Somali tribe in two, the Middle East mess of post–World War I boundaries, and the Kenya/Tanganyika (Tanzania) border cutting the Maasai in two.

Traditional territorial rights were ignored. In one case, back in colonial days in Kenya, a Maasai contender for the position of *laibon*, the chief seer, one *Olonana*, is said to have signed a treaty document handing over Maasai land to the British with a thumb print applied three days after his death. This loss of land has disrupted the balance of dry season and wet season grazing range because often the higher rainfall dry season reserve areas were seized for cropping by European settlers.

Of course, pre-colonial tribal land ownership by traditional rights had been the product of thousands of years of ebb and flow of tribal conflict. But that was indigenous against indigenous land-grabbing, not land-grabbing by an acquisitive foreign tribe with no conceivable land rights anywhere on the continent.

The land losses for the Maasai did not finish with the end of colonialism. Private or group ranches have been carved out of common lands. Ranches have been further subdivided into small private holdings, too small to enable communal responses to the seasonal forage variations the way communal rangeland could. Only quite recently, one Maasai section in Tanzania, some of whom I believe were people who had been forced out of the Serengeti national park many years earlier, were under threat again of losing land to a private hunting lease. But at the time of this writing, this proposal seems to have been shelved.

Today the Maasai ceremonial and life-passage traditions are not easy to sustain with most of the children and youth attending school. For men, going through the full traditional *moran* training is not possible with school and exams. Fewer are learning how to read and write in Maa. Swahili is encroaching, and English. Some educated Maasai politicians have urged their people to give up what they see as primitive ways. But others work to find sensible compromises that will enable the pursuit of education while holding fast to the essential traditions.

It is difficult to forecast where this will all end; there are Maasai websites that discuss these challenges. And there are channels for helping them meet their goals. There is a fine tribal tradition here that needs to survive, but with Maasai-driven, not outsider-driven, accommodation to the ways of the modern world.

This is important not just for the sake of the Maasai themselves but because they are a piece of the rest of us, a uniquely bright tile in the great human mosaic.

ABORIGINAL DREAMING TRACKS

*White man got no dreaming. Him go
'nother way. White man, him go different.
Him got road belong himself.*

– Muta[43]

Moving from African farming and pastoralism towards one-time hunter gatherers (who might also have been early agriculturalists), Australian Aboriginal practices offer an intriguing contrast to our formulaic Western attitudes to origins and land. They offer a very different way; a deeply land-related spiritualism.

Modern man evolved in Africa. Migrations north and east from there seem to have brought aboriginals to Australia about 50,000 years ago; about the time complex language was developing. Those who didn't make it as far as crossing the land bridge to Australia evolved into modern-day Chinese, Indonesian, and other Far East peoples. At about this time, when Australian Aboriginals were first reaching Australia, the Neanderthal forms in Europe were well into their evolutionary demise and their inter-breeding dilution.

Among the artifacts I have accumulated over a lifetime of casual collecting is an aboriginal grinding stone made of sandstone; a *muller*. It was used for grinding seeds from grasses, shrubs, and trees to be baked into cakes. I picked it up many years ago from a plowed wheat paddock near Lockhart in New South Wales when I was talking to a farmer about his wheat crop. It has about the curvature of the bottom of a saucer and is a perfect fit for my right hand.

I like to turn it over and feel the sandpapery utilitarian shape of a tool that was used to feed a family perhaps as much as a thousand of years ago. I wonder whether it was dropped carelessly or abandoned in a hasty escape from marauding neighbors. I like the personal connection I can sense as I examine it; not just that it was used by a woman—less likely by a man, given the firmly-established family roles—but that the original owner was right-handed. I know this because it nestles in the right hand perfectly, with a chipped indentation for the thumb, but in the left awkwardly. Also, the angle of wear on the grinding face could only have come from a right-handed grinding action.

Back in the 1960s, for several weeks, I worked alongside five young Australian Aboriginal men on the farm at Berwicks, near Quirindi. They came from the Caroona Walhallow community. Our job was to pick up sticks on new wheat land recently cleared of trees and scrub by machinery. This land was likely part of their ancestors' tribal territory.[44]

Later, we worked together during the lamb-marking season. But because of the pace of the work, there was little time to really get to know them. In any case, the aboriginal culture does not open easily to my tribe's direct Western approach to social interaction; for them, opening up to others is more like, well, like gathering sticks in a wheat paddock; the pile grows slowly.

Their culture responds, wisely, to a cumulative sharing of beliefs and histories. I had heard of The Dreamings and their Dreaming Tracks in those days, but I knew little about them until doing some reading and literature research many years later.

Aboriginal beliefs revolve around The Dreamings, sometimes referred to as the Dreamtime. This is often erroneously considered by outsiders to represent merely beliefs and legends about the time of creation. But these English terms are found by Aboriginals to be poor representations of the concept. At the heart is a more complex web of beliefs and connections to the real world. These have sometimes been encapsulated in the word *Every-when*, which may be the best we can do within the limitations of English. This construct of The Dreamings blends many notions: notions of creation, religion, physical location, symbols, moral codes, rules for managing country, the past, the present, the future, spirits, ancestors, cosmology, soul, life-force, and many other notions. It seems to me to be akin to modern poetry in which the words and syntax are elusive, yet the sense of the whole left behind is satisfying and palpable.

Dreaming Tracks, sometimes called *Songlines*,[45] and linked to The Dreamings, are sacred stories, songs, and dances about events often built around people, spirits, land, and stars. Dreaming Track stories are so revered that exposing the full meaning to outsiders is often frowned upon. There should remain a measure of concealed mystery.

Dreaming Tracks are a record of routes followed by creator-beings when the world was sung into being. Some are records of ancestral involvement in early events. They can be used for finding a route across country, but that would depend on the route and the purpose of the travel; many Dreaming Tracks, if taken from start to finish, are far from the shortest routes between two places; they follow the convoluted route of the story line which was influenced by, and influenced, the land features and terrain.

Each Dreaming Track is built around a saga. In European culture, we might treat them as fairy tales or legends, but they are entirely real and immediate to the tribe that owns the story; they are not seen *at all* as fiction or allegory. They describe the landscape, the ranges, the outcrops, the trees, the dry riverbeds, the rocks, and the billabongs.[46] They explain the events that are believed to have created these features. And these stories are much more than a handy ancient GPS system or a memory trick using association hooks as applied in modern memory competitions. They are cultural and religious, even creationist, biblical types of passages.

One of the most widely known is the "Seven Sisters Dreaming Track."[47] It is linked to the *Pleiades* star cluster, known in Greek mythology as the seven daughters of Atlas, the strong man who held up the world. Variations of this are known in several parts of Australia.

The story tells of the seven sisters being chased by a sorcerer spirit *Yarlu* (the name in one aboriginal language) who keeps catching up with them. Yarlu has an impressively long "member" which at one point he wraps around his waist. This is no delightful fairy tale for bedtime reading to your six-year-old. There is danger, pursuit, evasion, magic, lust, rape, violence and eroticism, all of it with links to locations or events such as the place where the fleeing sisters set up camp and only narrowly escaped the rampant Yarlu, who crept up on them with the help of his magical powers.

There is cultural persistence in Dreaming Tracks, too; the songs must be sung regularly to keep the land alive, to sustain the original creation. Without this reinvigoration, the original creation will fade. Land became sacred through these stories and, with repetition, this reverence is sustained.

As in Africa, there are traditional land stewardship practices, although Aboriginals never herded livestock—blame the refractory kangaroo for that. Vegetation management plays a key role in the cultures of Aboriginals, just as it does for African tribes. I do not have space to follow this lead further but Aboriginal knowledge of edible plants, their positive use of fire to manage vegetation, and other survival practices including managing bird pests have similarities to African practices evolved from a similar environment. It is now thought that Aboriginals may even have been the first agriculturalists, tending sown millet crops, probably sown by broadcasting seed before rains, followed by later protection of the crop stands. This is practiced by African tribes in drier areas today.

Those Aboriginals who still know the sacred stories, songs and dances, and who appreciate their cultural significance, are aware that the modern world is threatening. But they have also realized that that same world, in which their children use iPhones and the Internet, offers a technology to stem the leakage and to collect and record stories and traditions in electronic records. So all is not lost in the preservation of The Dreamings, although there has undoubtedly been significant erosion since Captain Cook's fateful landing at Botany Bay on April 29, 1770.

It is difficult to think of any connection to the land in other cultures that reaches the depth and the cultural and religious meaning of Dreaming Tracks. Somehow, we in the West never found, or perhaps we lost, the pulse of the land; the art of weaving our explorations into our origins and beliefs. The nearest that other cultures have come to such reverence of place that I can think of is the Hindu pilgrimage in India from source to sea and back around the sacred Narmada river in the Narmada Parikrama, with its connections to the earliest Hindu stories and literature. Australian Aboriginal dreaming tracks seem to me to reflect a saying attributed to Gautama Buddha, "You cannot travel the path until you have become the path itself."

AMERICA
THE PRECARIOUS

America, thou half-brother of the world;
with something good and bad of every land.

– Philip James Bailey

My first introduction to America was in the early 1960s. The British National Union of Students had cheap summer charter flights to New York. I teamed up with fellow students, Colin and Ursula, both from my university at Wye College. At that time, for students seeking temporary work, it was easier to go through the process of getting a "green card" than a temporary worker's permit.

Some weeks after filing the forms, I was summoned to the American Embassy in London for my interview. The official was a steely-eyed and intimidating woman. But at moments when she let her guard down, there were hints of a human lurking beneath the veneer. Presumably the strategy was that if you were intent on getting up to no good in America, her interrogation would break you and you would run for the door. Among other things, I had been required in the forms to declare that I was not entering the United States for the purposes of prostitution or living off the earnings of said trade.

Despite some preparation on my part on the question of the prostitution industry, my interviewer focused more on my possible links to communism. I was about to assure her that, despite a wayward great aunt who, in 1903, had thoughtlessly gone off and married the communist "Red Dean" of Canterbury, I was an improbable candidate for such political deviance, particularly given my father's recent role in the RAF's Cold War deterrence. But I decided not to push my luck with cheeky responses and offered, instead, some suitably grimaced negatives.

Eventually, she passed on to my earnings potential, which was by no means stellar—just a first contact with a California farming family. Her concern was that I might become a cost to the state. My employment competition seemed likely to be Mexican migrant labor, probably very skilled and far more suited to California's small, intensive fruit farms than my Australian experience of doing unpleasant things to sheep on farms that claimed a fair chunk of the horizon.

Well into what seemed to me to be a rather aggressive interview with weak responses from my side, and as I was starting to re-plan my summer towards something less testing, like mucking out Lincolnshire pig pens, she leaped to her feet and brusquely instructed me, "Please stand and raise your right hand." She rattled off several things that I had to swear to, much too fast for me to take them in. There was a carved eagle behind her chair that, from my angle, looked like it was perched on her shoulder, but I was able to keep a straight face long enough to get to the finishing line with the promise of a green card.

To get to California from New York after our charter flight across the pond, we purchased the British student stand-by—a "ninety-nine-dollars-for-ninety-nine-days" Greyhound Bus pass; an extraordinary deal. Other students on this migration bought beaten-up jalopies with six alarmingly mature figures on the odometer, dangerously threadbare tires, and an unpromising odor of transmission oil for a few hundred dollars and hoped their heap would hang together—with the aid of a big hammer and Midwest baler-twine—for the drive across America and back.

At the end of the summer, those few who limped back into New York, having entirely depleted their assets, joined others—license plates removed—in the airport parking lot as their fickle masters climbed the steps of a Boeing 707 headed back across the pond.

We three more cautious amigos took the Greyhound bus routes down through Washington D.C., Atlanta, New Orleans, through a crackling dry stretch of Texas, up to Colorado Springs, and across to San Francisco. Impecunious, we sought out barely habitable dumps to sleep in.

These were usually paint-peeled rooms hung with rusty pipes and enlivened by the cacophony of bus, truck, train and puking drunk. Such establishments were not hard to find near Greyhound bus stations; in fact, Greyhound travelers were their main prey! One or two nights we slept on the bus, saving on lodging and missing scenery but gaining the entirely different human interaction of a night ride. Traveling by bus gave us the opportunity to meet some fine middle and lower-income Americans who were exceptionally kind.

On one leg out of New Orleans, I sat next to a very leaky hobo. I was not sure if he was trying to get somewhere, to run away from somewhere or someone, or was simply using the bus as a place to sleep. In his pocket was an unlabeled bottle of clear liquid. His armpit and mouth vapors suggested that it had a generous share of the methyl fraction. After a couple of hours of unintelligible mumblings triggered by some flashing light on a highway or the glance of an ample-breasted woman on a sidewalk, he started jabbing me in the ribs with a sharp elbow muttering, "Ya gotta gun. Ya gotta gun."

"No. I have never owned a gun. Look!" I turned out my pockets and a piece of chewing gum fell out. I offered it to him. He accepted it, surprisingly graciously. He was not quite as rough as he seemed.

My two traveling companions found the one-act play behind them entertaining. I feared I was stuck with this geezer all the way to Santa Fe, since that is where he said he was headed. But at some short pit-stop along the way he got off and presumably forgot to get back on again. Nobody could find him, so the bus went without him. I was left with an empty seat beside me sporting a large wet patch.

As we drove on through the cool desert night, I found myself envying the freedom of a man who could forget to get back on a bus and miss absolutely nothing and nobody. No responsibilities. No tiresome objectives. No people to worry about. But then it occurred to me that perhaps he *did* have people to worry about and that perhaps they were worrying about him. It also dawned on me, too late, that he probably owned an intriguing human story and I had missed the opportunity to coax it out of him. A lost novel? That English reserve, I suppose.

Later in the trip, pulling into Rawlins, Wyoming, one evening, we found an old row-house hotel near the bus station. We went up the steep stone steps and knocked on the door. A hard-looking woman with black tangled hair and a cigarette dangling from her lipstick-smeared mouth looked down at us, puzzled.

We asked for a room. She peered at Ursula, then at me, then at Colin and scanned back over us once again. Taking the cigarette out of her mouth and slowly blowing a cloud, she asked, "Er...what exactly is the relationship?"

Colin replied, "Pretty good, actually," his English accent exaggerated against her drawl.

She shook her head and said with a condescending smile, "Oh no, I'm sorry kids, this isn't a hotel."

We reversed awkwardly down the steps as though backing out of the Queen's presence and hurried off down the road to find a place that was.

At the prune farm near Geyserville, we became a part of a wonderful American family, Al and Alyce Cadd, Larry and Cindy, it seems for life— we are still in touch today, and two of the three of us have visited recently. Colin's boot, Ursula's sandal, and my leather glove, dusty and shriveled after more than half a century, are still nailed to the old prune shed wall as a memento of our invasion from the old country.

There was insufficient work when we first arrived at the Cadd Ranch.

The plums were not ready, so we went to pick pears for a German farmer down the road. There was the usual transient Mexican labor force there; quiet, polite, often entertaining. With our pale faces, we stood out like delicate intruding cantaloupes in a field of pumpkins. To distinguish us from the Mexicans, the farmer referred to us as, "The angle saxels." He would stride into the orchard looking down the rows to give us our next picking orders shouting, "Where are them goddamned angle saxels?" We would respond with a shout and heft our ladders to the next row.

Soon after the pears, the prunes were ready back at the Cadds. To harvest them, we knocked the plums off the trees onto ground sheets using long aluminum poles, picking off the lower, reachable ones by hand. We gathered them into boxes and brought them to the washer ahead of the oil-fired drying tunnel. Sometimes we used a new mechanized tree-shaking machine on two wheels. It had a trunk clamp, handles and control levers. It was supposed to physically shake the trunk to shake off the ripe prunes. It was a reminder of Newton's Third Law of Motion—that for every action there is an equal and opposite reaction. It seemed only marginally more effective at shaking the prunes off at the business end than shaking the operator's balls off at the control end. After you stopped, your body tingled, you saw double, and you vowed next time to wear tight underpants.

There was a migrant Mexican family on the farm who came every year following the harvesting work up through California. They were an eye-opener to us Brits on what it meant to be poor in America. They lived in an adequate but basic wooden house, better than many Brits had at that time. They had few belongings since they migrated with the seasonal work and needed to travel light. But, amazing to us, they owned two vehicles.

At that time in England, if you were in the lower income bracket, it was unusual to have even a small old car. You would have a bicycle or motorbike and travel the longer distances by train. This Mexican family had a pick-up to transport their belongings and a somewhat battered but serviceable saloon car for the older son to take out his girlfriend. Their saloon car could have gobbled up two British minis and had room left for dessert.

After a blissful summer at the Cadd Ranch, we headed home. On the flight back to London from America, there was a collection of money for a student from our university who had been shot during his visit. He had arrived in a city late at night; I think it was New Orleans.

He had spotted a cheap motel near the Greyhound bus station and pushed open a door that was ajar, thinking it was the office. It wasn't. It was a motel room. A shot rang out. The man in the room had been sleeping with the door open and a loaded revolver under his pillow. The student was paralyzed for life. That was my first encounter with the American gun culture—a phenomenon that still puzzles the rest of the world to this day.

My first experience of living more permanently in America came in 1980, after moving from Kenya to Washington D.C. It's hard for me to imagine now, but for the first year, I found America oppressive. A British friend of mine, also newly arrived from Africa, felt it more acutely, couldn't handle it, and fled overseas again.

The oppression we both sensed was of Big Brother watching us. We had come from the disorganization of Africa, where law and order and regulations—or at least their application—were minimal. Yes, in Africa there were laws, such as speed limits on the roads, but in many African countries at that time, if you'd developed a yearning for a speeding ticket, you would have had to take a can of gasoline to the police so that their vehicle—if it started—could catch you.

If you wanted to get your home telephone connected, you'd have to find the right person, put the pressure on, perhaps get some leverage from the right quarter, and then sit back patiently and wait for your connection. It was aggravating, yes, but it also, paradoxically, left a strange sense of freedom, this absence of being boxed in by the way things were supposed to be. You settled into a freewheeling existence, taking frustrations as they came.

In America, one quickly learned about the high prison population, although it was lower at that time than it is today. For a newcomer, this added to the feeling that you were under scrutiny for any misstep. At the airport and in offices, instead of pushing and shoving to hold your place as you might in Africa or Asia, there were *rules*. There was a painted line on the ground at the immigration kiosk behind which you were supposed to stand to take your turn. If your children ran while at the club swimming pool, a life guard positioned high up on a stool would sternly—and loudly—tell them to stop running. (The fear being, of course, that they might fall over and break a leg, prompting a possible, if not probable, law suit filing by the parents.) In Africa, if your child broke his or her leg at the pool, it was *your* problem. Each rule in America could be argued to make sense—if one thought about it. But why should one have to think about it?

I felt that, in some respects, what I had come from in Africa was a greater freedom; the freedom of benign chaos along with the camaraderie that came from dealing with it. It took a year or two before I fell into line in America and felt less watched, and another year or two before I began to welcome the comparative orderliness.

So these were the strange effects of tribal differences and cultural tuning. Now, three decades on, I am happy in America. The system won, I suppose. America is a powerful country in more ways than one.

So is America "exceptional?" It's an immature question, begging an immature answer. If compelled to nominate a winner in a global exceptionalism stakes, I think I would rank New Zealand, Norway and Denmark well up there. They regularly excel in the annual happiness stakes surveys, if that is a valid test.

No, America seems to me to be best characterized as a "contrary" country, which in some but not all respects can be endearing. Contrary, for example, in being one of the most creative and innovative in technology, yet with surprisingly weak science knowledge among the general population[48] and an extraordinarily large share of people who believe the world was created a few thousand years ago.

Contrary in being vehemently committed to individual freedoms, yet, compared to similar developed countries, having by far the largest number of people in prison. Contrary in believing that owning and being prepared to use a gun is a freedom when the use of guns robs potential and actual, mostly innocent, victims of their freedom. Contrary in having the most evolved and mature edifice of constitutional rights ever devised by man— surely an assurance of responsible governance—yet having a large share of the population avowedly prepared to overthrow the government by force of arms should this arrangement not deliver to their tribe's satisfaction.

Yet, setting aside this rather puzzling, multi-colored cloak of contrariness, this is what I tell people about America:

I met a man in North Carolina who lived out of his truck. He worked as a chef to refine his craft and to save enough to buy his own restaurant. He was prepared to deprive himself today to attain his vision of tomorrow. He was dedicated to becoming the best.

I met a young man in Northern Virginia who worked ten hours a day pumping septic tanks for eight months of the year so he could save enough to travel four months of the year to live rough in poor countries and learn about the world. He had a passion for other cultures. He wanted to understand them; it helped him to understand himself, he said.

I have a good friend Larry in Northern Virginia who has a Ph.D. but did not find a job in his field that he felt sufficiently rewarding. He became a baker; a specialized baker. His eyes light up when he talks of flour, dough, consistency, and crust. It became a calling. He became the best.

I knew a man at the Outer Banks of North Carolina who didn't feel driven to work full-time so he opted for temporary jobs that would pay him enough to provide him with beer, simple food, a tiny rental house, and a temperamental truck. He marched to his own drummer. He preferred to go fishing than to change the world. As far as I know, he had never sponged off anybody or cost social services a penny. Indeed, I once tried to help him file some Medicaid registration forms which I don't think he ever signed. His was a freedom lived. I admired his choice and I acknowledged his freedom to choose.

I once met a young woman at the Outer Banks walking north with a backpack, a seraphic smile on her face. It turned out she was on the last ten miles of a one-thousand-mile walk. Her mother's small house up the road was her destination. She looked forward to a shower. She had accepted no lifts from any vehicle and slept always in her tent. I asked her why she'd done it; what was her reason for such a trek?

"Oh, nothing," she replied easily, "I just wanted to see if I could do it." It had taken her about two months. She had had many adventures along the way, but spoke mostly of meeting interesting people. She was okay with getting back to the grind, but she planned other adventures in the future to break from a life of routine. Her walk had taught her how cheaply she could live if necessary. It was a valuable Plan B, a now acceptable fallback if finding jobs went against her. Here was a young woman who was truly "the master of her fate, the captain of her soul."[49]

I met a woman from California in a small restaurant in Tanzania on the slopes of Mount Kilimanjaro. She was travelling alone. She had made money in the tech industry and wanted to do something for Africa. She had started a small NGO that she was supporting with her own money and, I think, some contributions from friends and colleagues. She had employed a couple of Tanzanians. They were trying to help a small number of Maa-sai settlements with services including health, education and water. She wanted my advice. There were some options in the livestock business and veterinary services and possibly in agriculture. This program had given meaning to her life. She was new to the rural development business but was learning fast.

I have rarely met people like this anywhere in the world. In America, you can still make it with inspiration and perspiration—or you can take the less frenetic path and cruise through life and drink beer. Despite the hardships of sudden and unpredictable economic downturns, I have met very few people who want to sponge off the system or who believe that the government owes them a living—a not uncommon attitude in Europe. I respect that.

So why, then, title the chapter *America the Precarious*? There is a creeping internal crisis today including: the recent retreat from a leadership role in the world, politicians increasingly bought with huge funding, an archaic Electoral College skewing one-person-one-vote rights, gerrymandered electoral boundaries, and a Supreme Court increasingly stacked and politicized.

And recently, it has become apparent that the Founding Fathers made a significant mistake: They built a fine archway of a Constitution, but left out the keystone holding it together at the peak. They forgot to affirm that to sustain the balance of the co-equal branches of government and to ensure the ultimate predominance of justice required the president, at the peak of the arch, to be held to exactly the same laws as any citizen and to have no power to pardon, least of all himself.

The recent emergence of institutional flaws is playing out against a gathering storm of outside threats, including likely catastrophic climate change, political disarray in Europe leaving little backup to fill the void left by America, an increasing number of unstable nuclear powers around the world, and a parlous situation in the Middle East and the Afghanistan Pakistan arena. In these parts of the world, there is potential for explosive and disruptive change due to unemployment, oil income decline, the perception of social media as being threatening, unresolved Israeli and Palestinian issues, internal Islamic strife, and the welcome (but by many Muslim men *unwelcome*) rise of women's power. So, the outside challenges today are immense.

America may be sailing towards the perfect storm…but with torn sails and a damaged rudder.

INDIA
THE BRILLIANTLY MAD

Be as intellectual as you like about it, but India is brilliantly mad. And if you want to love it, you have to hate it first.

— Simon Dring[50]

At first encounter, India is a phantasmagoria of prancing gods, a theatre-in-the-round of poverty, progress, politics and privilege. Looking deeper, there are ranks of scenery flats behind all that, displaying a sumptuous and deeply intellectual ancient history. India—if there really is such an entity at all—publicly thinks it knows where it's going, but privately is less than sure.

But a lot of good things have happened. The number of people in India living in extreme poverty today is down to about 6%. The total number of the extreme poor has fallen below that of Nigeria. This would have been unthinkable thirty years ago. It has come about partly due to the increase in agricultural production with the Green Revolution crop varieties and fertilizer. Take that away and you have famine at horrendous scale. If there is any one country in the world to keep an eye on for exceptional achievement in the next quarter century, it is surely India.

For this chapter, I draw from a time in the 1990s when I lived in Delhi for nearly five years, updated through more recent visits. First, I indulge in a lighter swing through some of India's entertaining quirks, but then I shift to some weightier observations.

While taxis in India have improved in recent years, in the 1990s, a taxi was a lottery. You could get lucky and pick one that was more or less functional, or you could end up in a battered crate of reconditioned parts trying earnestly but failing to cooperate.

I recall one nighttime taxi drive when almost every part of the vehicle was dysfunctional. The clutch was nearing its final death-squeal. The steering felt like a broken boat rudder. My driver worked the horn by shorting a dangling, bare wire onto the metal of the dash. At the rear, the roof lining had given up the struggle of clinging to the roof, so I was hunched under a collapsed Arabian tent of musty, monsoon-damp felt.

For all of this, every few minutes, the driver would humbly apologize. There was a squadron of mosquitoes inside that would have slipped aboard as the driver slept with open doors waiting for his turn in the line. Soon after we set off, he had made the usual pit stop for a gallon of gasoline. This was enough to enable him to freewheel down the slope to my destination hotel, drop me off, and just make it with his next passenger to the nearest gas station for his next parsimonious squirt.

The economic theory here is that, with extreme shortage of cash and the need to eat, one should carry the minimum of fuel inventory. I had to admire his astute volumetric intuition, given the dangling needle behind the cracked fuel gauge glass inanely pointing at a dead fly.

After ten minutes of driving, we ran into rain. This tested him further. Up to that point, one hand had been used to steer and the other had darted from working the hanging horn wire to changing gears. Now he reached out through the window and started up his hand as a windshield wiper.

He had a surprisingly flexible wrist and metronomic timing, but now *four* hands were needed—one to honk the horn, one to change gears, one to wipe the windshield, and one to steer!

I prayed that he had done his Hindu *puja* (prayers) and was in the good books of one of the many-armed gods—preferably Vishnu the Preserver. In the absence of divine intervention, his hands began a Bollywood dance. He dispensed with all but essential gear-changes and started to steer with an alarmingly bony, low-friction, knee. Being a bustling evening rush hour, the threatening traffic still required his use of the dangling horn wire. After two unavoidable protesting gear changes, and after forcing a passage through several circus-like roundabouts, I arrived at my hotel unscathed, although mildly gassed from inhaling the fumes from the cracked exhaust.

After pushing out from under the felt tent, paying him, and getting out with my bag, I walked around in front and realized that, despite the rain and darkness, he had never turned on the headlights. But why would he? There were no bulbs.

Stopping at red lights in most Indian cities used to be treated as optional, except when police were having one of their desultory "safety campaigns" which was obvious from their clustered presence at busy crossings.

At the traffic lights near our house in Delhi, buses and trucks frequently shot the red light. The more decrepit cars nearly always did. Taxi drivers with passengers sometimes deferred to the perceived wishes of a picky passenger, generally a jaw-clenched tourist. As my wife Laila experienced on more than one occasion, military cars were particularly averse to red lights and were adept at cutting you off when changing whatever lanes had inadvertently formed. Presumably red lights were considered unwarranted civilian interference. Her retaliation after one near miss was to pull up close alongside at the next traffic stop, thump fiercely on the door of a flag-flying general's limo and shout at him as he wound down his rear window revealing a chest full of medals, "You have a terrible driver!"

Ox carts were exempt too. Cows, of course, had right of way over everything, from the President's motorcade to a decked-out elephant. If a cow strolled through a red light it appeared that, in its exalted world, the light was always green. But to be fair to cows, they are color-blind to both red and green, so perhaps they should be given a pass!

Almost every day, near our house, lay a large brown cow with a withering glare. Like a deity, it commanded the middle of the road. It was always in the same spot and was always lying on precisely the same compass bearing. It seemed to hold a lifetime reservation. Drivers treated it as a roundabout. It dutifully went home at dusk so was only a daytime hazard. It was in good condition and showed barely a scratch. In all my years in India, I never witnessed a cow struck by a vehicle, although I came across numerous accidents where *humans* had been injured and in one case, even killed.

Some States in India are dry; no alcohol permitted. Many years ago, if you wanted a drink in a hotel in *Gujarat*, Gandhi's home territory, you had to answer questions on a detailed form effectively certifying yourself to be an irredeemable alcoholic. I think some jurisdictions in India at that time required your tame doctor's authenticated certification of your embarrassing condition.

Nowadays, you just get a one-month pass after showing identification documents that indicate you are a visitor. In Gujarat, this gives you, if I remember correctly, two 750 ml bottles a day for not more than ten days of purchases. After that, you need to either sober up or move to another state. The towns in wet states, just over a dry state border, have made good money out of these alcohol access gradients.

The delivery technique for alcohol in Gujarat hotels for guests with permits was a well-practiced ritual. Having shown the reception your required drunkards' chit, you would order your double shot of gin and tonic. It would be delivered to your room in a teapot beside an empty teacup on a saucer, with no bottle or any other evidence of alcohol to sully the presentation.

Going back a few years, for even greater authenticity, your teapot of gin might even have a blank teabag string with the tag hanging out of it. The string would be jammed under the lid, but with no teabag inside to taint your grog. Deception lies in the detail! You were not simply proper, but you were seen to be proper. One of the older waiters in my Gujarat hotel always showed utter distaste as he set the tray down at arm's length and hurried out. A younger waiter treated the game as routine, even with enthusiasm, perhaps hoping I would leave my tea unfinished.

You often hear criticism that India has too many useless cows. There are retirement homes for cows run at considerable cost to the taxpayer. The fact that Hindus do not eat beef and Muslims do triggers religious conflict, including cow riots against Muslims. The exalted stature of the cow raises the question of whether, in both religion and culture, Hindu cow reverence grew from some underlying economic purpose. There are several angles.

Looking at the benefit side, for those cows that are privately owned, the average milk production is low; a pint or two a day for the roadside scroungers. Many cows on the streets are so skinny as to have little useable meat even if it was acceptable to kill them. But there are still some potential benefits.

First, even an emaciated cow can rebound physically with improved forage after a spell of good rainfall. It may once again start producing calves and milk, both significant income providers. So keeping a cow till it almost drops is an insurance policy of sorts.

Second, apart from milk and calves, cows produce dung. It is collected by the *Dalits* and made into dung patties which require about three days of sunshine to get crispy and attain the desired product standard. It is a preferred fuel for the slow, controlled cooking of Indian cuisine and is also used in religious ceremonies. It is believed that cow dung purifies the air in a house.

Incidentally, the dung patty trade has recently been elevated. On E-Bay in India you can get a nicely-packaged pack of 24 uniformly hand-shaped patties for 280 rupees, free delivery. The product description on one website runs: "New. A brand-new, unused and undamaged item that is fully operational and functions as intended."

So a cow wandering the streets and eating off the roadside vegetation and discarded vegetable scraps, even if not producing milk, is, at a minimum, a dung dispenser. Quality cow urine can be bought online, too. It is said to have medicinal properties and to be good for diabetes, blood pressure, skin diseases and arthritis. Nothing in India goes to waste. Not even waste.

Those are some of the benefits of the Indian urban cow, but what about the costs? One argument is that the cows on streets are eating vegetation from urban land that is not used for farming and are cleaning up vegetable trash. So the fodder has what economists call a "zero opportunity cost;" it has no productive alternative use. Moreover, some cows are owned by the poorest families. A cow may be all they have for a small income. So these cultural and religious practices may have some origin in economics.

However, another argument is that retirement homes for cows is going too far. The land could be used for more productive livestock, such as good-quality milking cows or work buffalo for plowing. So while there may be some economic benefits from stray cows, there are high costs to sustaining them on publicly funded retirement home farms when so many are walking skeletons.

Speaking of dung, public toilets at railway stations and on trains have advanced considerably in India since the days of the British Raj, although they are still often quite basic. Here is the text of a letter of complaint written by one Okhil Chandra Sen in 1909, to the Indian Railways. It was, and perhaps still is, displayed in the New Delhi Railway Museum. It was written shortly before train carriages in India changed to having on-board toilets. (For translation, a *lotah* is the necessary water-bottle used for, well, you know what. A *doti* is the rectangular cloth traditionally worn by men in India loosely wrapped around the lower part of the body.)

Dear Sir

I am arrive by passenger train Ahmedpur Station and my belly is too much swelling with jackfruit. I am therefore went to privy. Just I doing the nuisance that guard making whistle blow for train to go off and I am running with lotah in one hand and doti in next when I am fall over and expose all my shocking to man and female women on platform. I am got leaved Ahmedpur Station.

This too much bad if passenger go to make dung that dam guard not wait train minutes for him. I am therefore pray your honor to make a big fine on that guard for public sake. Otherwise I am making big report to papers.

Yours faithfully servant
Okhil Ch. Sen

Much human excrement in India is still deposited outside on the fields or on wasteland plots in cities. It had always seemed to me that a principle of equidistant distribution could be observed. The latest deposition, as one might expect, was added as far away from the existing deposits as possible. In other words, a latecomer squatter would opt to maximize separation.

At one time, third-class railway station toilets consisted of a large, slightly sloped, concrete floor with a drainage gutter at the lower end.

At the end of the day, they would be hosed clean. So the first users of the day had the luxury of space, a luxury gradually lost as more deposits were introduced.

But in India today, there is a major drive to fix the problem of pooping out in the open. Led by the Prime Minister, the government has instituted national and state programs. I have met staff of dedicated NGOs working on providing toilet facilities in villages to help improve sanitation. They know from surveys that one of the main reasons people still go out in the open is the unpleasant state of the few available toilets in villages and towns. I can relate to that.

Sooner or later, the expatriate resident in India becomes familiar with cremations. In Delhi, this was held down at the *ghats* (steps and cremation platforms) by the Yamuna River. Nowadays there are electric or oil-fired crematoria for those who want to save money and break with tradition, but wood is traditional. At the first cremation I attended, for a person I had not known personally, the body was laid out on a platform wrapped in cloth with lengths of firewood carefully stacked over it.

The toes and thumbs are tied together to keep the limbs from shifting and a cloth binds the mouth shut, but this was barely visible through the wood. After a ceremonial lighting of the wood by a relative, the flames licked up around the body. It was enveloped first in clear flame and then gradually in smoky flame. The mourners stood around and spoke quietly amongst themselves as they might at a Christian burial.

After about half an hour, as the fire subsided, I enquired discretely from an Indian colleague at what point in the ceremony it would be acceptable for me to slip away. I didn't want to be rude or unsympathetic, but I had not known the person and I had several urgent deadlines to meet that day. I was told that non-family would be expected to stay until the head "popped." It is at that point that the soul is released for the next stage of its journey. Sure enough, quite soon there was a "pop" that sounded like a muffled champagne cork. I stayed for another ten minutes, offered my final condolences to the family, and slipped away. In some ceremonies, a clay pot is ceremonially dropped, I believe to simulate the pop because the actual sound may be inaudible. In some ceremonies, as the pyre burns down, a close relative with a long stick will hit the skull to crack it open. In this way, a family member plays a role in helping release the soul on the next leg of its journey.

But now for a handful of the weightier themes.

Bribery is still one of India's dead-weight handicaps. I prefer the word *bribery* to *corruption*. Corruption is too sanitized—although I realize the meaning is broader. Transparency International ratings show India to be about the middle of the pack in corruption—not good for a huge country competing globally for business.

As an example of the problem, admittedly going back a few years, a small appliance manufacturing factory owner once told me, "I have twelve government inspectors on my payroll." He explained how he had finally refused to continue buying off an excessively greedy cafeteria inspector. He thought this man had been raising his demands unreasonably and decided to call his bluff.

In retaliation, while the owner was away, the inspector visited the cafeteria and demanded some herbs from one of the containers in the kitchen. He had it analyzed and claimed that it contained only 99.5% of the herb on the label with, of course, a tiny amount of the usual harmless vegetable matter from the fields, assuming it was not added by the inspector himself! On the strength of this analysis, he had the cafeteria manager arrested. The owner fought it in court and got his man out after two or three days. But it cost him far more than the bribe including, of course, the necessary reward for his hapless cafeteria manager.

However, corruption is only one facet of the Indian business and public sector scene. Despite this drag, there is huge development potential. A stable country with well over a billion people of exceptional talent, still asking modest wages but with a growing middle class of consumers; what more could an investor ask for?

Corruption must be tackled and, it seems, is being tackled—there is a substantial corruption grievance system now. Further policy changes are needed—the justice system still moves like a crippled tortoise, and it could still be easier to open and run a business, but, for development potential, India is now one of the most promising countries in the world.

Poverty in India is still closely linked to social strata. *Dalits* is the name often used for those who were referred to as the "untouchables" or, by Gandhi, as the *Harijans*, Children of God, now considered derogatory and patronizing.

Dalits are a "caste" that, in the past, were considered technically caste-less. The four ancient castes—described long ago in Sanskrit texts, the Laws of Manu—were: 1. Priestly People (regardless of wealth, note); 2. Warriors, Rulers and Administrators; 3. Merchants; and, 4. Farmers, Artisans and Laborers, but the Dalits traditionally were hanging off the bottom of this pyramid as a sort of basement category.

Nowadays, they are grouped in legislation for support under the Scheduled Castes (different from the Scheduled Tribes). Legislation has provided for affirmative action programs and regulations protecting both Scheduled Castes and Scheduled Tribes. This includes reserved places in legislative and local bodies and in educational institutions.

In some respects, Dalits, who are about fifteen percent of the population, have come quite a long way since Indian independence from Britain. India has tackled poverty creatively and aggressively. But still, socially, the old discriminations—racism to be blunt—remain. Dalits' work was considered unclean work. It involved collecting cow dung and human excrement, curing hides, dealing with cremations and human bodies, cleaning drains or toilets, and sweeping streets.

Traditionally, they were expected to "know their place." Their shadow was not supposed to fall on a Brahmin; a priestly person. Some were required to drag a brush behind them, tied from the waist, to erase their "unclean" footprints. They were required to use reserved village wells so as not to pollute higher caste water sources. Still today they are often badly treated, sometimes being attacked by higher caste Hindus, for example, for taking part in cow slaughter.

While the British colonial authorities made some attempts to outlaw caste discrimination, some of their policies ended up exacerbating it. It has been argued that the British Raj system of land taxing contributed to pressures on higher castes to increase their incomes to help pay these taxes resulting in the knock-on effect of seizing land from the lower caste Dalits, often through calculated creation of indebtedness.

At independence, the improvement of their lot looked promising when a revered, highly educated Dalit, Dr. B. R. Ambedkar, one of the drafters of the Indian Constitution and a member of Nehru's cabinet, was able to fight for their rights. But he was unable to achieve his goals and later resigned.

The Dalits did not take their oppression lying down. Some tried to escape the Hindu caste hierarchy by converting to Christianity or Buddhism. Some looked to communism. As we see across the debris fields of history, the oppressed will rise, the only question is when, where, and how, and what will be the cost in human suffering.

With some similarities of condition to the Dalits, but probably with Gypsy connections, the *Dom* tribe, while technically outside the Brahminic hierarchy of castes, also perform "untouchable" types of work.

In the city of Varanasi, on the banks of the Ganges, they manage and control cremations. Here, in the ultimate business of death, the Doms have had the opportunity to fleece other castes. When I first went there, there used to be a sort of paramount chief, a single Dom Raja, who held ownership of most of the main cremation grounds, the *ghats,* in Varanasi. He also managed the "eternal flame" from which all pyres were lit—said to have been burning for 3,500 years. Imagine the awful responsibility of tending that!

The Dom Raja used to ask whatever price he thought he could get for a cremation, your wealth and origin being the yardstick. The old Dom Raja died some years ago and there was a succession battle. The extended family was unable to agree on a successor, so now, I believe, there are about five family Dom Rajas who hold a looser monopoly. Despite the family fissure, they still have a firm grip on the death industry. Other Doms have cornered smaller bits of the market, like sifting mud and ashes by the banks of the Ganges for gold tooth fillings or gold jewelry left on bodies.

One reason not to underestimate India is the strength of the women's movement which has been growing for many years, supported, among others, by the dedicated Self-Employed Women's Association (SEWA). Women's groups today—and indeed, women *themselves*—are transforming rural society. Support comes from governments, both federal and state, donors and many dedicated NGOs and individuals. Let me invite you to a women's group meeting:

I am sitting cross-legged on a mat in a small village house, part concrete part wood, with a group of fourteen rural women, all married. It is the house of one of the somewhat better-off members, her turn to host the meeting. They are wearing colorful saris, not everyday working ones. They have dressed up a little.

About half of the members are below the official national poverty line. Everyone knows each member's approximate rank on the poverty scale, but they don't make a big thing about it; there is collective commitment to pull everyone up. Every woman is equal as a member but there are two less poor ladies who seem to hold more command. One is their elected chairperson.

Last year she was also elected to the village council.

They meet every week, more often than most groups. They borrow as a group from a local bank and share out the loan. They save as a group each week and put money into a savings account for bad times and for loan collateral. For distributing their borrowed bank money, the best business ideas are selected from all their members' proposals. But over time, everyone gets a shot to borrow. This group has never had a repayment problem except when a member died—and even then, they all chipped in to make up the payment when the widower couldn't.

They show me their account book, neatly kept. They have an accounts clerk funded by a project who helps them keep the books. Next year they will pay him themselves, but they think that soon they will not need him. Two of them say they already know how to do it.

One woman bought a cow with her loan. She later takes me to see it. It looks healthy, has given the calf it was pregnant with and is milking well. It is fed in a shed with cut hay and bought concentrate feed pellets but sometimes grazes on common land. She sells some of the milk to the cooperative and keeps the rest for her family.

Another woman used her loan to pay for some fertilizer and rice seed, a new variety of rice, supposed to be more productive. She tells me it was. Another used hers to stock her village kiosk with cigarettes, soda, and other small goods. Another says she paid for medicine for a child. Health must come first she says. They all nod.

But they do more than borrow money. The state government has child health and maternity classes open to them. They encourage pregnant members to attend, especially the younger ones. They learn about child nutrition. The group has been helping a young mother who is struggling. She is sitting a little back from the circle. She married in from another district and has been finding it difficult with her demanding mother-in-law. They are trying to help her, but it's a juggling act because, if they don't do it right, things could get worse for her.

They get help in negotiating their bank loans from a young, well-educated woman who has been trained to properly complete the complicated bank forms. For each loan, they must present a group plan for what they will do with the money. Also, the group has joined a state government pension scheme. It doesn't pay a lot, but it gives them a little security.

They have organized themselves as a group to fight violence in the home from abusive husbands; one woman is in tears. She has a sad story. In one case they tell me about, they were prepared to turn up as a group and make it clear to a husband that his abusive behavior must stop. They are prepared to act through the law if they must, but they prefer to settle the matter amicably. Again, a heavy hand could make it worse.

After finishing our discussion, there are thanks all around and they have some lighter questions for me. We stand on a muddy village road. One stretch further up the hill has been repaired by project funds, but not this stretch; it is rough and slippery after rain. Two foraging buffalo with a child herder stare at me with curiosity.

There is a group of five men who I saw had been trying to edge close enough to catch snatches of our discussion. I wander over and ask them whether they have ever considered forming a men's group for farming activities like group borrowing for buying seed or fertilizer or for marketing. They look embarrassed. The oldest admits that they had a men's marketing group two years ago, but it didn't last. He says there were a lot of disagreements, several members lost interest, and there were not enough volunteers to organize meetings. They look uncomfortable.

Walking up the street with the women's group, I ask, "Why don't men form groups or keep them going?"

They all burst out laughing, some doubled-up with hilarity, and one of them shrieks, "Men? Men? They can't organize groups! They always fight! They can't agree!"

"And they are lazy!" another one chips in, "Only women can work in groups!" She turns back to her group holding out her hands, "Men's groups? Men!" They all collapse laughing again. I feel almost foolish for asking such a silly question, although elsewhere in India I have spoken with men's groups that did work, though rarely as well as women's groups.

If I was lending my own money to reduce poverty and if I wanted my money to be repaid so that I could lend it again to others, I would lend only to women. They repay. They care. They nurture the next generation. They support each other. They are strong. They are the future. In India, as elsewhere, women's time is now.

I owe a debt to my friend and colleague Balasubramanian, for introducing me to Hinduism. I gained a respect for a religion that is often regarded by others as quasi-pagan or just plain weird. Many non-Hindus look askance at the panoply of many-armed gods, giant phalluses, vulvas that could swallow a goat, and animal-drawn vehicles of the gods. But, again, it helps to apply a wide lens.

There has been much debate about whether Hinduism is polytheistic, monotheistic or pantheistic. The differences of perception say as much about the beliefs of the observer as about Hinduism. I find Hinduism closer to monotheism, or perhaps to a lack of a distinction between God and the world—God being present in everything. To most Hindus, the debate about what sort of "theism" they own is a problem for the outsider to fuss about. They grasp it even if we don't. They believe there are many paths to truth and they understand that there is room for various interpretations without collapsing the essence. Christianity and Islam could learn from this.

I find that there are differences in Hindu interpretation between the more sophisticated urban cultures, with a more nuanced, more monotheistic, interpretation, and the rural culture with a more polytheistic interpretation.[51] If you spend time in Indian villages, it will seem, at first sight, to be wholly polytheistic, with different castes propitiating different caste gods and different families propitiating different family gods, sometimes evident from the paintings on their house walls. Deity loyalties may shift if misfortune befalls. A family I met in the south told me, "We think that our youngest child died because we neglected a god who was good to a neighboring family. They had a sick child that lived." So they took up worshipping the neighbor's god too, as an insurance.

But even in these more traditional villages, underneath this superficial polytheism, one senses a deeper vein connected to a universal truth with the lesser gods acting more as manifestations at levels below the ultimate godhead. A clue is that in Hinduism there are associations between gods and moods and between gods and aspirations.

Christianity has a form of poly-manifestation in the notion of the trinity, God the Father, God the Son, and God the Holy Ghost—a concept, by the way, that Islam rejects as belittling the one God. Hinduism has its trinity in Vishnu, Brahma and Shiva, Buddha being considered a ninth incarnation of Vishnu.

Hinduism's Supreme Being, if definable at all, is Brahman, really a concept rather than a godhead. Brahman is more embracing than the godhead of the Abrahamic religions of Christianity, Judaism, and Islam that believe in a God generally conceived as male and, in one case, a God who was made manifest in a human body and lent to the people of earth. Brahman (not the same as Brahma the Creator, although linked) is perceived as being above and beyond man-conceived characterizations, a higher reality, the creative principle, an elusive yet pervasive influence on the universe, difficult to approach but impossible to ignore—the ultimate in oneness.

To better appreciate the nature of Hindu theism, one can think of our European fairy tales with stories of princes and princesses, witches and wizards, ogres and frogs, in which the strands of personalities parallel our own psyches. Jon Kabat-Zinn writes in his book *Wherever You Go, There You Are,*[52] in discussing the meaning of fairy tales, "It is worth seeking the altar where our own fragmented and isolated being-strands can find each other and marry..." At the deepest level, the Hindu gods, their strengths and their foibles, represent the personal being-strands that an enlightened life needs to explore and resolve in the search for ultimate truth.

So I submit that Hinduism offers real insight into our place in the world and how we should live in it. It is a legitimate faith with multiple facets of a unity—reflecting the range of human spiritual needs—rather than, in the shallowest interpretations, a motley mob of competing narcissistic deities. There is a difference.

FLY FISHING
AMONG ELEPHANTS

**Our tradition is that of the first man
who sneaked away to the creek when
the tribe did not really need fish.**

– Roderick Haig-Brown[53]

I suppose my passion for fishing came from my grandfather on my mother's side, Fred Taylor, mentioned earlier, whose best fish was a 735-pound Bluefin Tuna, 23 pounds short of the world record at the time, held by Zane Grey.

He caught it off Scarborough, England, in the early 1930s, from a rowing boat with one man on the oars and no motor, a real battle with fish and sea. My own fishing has been for lesser fry but sometimes in the territory of bigger land beasts.

The world can be divided into those who fish and those who don't, perhaps another Us-vs.-Them dichotomy, but a lighter matter. In any case, those who don't fish leave more river and fish for me and others who do, so while pitying their deprivation, I am inclined to applaud their indifference.

Fly fishing should have been invented by Leonardo da Vinci, but it wasn't. It seems to have been invented before his time by some creative fishermen in Macedonia. The technique of using crude feather representations of insects was reported from there by the Roman author Claudius Aelianus about the end of the second century. (Mind you, old Aelian may not have been the most reliable of observers. He is the one who reported that beavers, when hunted, bite off their own testicles and toss them out in front of hunters to put them off the chase—a whole new angle on having balls! But I digress.)

Having once surreptitiously caught—and returned—a trout taken on a short stick, two foot of nylon and a fly when I was illegally testing out a remote bush-hidden mountain cascade high in the Italian Dolomites, I can vouch for the presence of a trout species in Leonardo's corner of Europe.

But even though he didn't invent fly fishing, surely, as the consummate artist-scientist, he would have been fascinated by it. Fly fishing has everything that a Renaissance man sought; the artistry of an aerial line looping across a tapestry of streamside branches; the heavier-than-water artificial fly perched in defiance of gravity on a film of surface tension, and the entomological representation of the artificial fly that must look and behave like the diaphanous living mayfly.

A trout fly is both a delicate piece of art and a cruel deception. Each fly bears traces of its designer's story. Fly fishing, at least traditionally, culminates in a death, a death that seems somehow right, almost an act of nature, but not quite. And fly fishing offers the most erudite and philosophical literature of any sport.

The first piece of fly fishing literature seems to have been written by a woman, a prioress in England, Dame Juliana Berners. The evidence that she was the author is not entirely watertight, but it seems more than plausible; the language displays delicacy with practicality. It was printed in 1496 by an apprentice of the great Caxton under the title *A Treatyse of Fysshynge wyth an Angle*.

How I would have liked to have prevailed upon Dame Juliana to stroll a streamside path with me with rod and line and to entice her to spill her secrets! And how I would have liked to have instructed her in our modern fly fishing techniques to get her reaction. I think she would have approved.

In her book, she describes how to make a rod, how to make horse hair line, and how to dub flies on a hook with wool. She writes to us down the centuries of how to tie flies with hen hackle and peacock, materials I still use to this day. She suggested flies for each month. It is a remarkable work and it was published a whole one-and-a-half centuries in advance of the next major work, Isaak Walton's classic *The Compleat Angler,* published in 1653.

Dame Juliana has been considered by some to be the first environmentalist. At the end of her book she urges preservation of the fish stock by not taking more than you need. She talks about other ways to protect the environment and urges those who fish not to cause problems for landowners. What a dame!

I had fly fished once or twice in England in my youth, but I first started fly fishing seriously in Kenya in 1971. It became an addiction really; a sickness. I devoured every book on fly fishing that I could lay my hands on and learned how to tie flies. At night in bed, I would lie awake plotting my next assault on a stream with a cut-away bank under a tree where I believed there was some monster lurking.

I fished rivers in Kenya with names like the Naro Moru, the Thego, the Sagana, the Thiba, the Nanyuki, the Gatamayu, the Chania and the Mathioya. In Kenya, a Royal Coachman wet fly was the most popular, a white-winged fly with a dash of red. I confess that, against the tenets of purism, not only did I mostly fish with sinking wet flies rather than dry floating ones, but sometimes, due to the tightness of casting space and the speed of water in mountain streams, I squeezed a tiny lead shot on the leader above the fly to help flick it around. Sacrilege on the hallowed chalk streams of old England!

In England, the nearest you can come to danger while trout fishing is a little shit of a terrier from a local farm or ripping your vulnerable parts getting over a barbed wire fence. Trout fishing in Africa offered the real spice of danger from wildlife, the threat of the hunter becoming the hunted. This closed the loop. It altered the way you went about fishing.

Those who fish in grizzly bear country in America know the feeling. Fishing the high country in Kenya in the Aberdare Park above the forest line where elephant, lion, leopard, and buffalo shared the streams with you, placed you inside the evolutionary bubble. You reverted to being merely a claimant species with no particular rights other than the primordial right to kill or be killed. Carrying a gun was not permitted. If you got into trouble with upset wildlife your carcass might never be found. How fitting!

But I confess, I lead you on a little. The risks were quite small if you knew wildlife and little more than modest if you didn't and relied on instinct. On these high-altitude moorlands a few miles from the equator, the tunnels through the six-foot-high streamside bushes had been forced by wildlife; the smallest by little antelopes such as *dik-dik* and by leopards; the larger passageways by medium antelope such as *bushbuck*. These also served as short-cuts or shade refuges for lions. The wider lanes, open to the sky, were made by buffalo or elephant.

You could generally see buffalo and elephant at a distance if you fought through the bushes standing upright holding the rod above your head so as not to get snagged; but if you were on hands and knees—sometimes the only option—you could only spot animals about five yards ahead. Crawling was sometimes unavoidable if the prize was a deeper pool surrounded by dense bush.

Just as stealth is needed in hunting to get close to a quarry, the way to avoid unwelcome wildlife encounters is to avoid stealth. Few wild animals opt for fight rather than flight. They will generally slither, crawl, walk, or run away, provided the age of their offspring allows them the luxury of fearfulness.

Before plunging into thick streamside bushes, I was always careful to take note of the direction and speed of movement of any of the large animals spotted at a distance; elephants can move surprisingly fast if they are bent on getting somewhere and are not browsing on the way. The Cape Buffalo is relatively harmless in a herd but unpredictable as a lone bull, particularly an old, cantankerous one.

The teenage son of a friend of mine was once charged by a bull buffalo on a bush track in the Maasai Mara. He was knocked to the ground with a powerful blow to the thigh. Fortunately, that one, which had been wounded by a hunter a few days earlier and so no doubt took a dim view of humans, didn't turn back to finish the job. From its open wound, it left a gob of congealed blood on the track.

One of the challenges of fly fishing on the East African moorlands, not unlike the Scottish Highlands, is the clarity of the water. It is exquisitely filtered by bush, bog and matted tussock grass. Even fine nylon leaders of one-pound breaking strain seem to slice the water like a ship's hawser. On the trout streams of Kenya so close to the equator, three or four cutting across it, the light in the middle of the day has greater penetration than on the Scottish Highlands or in Australia or New Zealand, making it difficult to fool wiser fish in deeper pools.

To find less clear, "colored" water, it was sometimes worth seeking out the elephants and waiting about four hundred yards downstream for the stirred-up water from their playing and bathing to come down to you; better still, waiting until it had almost passed and was just beginning to clear. The fly line leader was no longer so conspicuous and there might even be a few displaced nymphs or struggling beetles dislodged from bushes that would stir the fish into feeding. But apart from the challenge of finding elephants bathing at the right time and place, the passing of a pachyderm plume was usually a brief affair, sometimes too short for the trout to wake up to the changed conditions.

There was always a small risk in Kenya from snakes, some deadly. But there was less risk in the highland trout areas above the forest line than

213

there was at the warmer lower altitudes around lakes and rivers where I fished for stocked large-mouth bass in lakes or native catfish in rivers. The deadly puff adder was the biggest risk because it is arrogant and retreats reluctantly.

The secret to avoiding snakes is to make plenty of ground vibration and noise by thumping around like a drunk, not the best approach when stalking your wary fish, but you have to choose your priority. You also need to look out for snakes in the obvious places, under rocks and bushes or basking in a patch of sun on a track.

In those days we obviously had no cell phones. If you were bitten effectively by one of the many poisonous species, and if you were alone, your hours could be counted on one hand with several fingers to spare. Trying to walk or crawl to a road or track two or three miles away would have spread the venom very effectively.

In my early fishing days in Africa, I devoured all the trout fishing literature I could lay my hands on. I have about a hundred and twenty books on fly fishing on my shelves. Many of them were bought in the mid-1970s in, of all places, Dar es Salaam in Tanzania.

There was a used bookshop owned by an erudite Indian gentleman. His shop was in an old Arab trader's store not far from the harbor. It had thick stone walls and an aroma of spices, sandalwood, damp book bindings, and boat pitch. The humidity in his shop would have been intolerable if it had not been for the hidden gems I was seeking.

On one of my visits during a rainy season, the humidity was magnified by a bulging black plastic tarpaulin that had been tied from four corners to prevent rainwater from the leaking roof dripping onto the rows of book shelves. Like a giant dinosaur bladder, it was distended close to breaking point. Not only did this reservoir boost the humidity but it was providing an ideal nursery for mosquito larvae. The place hummed. But these tribulations were well worth it in a country where, for antiquarian English books, this was the only place to go.

He had accumulated his stock of trout fishing books because many white farmers from around Mount Kilimanjaro and across the border in Kenya had been selling up and leaving Africa, or simply dying off. Trout fishing had been a popular recreation for them and he had been buying up their libraries.

On my first visit, I thumped five large fishing books on the counter, including two tattered first editions. With his glasses on the end of his nose, he looked at them one by one, turning each over studiously and finally declared with a brief smile, "My God! A fishing maniac!"

As I thumb through them now, I am reminded that some of them have names, addresses, or dedications inscribed inside the front covers. I have always felt that clues of earlier owners in the front of old books add greatly to their value. Yet they also make me feel a discomfiting responsibility. What if I was the last person to know this person's name and his love of fly fishing? Who was this B. A. Bird, March 1910? Who was this fly fisherman Johnson whose address was neatly inscribed Kyambu, Kenya Colony? What was the event that caused the tea stain on page twenty-nine? Or was it whisky? Had there perhaps been an argument at home? Had he been drunk? Did he once fish the same rivers that I fished? And if I do have a responsibility, what is it exactly? To research his existence? To pass his book back to his descendants if I could trace them?

I wish more people would write in books. We can be sure that those who follow will find scribbled annotations interesting now that books are following the clay tablet into the middens of history. In this age of electronic readers, books have changed their nature. They are no longer merely records; they are artifacts.

Fly fishing in Australia in the fast mountain streams and, a little lower down, in the slower rivers coming off the Snowy Mountains, offers supreme solitude, even by the ridiculously generous Australian standards of elbow room. Perhaps less so now, but in the 1960s, it was uncommon to see another fisherman all day.

There were platypus[54] in these rivers. They were hard to spot unless you knew what to look for. Strange creatures. They lay eggs, have beaks, beaver tails and otter feet, and the male has a poisonous spur. When fly fishing, I would suddenly notice a smooth rock barely breaking the surface that I felt sure had not been there at my previous cast. Then I would conclude it must have been there and I would resume my casting. Then it would seem to move, and I would realize it had soap-slick fur. There would be a small whirl and it would vanish, only to pop up a minute later in another spot. I was always afraid I might snag one with my fly. On one occasion, my fly slid right over the back of a large one that had just surfaced, but fortunately, it was tied on a tiny hook and didn't take hold.

New Zealand has some monstrous trout. No country I have fished can compare. I fished there many years ago around Lake Taupo, in the North Island, but I was there at the wrong time of the year for catching trout in the rivers. It was summer and most of the trout in the warming tributary streams were back in the lake in deeper, cooler water. I have never enjoyed thrashing the still waters of a lake; it rewards modest skill too readily. So I decided to ask around to see what my options were for river fishing.

I asked a fisherman in a pub bar whether there was anywhere I might find trout in a stream. He thought for a while and said, "Well, mate, I don't fish much nowadays, but the place to go, if you're up to it, is below the dam at the Aratiatia rapids. But if you tell anyone I told you, I'll deny it."

He took a swig, frowned and paused with the beer hovering near his lips. "There's one slight problem. They let the water out at the dam three times a day to keep the river fed." He went on, "I think, I think, the time of the releases is about ten, twelve and two, but I'm not sure. They may have changed it."

He ordered another beer which I put on my tab. "But you'll know, you'll know, they blast a siren. I think they blast it about a minute before they open the gate."

I noted with some concern that there were a lot of "thinks" and "abouts" in his instructions.

He went on, "When they open the sluices, the gorge turns into a raging bloody torrent, mate. If yer down there at the bottom you'll be pummeled into…" he paused, searching for a word.

"Trout pellets?" I volunteered.

"Yea, trout pellets!" He smiled. *That* part he seemed to be quite sure of.

He looked into my eyes, "Let me repeat, it won't be good for your survival to be down there at the wrong time." I gulped and nodded.

This was starting to look a little more serious than taking the occasional risk with cantankerous elephants in Africa, but, well into my third beer, I said, "I'll give it a shot."

He gave me directions to a bend on a small road. I would see big red signs over a wire fence saying DANGER. DO NOT ENTER. He drew a rough map on a beer mat.

"You'll see a hole in the barbed wire fence under the signs, at least there used to be a hole. I haven't been there for a couple of years. Ignore all the 'Danger' signs, climb through the hole and crawl down through the tunnel in the bushes. You'll come out at the bottom beside the river on an exposed bank of pebbles."[55]

The following morning, I headed out with some trepidation. I found the hole in the fence. His directions turned out to be spot-on. Ignoring the danger signs as instructed, I crawled through with my fly rod. (Note to reader: DON'T EVER TRY THIS. Apart from the fact that it was silly back in the 1980s, it is even sillier now. A young woman drowned at this spot recently.)

I descended uneasily through the tunnel in the bushes. Partway down I reached a point where the bushes were wet. I stopped and hissed to myself, "Holy shit!" The place clearly turned into a mighty torrent. Soon after that, I came out on a small beach area of large river pebbles. It was just as he had said.

There were three trout of about four- to-five pounds swimming around in the clear pool. I surveyed the gorge towering over me and could see, from the height of the water line, what would happen when the gates opened. I would be tossed around like a discarded cigarette butt. I decided to practice a dry run for my escape in case I had misunderstood the times of opening and the siren warning.

Checking the second hand of my watch, I dropped my rod by the river's edge and ran up to the tunnel in the bushes, crawling as quickly as I could until I got above what seemed to be the high-water mark. It took about a minute. So if it was true that I had a minute from the siren, I reckoned I could probably make it out alive. Just.

I fished for about thirty minutes. The fish were not as easy as they looked. But eventually, after changing my fly to a popular local pattern, one of them broke from its group and dashed furiously at my fly at the edge of a patch of shadow. It fought fiercely. I thought perhaps this was because it got its gym exercise three times a day trying to hold position in the dam-release torrent.

I eventually beached it and whacked it on the head with the handle of my sheathed knife. I started casting again for one of the other two that had slipped into hiding. But after about ten minutes, I decided I had pushed my luck enough on the nagging question of water release. I had my one nice fish. I crawled back up the tunnel out of the gorge with my prize. As I was driving away, about a mile down the road, I heard the siren go. I did a U-turn, drove back, looked down into the gorge, and gulped.

ORCHESTRATED HELL

A kind of orchestrated hell—
a terrible symphony of light and flame.

– Edward R. Murrow, writing of a
Lancaster raid over Berlin, 1943

I go backward in history now to stories from before my time, but I suggest forward in history in contemplating the future of our species. War is the ultimate expression of mankind's Us–against-Them disorder. Yet paradoxically, it has on occasion brought the Us and the Thems together, or at least into new relationships. The impact of the First World War trenches on the English class system and on the officer to "other ranks" relationship was one example. I offer here only a few vignettes of war, but I hope collectively they build to an impression of a little more.

I never served in the armed forces, but nearly all my male forebears of two generations fought in at least one of the two world wars. As noted earlier, my father commanded a World War II bomber base. My grandfather Nelson fought in the Royal Navy in World War I at the Battle of Jutland and was recalled to the Admiralty in London for World War II. An uncle, Ivor Nelson, was a British officer in a Gurkha paratroop battalion of the Indian Army, and earlier in the Kurram Militia in the tribal areas of what is now Pakistan. Another uncle, Bobby Taylor, was a tank commander at the front of the British advance through France and Germany after D-Day. Still another uncle, Brain Taylor, served in Burma as a Provost Officer.

One of my great uncles helped raise a World War I Manchester Pals Regiment and served as Staff Captain. Only a handful of that regiment limped away from the Western Front. A great uncle fought at the Battle of Omdurman in Sudan, and in the Boer War, and later at Gallipoli. Shortly after leading a team of wire-cutters under heavy fire from Turkish forces on the heights, he was shot in the head. He survived, just, but was never the same person again. One of my great-grandfathers was a Royal Navy captain who fought in many naval engagements in the late 1800s in a battleship that had sails supplementing coal-powered engines.

Despite all this military service, by extraordinary good fortune, my family on both sides lost nobody. Less fortunate families lost every one of their men and boys. Every village and town memorial in Britain, in the Commonwealth countries, and in America speaks of the millions who "grew not old."[56]

To honor the sacrifice of those who lived and those who died, I believe every one of us should understand the toll of war. This is best done by looking at the smaller dramas rather than the broader sweep of colliding histories, but first I must offer briefly just one broader sweep for context and because it is not atypical.

THE BATTLE OF JUTLAND

The First World War was triggered by a spiral of descent into conflict that is still hard to fathom, even with a century of perspective. The players were caught up in a global version of an escalating ice hockey brawl. Greatly oversimplified, there was a series of events triggered by alliances.

After the assassination of Grand Duke Ferdinand and an ultimatum by Austria-Hungary to Serbia, a Russian treaty kicked in, then a German treaty, then a French treaty, then a British treaty, then other players' treaties, later, in 1917, drawing the United States into the quagmire. The sequence of events suggests that this war came about largely by ricochet.

However, behind the triggered alliances, there was a deeper cause; Germany and Britain had been drawn into a naval arms race, my grandfather's dreadnought battleship being one of the products. Churchill, as First Lord of the Admiralty, had foreseen the risks and had several times proposed a capital ship construction pause for Britain and Germany. The Germans were suspicious and the British case was not helped by the stick that Churchill held too close to the carrot he was proffering—that if the Germans rejected his pause, then for every ship Germany built, he would build two. Not the recommended way to get a handshake.

On May 31, 1916, at the Battle of Jutland off Denmark, in which the British fleet fought the German fleet for the first and last time, my grandfather was the second engineer on the super-dreadnought HMS *Warspite*, a Queen Elizabeth Class Battleship[57] with, among other armament, four huge, twin 15-inch guns, capable of firing nineteen miles.

Jutland was one of the largest naval engagements of all time measured by the total tonnage of warships. There were some two hundred and fifty ships arrayed against each other. *Warspite* was one of four battleships that had recently been assigned to the 5th Battle Squadron alongside Captain Beatty's faster battle cruisers, vessels of similar size, but lighter. To some tacticians, this was an error of disposition—putting the lighter armored and faster ships with the more heavily armored slower ones. In any case, it turned out that the lighter battle cruisers suffered from a design flaw: To help save weight, they had insufficient baffling below the guns, allowing blast to force down the turret into the magazines. "There's something wrong with our bloody ships today," muttered Beatty after several blew up. There was.

Early in the battle, *Warspite*'s steering gear jammed due to a shell strike on the stern and a gear-stressing tight turn away from the enemy. She started making wide circuits within range of the German fleet. Each time she approached them, she took full broadsides at about eight thousand yards from five German battleships, eventually taking twenty-nine direct hits.

As I write, I have on my desk a jagged piece of shrapnel from one of those hits; if I have judged the rifled side curvature correctly, it was a thirteen-inch shell. My grandfather and his team struggled down below under very difficult conditions of smoke, fire, and shell impacts to repair the steering. After about twenty minutes and three circuits, the ship's guns blazing defiantly all the way, his team was successful, saving them from almost certain destruction.

She had taken such a pounding that she was ordered back to Rosyth in Scotland, narrowly escaping two submarine torpedo attacks, attempting to ram one of them which crash-dived. Sitting four-and-a-half feet lower in the water than normal, with several fires still being fought and carrying many horribly burned men, she sailed past the oblivious nesting puffins on the Isle of May into the safety of the Firth of Forth.

Jutland was an indecisive battle and one in which the British Fleet should probably have had more of an upper hand. However, the German fleet never ventured out in full force again, so it was tactically decisive in favor of Britain, despite the heavier losses of ships and men on the British side.

In the same battle squadron, not far from *Warspite,* a poignant drama of war that my grandfather once described to me was playing out involving a teenager, Jack Cornwell. He was sixteen years old, holding the rank of Boy 1st Class. He was from a poor working-class family in London. He was the sight-setter on the forward 5.5 inch gun of the Light Cruiser HMS *Chester.*

Through earphones, he would receive the bearing and elevation for firing the guns and would relay it to the gun crew. Early in the engagement, HMS *Chester* was sent forward to probe enemy lines. This attracted concentrated fire. Jack Cornwell's gun was hit and most of the members of his gun crew were killed or wounded. Until the end of the action, with shards of shrapnel in his chest and in great pain, he stood bravely at his post on the exposed foredeck, earphones still on his head, losing blood but awaiting any orders that might come through.

After some time, the ship's doctor was able to go forward and work on him and other wounded. The ship survived the battle. As young Cornwell was being brought into the hospital after returning to port at Grimsby, a nurse asked him how they had got on. He replied, "Oh we got on alright, ma'am." He died shortly before his mother arrived at the hospital off a train from London.

The ship's captain wrote to his mother: "...his gun would not bear on the enemy, all but two of the ten crew were killed or wounded, and he was the only one who was in such an exposed position. But he felt he might be needed—as indeed he might have been—so he stayed there, standing and waiting, under heavy fire, with just his own brave heart and God's help to support him..."

He was posthumously awarded the Victoria Cross, the highest British and Commonwealth award for gallantry. He was the youngest in the navy ever to receive it. His gun is on display at the Imperial War Museum in London. Court painter Frank Salisbury painted the scene. His fine gravestone at Manor Park Cemetery in London, reflecting the class consciousness of the day, is inscribed: *"It is not wealth or ancestry but honourable conduct and a noble disposition that maketh men great."*

THE YEARS BETWEEN

My father had some of his narrowest brushes with death outside of wartime between the First and Second World Wars. Flying in those days was a risky occupation. His closest call was on June 24, 1935, when he was flying a Fairey Seal configured as a float plane. He was towing drogues, large windsocks, for the navy to shoot at.

This day the practice was over the Solent, the stretch of water between the Isle of Wight and the English mainland. He was in the front cockpit and his telegrapher, Roberts, was in the rear. These were open cockpits and very cold, so the pilot often wore a scarf around his neck. A large drum was mounted between the cockpits carrying a cable shackled to the drogue.

On this day, a couple of shots passed too close. My father ordered Roberts to let out another hundred yards of cable. Roberts pulled the lever. As the drum slowly paid out, my father's scarf became trapped under the cable on the slowly revolving drum. It tightened around his neck, lifting him up out of his seat and throttling him against the drum. Roberts felt the aircraft go into a dive and realized something was wrong.

Taking considerable risk, he stood up out of his seat. Peering round the drum as they were diving seawards, he saw my father purple in the face and unresponsive. Roberts was not a pilot, so he had to act quickly. With a knife, he cut the scarf free. My father slumped forward over the controls. There was little altitude left. Roberts reached round further, lying along the top of the fuselage beside the drum and shook him and slapped his face. My father regained consciousness just in time to see the water coming up to meet them. He pulled back the stick, putting the aircraft down a little heavily on its floats in Portland Harbor and lost consciousness again.

He was in hospital for several days with bruises and neck burns. The newspapers reported the incident the following day: "FIGHT FOR LIFE IN AEROPLANE - Scarf Nearly Strangles Pilot." His pilot's log for that day reports drily, "Towing drogue. Forced landing Portland Harbour."

LANCASTERS OVER GERMANY

I was given my way of life, if not life itself, by an extraordinary generation who fought to defend Britain in World War II. One of the RAF pilots lost very early in the war was Ridley Bradford, after whom I am named, and to whom this book is dedicated. But many on the British side came from lands far from immediate threat, from Australia, Canada, New Zealand, India, and America. Without these and other allies including Poland and Russia, Britain would certainly have been overrun by another tribe, a tribe that had careened off track. My world would have never been the one I am now able to look back on from an armchair. I suppose I would have grown up fatherless, perhaps in some youth brigade, although I believe Hitler would have had great difficulty controlling an occupied Britain given the citizens' bloody mindedness.

Probably I would have grown up reading only permitted texts, mixing only with permitted people. Possibly I would have become an enthusiast; young minds are malleable. Whatever the outcome, I doubt I would have had the same opportunities nor been the same person. But who knows? T.S. Eliot understood the slipperiness of history, "History has many cunning passages, contrived corridors / And issues, deceives with whispering ambitions / Guides us by vanities."[58]

After a nearly three-year posting in Australia, and our return by convoy, my father took over command at RAF Elsham Wolds,[59] a Lancaster bomber station. The Lancaster bomber was an extraordinary aircraft carrying a bombload of about ten tons. It was quite fast, with a high effective ceiling and maneuverable enough to do a barrel roll. Towards the end of the war, they sometimes carried a single Grand Slam weighing 22,000 pounds. An American pilot peering up into the huge open Lancaster bomb-bay had remarked, "Goddamn it! It's a flying bomb-bay!"

On December 2, 1943, my father was on a raid over Berlin the same night that Edward R. Murrow, the American broadcaster, was flying with another crew from a nearby base. It turned out to be a difficult attack. The city was strongly defended and there was an incorrect wind forecast making it more challenging with many hundreds of aircraft pouring into the same target.

Murrow filed his report the day of return, describing what he saw as, "orchestrated hell, a terrible symphony of light and flame." His reports from London were instrumental in building sympathy for American involvement. To get this ride in a Lancaster, Murrow had reportedly begged his reluctant boss, "Let me ride in a bomber so I can know how a pilot feels when his tail has been shot off." It was seldom that journalists were taken, but there were four foreign journalists on four different aircraft that night; two out of the four did not return. Murrow was one of the lucky two.

It was on that same night that my father had his closest wartime brush with death. He recorded in red ink in his pilot's log, "Just missed exploding Lancaster." The RAF Bomber Command losses on that raid entered in his log book were 9.09%, with later adjustments now listed officially as 8.7%. It was one of the costliest mass raids of the war. From his squadron, out of the eight aircraft flying that night, three failed to return and two had to land short of their base due to heavy damage and hydraulic failure.

Having climbed around inside Lancasters as a young boy, and having seen them flying, I can picture the attack. A German gunner is dug in among sandbags on the edge of Berlin surrounded by blazing buildings, his ears ringing from the whistle and crump of bombs. His face and hands are feeling the warmth from spreading fires. He peers upwards, panning his flak cannon. He spots a Lancaster caught for a moment in a searchlight cone.

There is another faint outline of an aircraft outside the beam. He fires several bursts. He sees a hit on a wing and lets out a shout. Far above, the pilot of the Lancaster feels the impact and sees an engine ablaze. He wrenches at failing controls. Then another hit, and my father and his crew see their neighbor's bomb load detonate. That night they are the fortunate ones; they make it back home to record in their logs the other's final moment.

Meanwhile, in the early hours, with me tucked in my cot, my mother waits for the different-sounding knock at the door; for the muffled, nervous voices. But this night, for us, it doesn't come. It comes for others down the road. This time, once more, the sound is familiar. The brass doorknob turns. My father calls up from the hallway.

How foolish, I never asked my mother what she was occupying herself with through those stretched nights. She wouldn't have had notice of planned raids for secrecy reasons. My father would have simply told her not to wait up. But the roar of thousands of Rolls Royce Merlin engines rising and falling across the Lincolnshire night air would have been unmistakable. Some of the aircraft would have passed directly overhead on their sickeningly shallow climb to assigned altitude.

Those shallow climbs could occasionally turn out to be an imperceptible descent, with an aircraft flying back into the ground and exploding. On April 30, 1944, a Lancaster from Elsham was taking off from their shortest runway. Despite full power built until the brakes couldn't hold, it failed to get enough speed.

They just scraped over the end of the runway, but as the wheels were being raised there was a crunch and a lurch. In the cross-wind, they had drifted and hit a guidance pylon off the side of the runway. The pilot managed to stay airborne and gradually gained altitude. A look at the undercarriage showed a partly retracted and damaged starboard wheel. Hydraulic fluid to the wheel was gone. There was radio discussion with the Ops Room about what to do. To avoid sending a crew over Germany with no chance of making a safe landing, and with not enough fuel to return anyway due to the drag of the wheel, it was decided to order them to fly around and dump fuel until there was exactly enough fuel to reach Hamburg.

The pilot was told to order his crew to jump out over Norfolk. They each shook his hand and jumped. As instructed, he set the aircraft on automatic pilot on a bearing for Hamburg allowing for wind track, but at a lower altitude than other aircraft. He left the lights on so other RAF aircraft could stay clear, and then jumped himself. As far as I know, it was never learned where this pilotless Lancaster cut out and spun from the sky with its load of bombs.

BILL EDDY'S STORY

My father had a very close friend in 103 Squadron, Bill Eddy, a British Argentinian farmer who had a ranch in Patagonia.[60] I tell what I know of his story because I don't think anyone else has.

On the night of February 25, 1944, Bill and his crew, after the usual banter with the parachute store ladies, climbed aboard their Lancaster. They were sitting in their aircraft waiting for take-off clearance when my father drove up waving a telegram. He got out and shouted the telegram message up to Bill in the cockpit.

Bill's wife, whose nickname was "Blackie," had had a baby boy! Bill asked my father to tell her congratulations and that he would be back the next morning and now with a whole week's maternity leave to boot! As they sat waiting for clearance to roll, the crew tossed around possible names. Their faithful Lancaster's call sign was P for Peter, so they went with Peter. Whether Bill's wife ever got a say, I don't know!

After delivering their bombs over Augsburg, on the return trip near the Vosges Mountains, they were hit by flak and badly damaged. Fire in the navigator's area had burned one of the crews 'chutes, so Bill handed him his. This meant that his only chance was to put the aircraft down on the snow in the foothills of the mountains. The fuel tanks were holed and they were losing engines.

When they were down to the last engine, Bill ordered his crew to jump. They were loath to leave him to go down alone with little chance of landing safely, but he ordered them out. As he was looking for a landing spot, Bill noticed that one of them was still there, fussing about behind the cockpit, hunting for his civilian shoes, useful to avoid capture.

Bill shouted at him, "To hell with your bloody civvy shoes. Get out of the bloody aircraft! We're going down!" So his last man jumped. With one faltering engine, flaps down, wheels up, Bill put the aircraft down perfectly in fresh snow. Lancasters were known to belly land well, but he was a superb pilot. There was no fire and he had no injury, although he believed he was concussed for a couple of minutes.

Once he came around, he completed his required chores, destroying documents and getting his own civvy gear together. He climbed out into eighteen inches of snow. He walked backwards and messed up the area to make it harder for the Germans to track him.

The first farmhouse he approached, he knocked on the door. A woman with a young girl opened the door. He told her who he was and that he would like help. Before she answered he stopped her and carefully explained that she and her family would be in grave danger if they gave him any assistance whatsoever. He told her that he himself, if caught, would merely be sent to a prisoner of war camp for the duration of the war, but, for them, the consequences would be much more serious. She needed to understand that. The lady nodded bravely. She understood what they were getting themselves into.

From there, with help from the French Resistance, and what was known as the "Comet Line," he got into Belgium and then France. (The crash site had been near the border.) For a while, he joined up with an American downed pilot whose name I never knew. But being both ebullient characters and great story-tellers, especially after a bottle or two of French vino, their fame spread through the villages. After a couple of days, they were taken aside by an experienced French Resistance leader and told very firmly that, as a pair, they were becoming too well-known; word of them was spreading. Unless they split up and travelled separately, their chances of being caught were very high. They accepted his advice and split up. With help from many brave French men and women, some very young, Bill was passed on down the Comet Line towards Spain, mostly by train.

At one stage, they arranged for a steam train to pull up with the engine a little beyond the platform. He and a Resistance fighter who worked for the railways, both dressed in engine drivers' gear, climbed into the engine on one side while the regular crew slipped out the other side. The German guards barely glanced at the new crew as they marched along the train. This got him far to the south.

He was then guided to the Spanish border by a well-known Free French Forces Resistance woman named Michele. I believe this was probably Michele de Ducla, a formidable five-foot-one-inch, convent-educated young lady, recently trained to kill, who had been parachuted into France from England. Remarkably, she did not end up in front of a firing squad. She survived the war and was later awarded a U.S. Bronze Star and married an RAF officer.

At the border, Bill slipped in and from there got further help travelling through neutral, but still risky, Spain. His fluent Spanish helped. With necessarily arm's-length help from the British Embassy there, he was smuggled aboard a Swedish ship out of Spain. The ship slowed down off Gibraltar, lowered him in a dinghy, and he rowed himself ashore.

From there, about two months after taking off from Elsham Wolds in P for Peter, he flew home in a DC3 to his wife and to see his son for the first time. He arrived back from his adventure to a great reception the night of my father's farewell party. My father had been transferred to another bomber station. Bill Eddy survived the war, remarkable for a bomber pilot who had, I think, been operational for nearly three years.

TO CAUSE MAXIMUM

War has not only changed enormously in the last half century in terms of precision of striking, but in terms of attitudes and strategies. Still folded in my father's log book is a briefing sheet for his Lancaster squadron covering that same December 1943 Berlin operation.

On the cyclostyled operations sheet of aircraft numbers and crew names—a number of them listed for the last time—there is a box at the top of the form headed "DUTY". This was for the mission objective statement. Entered on this sheet are three words: "To cause maximum." Note that there is no object in the sentence. It is not, "To cause maximum loss of life." It is not, "To cause maximum destruction of factories." It is not, "To cause maximum damage to a particular railway siding." It is simply: "To cause maximum."

What else could it say? Omitting the object left open the question of where the bombs might fall. RAF Lancasters were bombing at night under heavy fire with no possibility of precision; they were aiming as best they could at colored flares dropped earlier by the Pathfinder Squadrons flying the almost uncatchable twin-engine Mosquito.

The Lancaster's heavy bomb load came at the cost of almost no armored protection, save for a steel plate immediately behind the pilot's head—the pilot's head being deemed the most critical item on board. Except for very specialized night actions, such as the Dambusters low-level Lancaster raid with the bouncing bombs on the Mohne and Eder dams by 617 Squadron, only highly risky, extremely low-level, daytime raids could target with any precision. Such operations were reserved mainly for high-value railway sidings, specialized factories, and U-boat pens.

These daylight raids were at great risk to their crews. A friend and colleague of my father, an Australian, Hughie Edwards, later an Air Commodore, won a Victoria Cross for leading his twelve Blenheim bombers on a daylight raid on the port of Bremen, one of the most heavily defended towns in Germany.

He brought them in at fifty feet through a hail of fire and a formidable balloon barrage, even flying under high-tension power cables and carrying home lengths of telephone wire on their wings. All his aircraft were hit, and four were lost. His own aircraft took over twenty hits. That was the cost of precision.

But to fully understand the cost of war one must look even closer—at the glory, yes perhaps, but particularly at the unspeakable horror.

War is not only feats of gallantry like surviving Victoria Cross winner,

Rifleman Gurung of the 8th Gurkha Rifles in Burma who, as the last alive in his trench, screamed at the closing Japanese, "Come and fight a Gurkha!"

With a shattered right arm from throwing back a little too late the third incoming grenade, he repelled wave after wave of attackers for four hours. He had to load and fire his rifle with one hand. The relief force found piles of enemy dead right up to the lip of his trench. He had repeatedly held his fire to the last seconds to be sure of a kill.

But war is also the horribly burned men on my grandfather's dreadnought at the Battle of Jutland. A surgeon described, "flash burns making the face swell…the eyes invisible through the swelling of the lids, the lips enormous jelly-like masses, in the center of which a button-like mouth appears…The great cry was for water…They die very rapidly."[61]

And war is also the terribly injured soldier of a Manchester Pals regiment, a sister regiment to my great uncle's, found dying in the devastated moonscape of Ypres, an arm and a leg blown off, an eyeball hanging by his cheek, still pulsing weakly, who was shot in compassion by a fellow soldier.

In the contemplation of military action, those who make decisions on our behalf must weigh the strategic sweep against the thousands, sometimes millions, of lives that will never again be the same, for both attacker and defender. I count myself fortunate that, not only have I never had to go to war, but I have never had to make such calls. Those who must need to be our wisest and our most mature.

WINKIE'S STORY

I was going to end this chapter there, but since this is mostly a light-hearted memoir, let me finish with something more uplifting: Winkie's story.

The night of February 23, 1942, Winkie was on board a *Bristol Beaufort* bomber that ditched in the North Sea after being badly shot up on a mission to Norway. Winkie was a female carrier pigeon serving with the RAF.

As the crew scrambled desperately to leave their sinking aircraft on the bitterly cold North Sea, they managed, only just, to release her from her box. She was their only hope for survival.

Carrier pigeons were used by the RAF because radio contact was often impossible from a crippled aircraft going down. When released, Winkie was coated in oil, presumably from fire in the fuselage and was probably suffering from smoke inhalation. But she bravely flew the 120 miles back to her owner, George Ross, near Dundee, Scotland, arriving exhausted.

Ross immediately phoned the RAF base at Leuchars and they were able to quickly triangulate the aircraft's position using its probable flight path, the time of Winkie's arrival, and her estimated flight speed in her handicapped condition. Remarkably, they got the location spot-on, and the crew was picked up exactly where predicted within an hour of her arrival.

Some weeks later, Winkie, fully recovered from her ordeal, was the guest of honor at a squadron dinner with the rescued crew. You may be sure they drank more than one toast to her and gave her some treats of corn and split peas. She was awarded the Dickin Medal, the animals' equivalent of the Victoria Cross. The citation reads, "For delivering a message under exceptional difficulties and so contributing to the rescue of an Air Crew while serving with the RAF in February 1942."

The medal carries the words, "For Gallantry. We also serve." When brave Winkie eventually succumbed to old age, she was stuffed and mounted and is on display, I believe, in Dundee, her hometown in Scotland.[62, 63]

EXIT STAGE LEFT

**Life has meaning only if one barters it day
by day for something other than itself.**

– Antoine de Saint-Exupéry

It may be pure arrogance, but I feel I owe some sort of a "so what?" contemplative chapter here at the end; a chapter that provides something of a philosophical wrap-up; a final glass of port, as it were.

Socrates' dictum at his trial, "The unexamined life is not worth living," must occur to many of us who start to fossick in the slurry of our recollections. Of course, we should have got the panning tray out earlier, and then again when roads diverged in Robert Frost's yellow wood.

There is surely value in self-examination at any time, but especially on the final legs. I have never been quite as cynical as the late Kurt Vonnegut who quipped, "But what if the examined life turns out to be a clunker as well?"[64]

Looking back on my, in the grand scheme of things, utterly inconsequential life, I like to think of it as reflecting Richard Feynman's sum-over-histories idea about quantum particles. This draws from the renowned two-slit trick where particles fired at two slits produce a pattern on the screen behind, showing that each particle went through both slits at the same time as a wave, yet, when we try to catch them doing it by looking at them en route, they slyly revert to passing through only one slit.

Feynman's proposition was that a particle potentially takes all possible paths to the destination screen but that these cancel each other out until only the path observed survives. I like to imagine that my own life left behind many such "shadow" lives taking entirely different paths. But I prefer to think that, rather than being cancelled out, they were recorded in a parallel universe open to scrutiny. A load of old cobblers? Probably. But I find it to be a thought experiment that aids perspective.

It has been said that those who spend a life traveling are running away from something. But then surely those who stay at home are hiding from something. Certainly, itinerant expatriates never really have a home. But then people who don't roam—at least a little and with intent—seem to me to lack perspective on the home they cling to, missing the backyard lives they have allowed to slip past the train window. I have sometimes regretted the lack of a true home, but I have never regretted the doors that opened to me through which I could glimpse, if only through a chink, the way other tribes negotiate their lives.

People travel for many reasons. I have travelled not so much to reach a destination as to explore a trail. This is not a new idea of course. It shows up in T.S. Eliot's "We shall not cease from exploration. / And the end of all our exploring / Will be to arrive where we started / And know the place for the first time."[65]

What soon becomes clear when we travel is Joshua Greene's contention that there are three players or collectives of players in the world, the Me, the Us and the Them.[66] The Me tends to be selfish and self-centered, but has evolved a moderate degree of altruism to enable the Us to be collectively competitive. The Us is the bundle of all the Me units that make up our own tribe—say, the Kikuyu tribe of Kenya or, on a different plane, the British Precast Concrete Federation.

But the trickiest player of the three categories for all of the Us is the Them—that fearsome *Them*. It's that old savanna enmity, elephant versus buffalo, cheetah versus hyena, rhino versus, well, everyone. The Them are the outsiders that many of the Me and the Us are at a loss to fathom, for example ISIS extremists or, more benignly, a barely contacted tribe such as the treehouse-dwelling Korowai in the West Papua New Guinea rainforest.

I have come across few people in my travels who do not sincerely believe in their culture's traditions, practices and religious beliefs and what they themselves stand for, even though outsiders may find some of their practices evil or incomprehensible. Like mushrooms, people grow true to their culture's spawn. Even in cases where things seem to have crossed an ethical line—say, female genital mutilation in Africa—those who practice it believe that, without it, their social fabric would be irretrievably torn. Sometimes they have a point. At least they have a point for their time and their place. This is not a justification for an unacceptable practice; just a reluctant acknowledgment of the panoply of values that can come into play.

As I have suggested along the way, understanding other tribes' cultures helps us to calibrate our own. It questions our hopes, our beliefs, our hatreds, and even our existence. Learning about others offers respite from our own dark tunnels and cultural fogs. It centers us, while tracing our boundaries.

There is an old African Bantu proverb, "The world is a beehive; we all enter by the same door, but we live in different cells."

We have indeed evolved into quite insulated creatures despite our common species name and our astonishingly similar DNA. We can grow from understanding what is playing out on other floors of the hive.

The Maasai cattle man who deftly jets a gob of snot onto the ground wondering to his fellow herdsman why the tourists like to save that stuff in a white cloth, is not simply demonstrating an alternative waste disposal option. He is offering the observer a slice of his culture while exposing us to a perspective on our own. He is showing that, in his society, bodily functions have been from childhood a thread of nature; that the earth has ancient ways of recycling and, more prosaically, that there are other things he would sooner carry with him across the plains than desiccating boogers.

The young Indian girl with a Ph.D. from Stanford who accepts an arranged marriage to an Indian boy back in Ahmedabad, despite only meeting him twice under an aunt's steely gaze, is living her rules of social survival even though we in the West find them unfathomable. She is revealing that family is everything to her and that, while love, she has observed, seems to be only fleetingly passionate, having a mate from the right caste and income bracket acceptable to her family is what will ultimately sustain her marriage. This is her reality, even if the chosen boy seems at first blush to be a bit of a slob. She is showing that she trusts other people's judgment at least as much as her own in an endeavor that, in America, applying an alternative selection protocol, delivers an abysmal fifty percent success rate.

The Aboriginal Australian, who has no interest in the available GPS apps to traverse his tribal area, and who uses an inherited Dreaming Track song, is declaring that the land is his ancestors' estate and that he wants to do more than walk from *Coonabarabran*, along the *Warrumbungle Range* to *Wallah Wallah Creek*. With rhythm and music, he wants to relearn an ancient, but still existent, saga of his land and, more importantly, to give back to his land and his tribe a new episode of that saga. In other words, to him, it is not just a trip.

Yet there are also surprising similarities between cultures, often not obvious at first. It seems we have all picked out our behavioral traits from a common global goody bag; they just manifest differently.

The old Maasai cattle trader I met on the Tanzania border with Kenya back in the 1970s, who bribed the guards with crates of beer, was traveling much further than any other cattleman I had ever encountered in Africa. He was a loner in his business. He had, I thought, very similar attitudes and ambitions to a middle-aged hippy I once met crossing the Landi Kotal border into Afghanistan at the top of the Khyber Pass in 1970. Only instead of cattle, the hippie was moving weed or worse. Both were loner adventurers taking risks. Both were reveling in new experiences, testing their beliefs and their environment's and culture's bounds, and growing with it.

In looking at mankind's performance with a long eye to the persistence of our species, it seems to me to be important to consider how we might be rated by an independent performance evaluation; one contracted, presumably, from some neutral alien observer civilization. What might a *Homo sapiens* report card really look like?

The evidence suggests that mankind does seem to have become more ethical, although only quite recently. Globally, deaths due to conflict are down. The world seems to be becoming a better place, and for the poor too—although still far too many are left behind. Wider education has surely been the main driver.

Looking back, the greatest global achievement in my lifetime—perhaps the supreme achievement in the history of mankind—has been the reduction of the percentage of people living below the absolute poverty line from 44% of the global population in 1981 to 13% in 2012, passing 10% in about 2015, with an aim to reach 3% by 2030. This was an unthinkable goal just a few decades ago and surely a notable ethical advance.

But how much has mankind truly *changed*, deep inside? The evidence suggests that the old donkey engine of cruelty is still there, ready to be cranked up with the right combustible mixture. Going back a little, my Australian Godfather, Cecil Middleton, who died in 1952, met a man who had been flogged as a convict.

He described how his back had looked like thousands of grains of rice. He asked, "What sort of people were we so few years ago?" Yet during his own lifetime some six million souls, including one million children, were culled—I use the word "culled" with precision—from the European population.

I do not see major differences in tribal values between the Germans and many other European nationalities. The Nazis had exceptional taste in the arts, the Luftwaffe often displayed great chivalry to their aviator opponents, and Germany produced some great humanist and religious thinkers. Yet something in Germany at that time snapped in the human soul. So it seems to me that as a species we remain, beneath the veneer, supremely capable monsters, particularly when misled en masse.

Despite the nagging of history (and here, perhaps I am abandoning common sense), I am inclined not to ditch optimism for the reason Aleksandr Solzhenitsyn identified—what he once referred to in his letter to three students as the "knocking inside us," our conscience. Solzhenitsyn saw that, "Justice is conscience, not a personal conscience but the conscience of the whole of humanity."[67]

The poet Anna Akhmatova, also Russian, seems to have held to a similar belief when she reportedly told Isaiah Berlin, "History can be made to bow before the sheer stubbornness of human conscience."

A tribe in Zimbabwe, the *Shona*, have a word for conscience, *hana*.[68] It is a cornerstone of their impressive edifice of desirable human traits. A person without *hana* is considered cruel. It means the inner feeling of right and wrong, the conscience, but it is also their word for "palpitation." So when feeling guilty, they are saying, "My conscience is palpitating, it is knocking." This palpitation signal may be built into all of us, even though it is often stashed behind the brooms in a cupboard during our shameful hours.

With weapons now far beyond anything conceivable a mere century ago, let's hope that history can indeed be made to bow before the collective conscience, otherwise Fermi's paradox (the paradox that, despite the very high probability of widespread intelligent life, so far we have had no communication) may turn out to look less of a paradox. We may, through our failure, have added another supporting case to show that the reason for the deafening silence out there is that, quite early in intelligent life, self-destruction through ethical failure has been almost universal.

Man's greatest challenge today, with the escalation of warfare technologies, with the ability to manipulate the biology of life, and with our accelerating global warming, will be managing the ethics of science while also exploiting it.

Superlative wisdom will be essential for our survival. Decisions will need to be in the wisest hands—not in the hands of lawyers in supreme courts or ephemeral politicians beholden to money. It is alarming that supreme judgmental bodies are composed of lawyers when most of the momentous decisions for our species are less matters of law than matters of our collective conscience.

Why should lawyers monopolize the commanding heights of societal refereeing? No, our decisions will need to be in the hands of ethicists, scientists, historians, and yes, even artists and poets—perhaps conceding a lawyer or two to patrol the legal boundaries. Societal referees will need to be discerning, to be widely respected, to have records of measured judgement, and to be prepared to draw lines between rightness and wrongness at contentious contours, and on slippery slopes.

Traditional African society had taken a shot at this long ago. The elders, responsible for the tribe's most crucial deliberations, were those widely acknowledged as wise men. There were two weaknesses, of course: One was that they were all men—no women, except in a few matrilineal societies. The second was that some of the elders were hereditary, including often the chief, although hereditary succession can help to provide a thread of tribal continuity.

In the end, the maturity of those who will adjudicate the great questions of our time will determine our species' longevity.

So, what about death, the "good career move" as Buddy Holly called it, the occupational shift that most of us get jittery about? Is it more than merely an unremarkable biological case of entropy; the inevitable collapse of an energy system into disorder?

My younger daughter Antonia, who I think was about four at the time, hadn't quite grasped my first bumbling explanation of faith and death. I had summed it up as positively as I could saying, "Most people believe that, after death, the soul goes up to heaven."

She nodded knowingly as she pulled a stretched sweater over her stuffed bear, and added, "Yes, and the feet!" I was more surprised that she knew the word sole for the bottom of the foot than that she was not quite there on the more elusive concept of the soul. I'm not sure that my elaboration enlightened her.

In what I consider to be my English home county of Lincolnshire, the old word for death used to be "gathered"—meaning harvested—as in, for illustration:

"Oh yez, old Billy Smith, 'e was gathered last year. Di'nt yer 'ear? Lot of them Smiths bin gathered rearcently. Sud really. But s'pose we all got ter push up't daisies sum day."

I like that word, *gathered*. It sheds a more benign light on the harsh medieval image of the grim reaper.

I count myself a Christian; a stumbling one. Whether I would pass the entry exam at St. Peter's portal I couldn't say. Doubts often nag. But they did for many, including Mother Teresa, so I suppose I am in good company. But if I have been too optimistic about the promise of an afterlife then, as a back-up, I might be inclined to go with Mark Twain's notion along the lines of: I was dead for millions of years before I was born and do not recall being inconvenienced by it. (Actually, Twain was rather more long-winded, and we have come further on the age of the universe since his time, but that was the gist of it.)

A starker way of contemplating immortality, but one that I try to avoid, comes from the British particle physicist Frank Close, who reminded us coldly, "You are made of stuff that is…one third as old as the universe, though this is the first time that those atoms have been gathered together such that they think that they are you."[69]

An eighteenth-century woman writer, the redoubtable Lady Mary Wortley Montagu, at her death in 1762, warranted the prize for phlegm (if not profundity) when she raised herself from her pillow, croaked, "Well, it has all been most interesting," then sank back and dutifully expired. I would not quarrel with her workmanlike wrapping up, but I am inclined to adorn it a bit.

Some years ago, in England, at a conference of headmasters of boys' private schools, a sample of the headmasters were asked by an attending Anglican minister what they prepared their boys for.[70]

If I remember the story correctly, one replied airily that he prepared his boys for life, another replied that he prepared them for the "professions," another, for the armed forces, and another prepared them to be good citizens. But one replied, "I prepare my boys for death."

This is not perhaps something a school head would want to blurt out to a prospective pupil's parents on their first visit, but his response surely displayed the greater depth. As the Buddhists have long known, if you don't come to understand death, you don't come to understand life.

There has always been a deep connection between the arts and death. Much of art and literature has roots in the mysterious unmapped caverns of mortality. Professor Hugh Kenner, the Canadian literary critic, had spotted this when he wrote back in 1955, "Art is a fake but when vital has death somewhere at its roots."[71] Art can take us a long way towards unravelling the tangled fishnet of the human condition, but not all the way surely. That, I think, lies in our own hands, in our minds, actually.

My own first witnessing of a human death was at the age of eleven. I was at a Battle of Britain commemoration air display at an RAF station at Coningsby in Lincolnshire, in 1953. I saw a Gloster Meteor, the first British jet fighter, explode as it executed a low-level run almost directly overhead.

My eyes happened to be on the aircraft at the instant of the blast. I felt the explosion in my chest. I saw a flash come from the nose of the aircraft right in front of the cockpit. A large chunk, I think the cockpit canopy, fell about ten yards from me. The two engine pods carried on for some distance towards the end of the airfield before breaking up, I suppose from the momentum and the kinetic spin of the turbine blades.

The spectators around me knocked over the folding canvas chairs in their rush to get away from the falling pieces. There were a few screams and gasps, but mostly just the crump of chunks of fuselage hitting the ground around me. I don't recall great fear for my own safety, although there was certainly the instinctive flight reflex; it all happened too quickly.

I recall more the horror afterwards at the obvious loss of a life. It was clear to me that the pilot, alive just a few seconds ago, had been blown to pieces. Arms, legs, bits of flesh could even be lying there on the grass around me. What seemed to be the shattered canopy a few yards away could even have blood on it.

I remember lying awake that night picturing someone informing the pilot's family and thinking I wouldn't like that job. Since my father sometimes flew the same type of aircraft, it was one of my first realizations of our vulnerability as a family. He had survived the war, but this brought it home that, even in peacetime, being a pilot was a risky business and seemingly random.

I once had an uncomfortably close call myself related to flying. A good friend and colleague, Tom Martin, died in a plane crash in Sudan taking off from a small airstrip, somewhere near the small town of El Obeid, I think it was. I frequently worked with Tom and might well have been on that mission, but I was sent for a couple of weeks to Tanzania instead.

They took off from a dirt airstrip, climbed to about fifty feet, and a desert dust-devil caught the Cessna from behind and stalled it into the ground. Two of the three on board died.

So, for me, here were those eternal questions that every generation has struggled with. Why them? Why not me? Why then? These were Thornton Wilder's *The Bridge of San Luis Rey* questions—why those five people of different backgrounds came to be on that flimsy rope bridge in Peru at the same time? Was it merely a roll of the dice? Or was it something more? Were their lives already inexorably intertwined in some way? Like entangled quantum particles? Did God have a purpose? And if so, what exactly?

That accident raised questions for me about what is ordained. It seemed to connect to the Buddhist insights on impermanence. But that still didn't offer an explanation, in fact rather the opposite, it called for the acceptance of what is with no expectation of a reason. Is it perhaps that acceptance and faith are the only realistic end points? The final philosophical cul-de-sac? One might ask how it could be any other way. If we knew the reasons for everything, there would be no journey for Lady Montagu to have found "most interesting."

Regrets? Yes, I regret I didn't take more of my own advice along the way, but that's the way experience works, As Søren Kierkegaard wrote, "Life can only be understood backwards; but it must be lived forwards."[72]

So I haven't myself spent too much time looking in the rearview mirror. But I especially regret that I never had the guts to walk away from our consuming lifestyle. Asceticism was never one of my stronger suits. Since, through my work, I suppose I have seen more deprivation than the average person in the West, I surely bear a greater burden of responsibility. I have been a card-carrying member of the consuming generations and, because of my frequent travels to impoverished places, have absolutely no excuse that I never noticed.

We in the rich countries consume far more than we need and many of us, including me, are deluded into thinking that we need what we want. I myself this year spent more than a poor family in Africa would have spent in a year on veterinary treatment for my dog. Obviously, something is out of whack—apart from my pooch.

Our consuming culture was epitomized for me recently by a family teaching moment I witnessed in America. An intense father, head thrust forward, was pacing eagerly in the direction of a display of expensive cars with his two young boys struggling to keep up. He was instructing them, "Now remember boys, it's all about brand recognition and model recognition." I fervently hoped that there would be other lessons for the day more important than brand and model recognition. But that is the way we have become, and I cannot pretend to be an innocent onlooker.

The message of the ascetics on this uncomfortable question of toys and possessions was best summed up by the inscription on the 16th century archway at Akbar the Great's abandoned city of Fatehpur Sikri, not far from the Taj Mahal. Purportedly a quote from Jesus, although this one seems to have been mislaid by Christianity, it reads, "The world is a bridge, pass over it, but build no houses upon it…"

This is quintessentially Buddhist, but Christian, Hindu and Islamist too, especially Sufi Islamist, but it is apparently hard to follow for most of us. We of the rich countries have become increasingly wedded to the prestige and comforts of our houses, our sports cars, our massage chairs, our heated car seats, our cell phones, and our other, plentiful, ego-stroking and body-stroking baubles. The shallow shall inherit the earth?

So, to pick up again from my long-ago musings during frosty nights driving a tractor, what about the purpose of life? Is it an answerable question? A pointless question? Or is it the only question? Surely, it is at least a valid question for a sentient life form to ask itself.

It seems to me that there should be two purposes in life—although who am I to say "should"? Neither of them is prosperity or the pursuit of happiness, at least not as end products with the patent-pending labels "Prosperity" and "Happiness."

The first of these purposes, espoused again by Solzhenitsyn, is to strive towards the maturity of the human soul. Expressing thanks for his enlightenment during his imprisonment, he wrote, "…For there, lying upon the rotting prison straw, I came to realize that the object of life is not prosperity…but the maturity of the human soul."[73]

(What timing! As I type these words, my Labrador just walked in and flopped down beside me. He reminds me that a faithful dog brings back to us our own soul licked clean and free from blemish.)

Plainly, mankind has failed to reach maturity collectively. We only need to look at the immaturity of current American politics. Or British. Or Venezuelan. Or the many forms of extremism in power and religion. True maturity of the human soul seems to me to have been approached by only a few individuals across history; superior beings like Mother Teresa, Mahatma Gandhi, Gautama Buddha, Socrates, St. Francis of Assisi, and Rumi.

But what is this collective maturity if it is not the call by Joshua Greene[74] that we strive to extend our cooperation within tribes to a wider cooperation *between* tribes? A pipe-dream? Possibly. But surely not one to tap out against a wall and walk away from.

I believe the Buddhists may have come closest to glimpsing the maturity of the human soul. You find it in their philosophy. You see it in their eyes. Some say you feel it even in the proximity of the Dalai Lama before you set eyes on him. The success of Buddhism in picking out the tangled knots of the human mind is surely because it draws from millennia of wisdom and experimentation with the mind going back well before Christ and even further before the Prophet Muhammad. The closest approach to Buddhism in other faiths seems to me to be the Sufi branch of Islam, where Rumi saw love and reflection as a direct route to the divine.

Buddhism offers something rather unsettling though; what would seem to be the ultimate release from rebirth, by snuffing out the cycling of the soul. Some interpretations seem not to care whether anything soul-like remains, setting it apart from most other religions. There is a reason, I believe, why the question of what eventually happens to the soul was treated ambivalently by Gautama Buddha. Permanency of the soul treads perilously close to placing too much value on continued existence. And Buddhism teaches that clinging to existence is part of our problem in the first place. Worth a lifetime of meditation perhaps?

The core message of Buddhism was best captured, surprisingly, by a non-Buddhist in the expression, "To look on the world with a quiet eye." The expression is first found in a poem by the English poet Eliza Cook (1818—1889), her poem entitled "The Quiet Eye," published in 1861.[75]

This notion of a "quiet eye" was picked up again in a poem by Frances

Shaw in 1917—a Great War year when there was a dire need for a quiet eye. Later, it was adapted and adopted by others, often, and unfortunately, without attribution to Eliza Cook.

The second purpose of life after the reach towards the maturity of the human soul, is, I suggest, the notion of Professor Raymond Tallis who, you may recall, in response to a question about the meaning of life replied, "I don't know about the meaning of life, but the purpose of life is to gather together as many meanings as possible and to explore and enrich them. Meaning changes: it is not prescribed."

The summons here surely is to be boundlessly curious. To advance meanings, we must reach across disciplines in the pursuit of associations and contrasts, taking those muddy lanes leading away from our own small paddocks.[76]

It seems to me that one of the tricks in the exploration of meaning is to never come back the same person—from anything. Even from buying a cauliflower. In an earlier draft, I had dropped this image as being too intense—not to mention disturbing for your grocer. But having recently reminded myself over a salad of the exquisite pattern of florets in a raw cauliflower head, I stick with my original inclination—I do indeed mean even from buying a cauliflower! Professor D'Arcy Thompson would have been delighted! Whoever may have written it—author Eden Phillpotts most likely—seems to have had this in mind when he wrote, "The world is full of magical things, patiently waiting for our senses to grow sharper."

And this now leads me back to that Inuit bone-carving metaphor that I promised to pick up on. Let me take it for a brief spin into life and towards the arts and sciences. I have always felt a deep sense that there is a trapped figure waiting to be carved out and released in every creative human endeavor.

Some poets and artists experience this sense that what they are searching for is a creation that somehow already exists and has existed since the dawn of time, waiting patiently to be uncovered. This is not to say that there is no creativity by the artist, merely the removal of extraneous matter; it is to say that the artist is an active participant in an interactive process with the materials and with life itself. The great artist is releasing a fresh creation in a way that nobody else could have released it.

Now in the physical sciences, this connection is more direct because releasing the trapped seal happens to be the core of the scientific process. Finding meaning in relationships between different bits of matter—relationships that have existed, hidden, since the first products of the Big Bang—is the essence of scientific endeavor.

But for the seeker of meaning and truth there is always risk. All human endeavor—painting, poetry, music, science, architecture, or, for that matter, cuisine—when taken to the highest level, involves pushing outwards towards new frontiers. The risk is that frontiers, by their very nature, lie close to the edge of a cliff. Fall over it and you are done. You have blown it. At least you have blown it for your time and your place. Tectonic movement may shift the location of the cliff, but that will be for another age, another time.

T.S. Eliot recognized this in his *The Art of Poetry:* "The poet is occupied with the frontiers of consciousness, beyond which words fail, though meanings still exist."[77] And frontiers are dark mysterious places, not for the faint-hearted.

Looked at in the light of another metaphor, the Tallis exploration of meaning is the expedition upstream towards the source of the Nile, towards Solzhenitsyn's maturity of the human soul. But such a search can only be fruitful with perspective. This calls for scanning upstream and down from the river bank, perhaps wading the river, even camping the night and looking again in the fresh light of dawn.

The eighteenth-century physicist Georg Lichtenberg realized that to reach understanding requires us to stand back the right distance from the subject. Distance and stance—that is, *perspective*—is indispensable in any quest for meaning. And standing back calls for us to stand back from ourselves. Rumi saw this when he wrote, "When you let go of who you are, you become who you might be."

And this is where travel to new countries and cultures comes in, because standing back, examining others from new angles, is thrust upon us when we travel; the lives we stumble upon urge it, their stories demand it. Through travel, we realize that parochialism has always been one of mankind's most pernicious inclinations. We achieve a measure of proximate depth by understanding our own history, but we achieve perspective and breadth by understanding the history of others.

But do philosophical quests for meaning really have much relevance for poor families in Africa or Asia eking out a subsistence living? Absolutely, they do! Farmers are applied scientists. They observe. They innovate. They adapt. They learn. They strive to advance their own local constellation of meanings. And many of them—I suspect due to their intimate connection with the soil—are strongly committed to a faith, whether it be Christianity, Islam or Hinduism.

They search, as do we all, for deeper truths. Significantly, within their traditional culture, they often focus a great deal on what is right and proper. Again, the Shona tribe in Zimbabwe have a set of generally accepted cardinal virtues:[78] truth, humility, love, sympathy, self-discipline, forgiveness, satisfaction with sufficiency, trust, generosity, courage, patience, unselfishness, and, interestingly, making others happy. Could one really do much better for a philosophy or code of conduct?

But there is still a loose end here. Any blueprint for attaining the maturity of the human soul, individually or collectively, is an architect's design on a scroll; admirable perhaps, but built solely in minds. This can never be the end of the pilgrimage. For an individual, thought without action is a Hamlet "To be or not to be" moment. Each of us, as a human being with inescapable responsibilities, whether of a humanist or religious bent, needs to be prepared to act on what we uncover. And acting includes not hiding behind walls of silence when evil is abroad.

So here, I take my leave and potter out to my vegetable garden to weed another year's crop of smothered onions. When will I learn to do it earlier?

If there is anything I would pass on as avuncular advice to a searching youth, or to anyone who is expecting reincarnation for another circuit of the track, it would be something along these lines:

- Life can only be understood backwards, but it must be lived forwards.

- Live to explore and enrich meanings.

- Be relentlessly curious, shaping ideas with insights from beyond your own barbed wire paddock.

- Use whatever intuition you have been gifted with, but, in the end, there is no substitute for the facts.

- Look on the world with a quiet eye.

- Go walkabout often and extend your dreaming tracks towards other tribes.

- ...Oh, and I nearly forgot, keep yer bloody tools sharp!

ENDNOTES

1   Zinsser, W, 1976. *On Writing Well*, Collins.

2   I jotted this down in a notebook many years ago from a television interview that Professor Raymond Tallis gave which, as far as I know, has no transcript. I was so struck by it that I grabbed my notebook and wrote it down immediately. I am confident that these were his exact words. However, just to be sure, I contacted him to check whether I had recorded it correctly. He said that, while he did not recall this particular statement, "it sounded Tallis." I am indebted.

3   Author of *On Growth and Form*, published in 1917.

4   A book published in Australia, *Wings at War* by Haughton-James and Manley (Berry Books, 1995), tells the story of the Evans Head base, the people, and the events of those days.

5   A world depth record was recently achieved in finding the *City of Cairo* where she lay at over 5,000 meters.

6   The U-boats, it is now known, were U-404 under Captain Otto Von Bulow, who was one of the top U-boat commanders of the war, and U-662 under Captain Heinz-Eberhard Muller.

7   Four months later U-662 was sunk after three days of aircraft attacks off the coast of Brazil. Müller repelled three attacks before a Catalina aircraft sunk his submarine. Müller and four men were thrown overboard when the depth charges exploded. One died and Müller and three others drifted on a raft dropped by the aircraft in shark infested waters for 16 days before being found by an American B-24 aircraft.

8   Laffage, Horace, editor. 2007. *Profiles in Polo*, McFarland. The piece on Sinclair Hill was written by the late Chris Ashton.

9   Polo ponies are actually horses, although rarely large ones, but are traditionally referred to as ponies.

10   At that time, I occasionally used my Australian godfather's stockwhip, then about fifty years old. Now, over a hundred years old, it hangs on my study wall, still remarkably supple but depleted in length from a crack-off due to aged leather plaits—what a story it could tell.

11   He was Air Vice Marshal Ronnie Ramsay Rae, an Australian. His wife was Rosemary. A wonderful couple. He was in the following Japanese camps 1943 to 1945: Garoet Gaol; Bicycle Camp; Maca-sura, Bandoeng, Batavia. His stories are available on Imperial War Museum recorded interviews.

12   Clapp, Susannah, 1997. *With Chatwin: Portrait of a Writer.* J. Cape.

13   Foer, Joshua, 2011. *Moonwalking with Einstein: The Art and Science of Remembering Everything.* Penguin Books.

14   For those familiar with the area, I believe it was not the White Hart at Brasted, which has an intriguing history of its own with connections to fighter pilots, famous people, MI5 and even murders. I am still not certain which pub it was.

15   Some of these and other traits are well documented in *Watching the English* by Kate Fox, published by Hodder and Stoughton, 2014.

16   I may be indebted to Julian Blackwood for this one, and possibly also for one or two other stories whose origins I have forgotten.

17   Elements of this idea come from numerous sources including, Joshua Greene, *Moral Tribes*, Penguin Press, 2013, cited again later.

18   Scott, J. C., 1999. *Seeing Like a State*, Yale University Press.

19   Lofchie, M.F., 1978. *Agrarian Crisis and Economic Liberalization in Tanzania.* Journal of African Studies, 16, no.3.

20   I am indebted to my one-time colleague in Tanzania, David Pudsey, for this one.

21 For simplicity, I stick to the English convention referring to the tribe and language as Sukuma. They call themselves the Basukuma, meaning the people of Sukuma (meaning the north) and, in Swahili, Wasukuma. The language is referred to in Swahili as Kisukuma.

22 It is just possible that this story came to me second-hand through someone else. I believe I recall a conversation I had with one of the White Fathers about this, but I may be transposing.

23 The Liemba is still doing the circuit of Lake Tanganyika and reached its hundredth birthday in 2013. It is said to have been the model for the German ship in the Bogart–Hepburn movie *The African Queen*. It had been scuttled by the Germans during World War I to keep it out of British hands and was later raised and renovated. A historic vessel.

24 In Swahili a *rungu*.

25 Isak Dinesen (Karen Blixen), 1937. *Out of Africa*, Putnam, London.

26 Chadwick, Douglas, 1994. *The Fate of the Elephant*. Sierra Club Books.

27 Poole, Joyce, 1996. *Coming of Age with Elephants*, Hyperion, for one version, but it has been told in other sources too, I believe.

28 Chambers, Robert, 1983. *Rural Development: Putting the Last First*, Harlow, Prentice Hall.

29 Carr, Stephen, 2004. *Surprised by Laughter*, Memoir Club.

30 Johnston, B., and Clark, W., 1982. *Redesigning Rural Development*, The Johns Hopkins University Press.

31 It was Leakey who fostered the research of Jane Goodall (chimpanzees), Dian Fossey (gorillas), and Birute Galdkas (orangutans) who all did research on primates. Leakey used to refer to them as "The Trimates"!

32 Colin is the elder half-brother of Richard Leakey.

33 In the U.S., based on my own research, the average cost of diesel per liter from 2008 to 2012 was about $0.84 (within limits, the precision of these numbers is not important, it's the principle that I am trying to convey); in Kenya over that period, diesel was about $1.27. The average wage for a farm worker was about $7 an hour in the U.S. but only about 20 U.S. cents in Kenya.

34   The risk of drought has always been a threat for dryland ranchers in America and Australia, too. Patrick Durack, the Irish outback cattle pioneer of the early days of European settlement in Australia, wrote in 1878, "Cattle kings ye call us, then we are kings in grass castles that may be blown away upon a puff of wind." Relying on rainfall has always been a risky business.

35   Hardin, G., 1968. *The Tragedy of the Commons.* Science. 162 (3859): 1243–1248.

36   Greene, Joshua, 2013. *Moral Tribes: Emotion, Reason, and the Gap between us and them.* Penguin Press.

37   Mearns, R., 1996. *When Livestock Are Good for Environment Benefit Sharing of Environmental Goods and Services,* World Bank/FAO Workshop.

38   Ole Sankan, S. S., 1971. *The Maasai.* East African Literature Bureau, Nairobi.

39   Moll, F., 1978. *A Dictionary of the Maasai Language and Folklore,* Marketing and Publishing Ltd, Nairobi.

40   Father Frans Mol, again, *Maa Dictionary.*

41   Sheep and goats were collectively enumerated as "shoats," or sometimes "geeps," in our farm and livestock surveys in Africa when we didn't need to differentiate between the two.

42   Again, S.S. Ole Sankan, 1971. *The Maasai.* East African Literature Bureau. Nairobi.

43   Muta, a Murinbata tribe man, quoted in W.E.H. Stanner *White Man Got No Dreaming Essays 1938 - 1973.* Australian National University Press, Canberra, 1979, p. iv.

44   I have not attempted to review or comment on the sad history of colonial and later impact on the Australian Aboriginal people; I am not qualified to do it justice.

45   Chatwin, Bruce, 1987. *The Songlines.* Penguin Books.

46   A *billabong* is a section of a river meander, formed in flood, but cut off in dry times into a stretch of pools, sometimes like an oxbow lake.

47   *Songlines—Tracking the Seven Sisters*, edited by Margo Neale, 2017, National Museum Australia.

48   Americans aged 15 in 2105 ranked a little above half way placing 19th in science out of 35 OECD countries on the PISA test.

49   Adapted from the poem *Invictus* by William Henley.

50   Dring, Simon, 1993. *On the Road Again: Thirty Years on the Traveller's Trail to India.* BBC broadcast.

51   But note that India has always been enormously diverse. There are many originally forest tribes in India, for example, the *Birjia*, who have more animist beliefs, mostly built around propitiating spirits that guide their life. Some spirits are malevolent some harmless. The godhead for the Birjia is the Sun, who created all humans. Their personal ancestral spirits are mostly benevolent and welcomed except that people who had an unnatural death are believed to turn into malevolent spirits.

52   Kabat-Zinn, Jon, 1994. *Wherever You Go, There You Are.* Hyperion Books.

53   Haig-Brown, R., 1991. *A River Never Sleeps.* Lyons Press. First published 1944.

54   In case you are lexicographically inclined, the word platypus is singular and generally used for the plural, the sometimes seen purported plural platypi is incorrect because it is not a Latin word, it is Greek. Platypodes would be correct but platypus or platypuses is generally used.

55   I believe this is near the stretch of the rapids where, many years later, the escape of the dwarves through the rapids from their captor Elves in the movie *The Hobbit* was filmed.

56   Binyon, Laurence, 1914. *For the Fallen.* First published in The Times. Often recited at Remembrance Day services in UK.

57   *Warspite* carried on into the Second World War and by then was known affectionately as "The Grand Old Lady." By the time of her demobilization, she was the Royal Navy ship with the greatest number of battle honors ever awarded.

58   Eliot, T. S., 1920. *Gerontion*.

59   Elsham happened to be the home of a very special aircraft, Lancaster ED888, which went on to hold the record of 140 missions by the war's end and was never shot down. Sadly, it was not preserved.

60   Bill Eddy's story here is a summary of some notes in my possession that he gave my father many years ago. I don't know if it has been told elsewhere, but I believe not.

61   Massie, R. K., 2003. *Castles of Steel*. Random House.

62   Wikipedia. Winkie (pigeon).

63   Currie, Jack, 2004. *Lancaster Target*, Crecy Publishing. There is an earlier published version. Currie was a friend of my father although, as far as I know, they never flew together. Currie did once take my Gurkha paratrooper uncle Major Ivor Nelson up for a deliberately wild spin—on my father's instructions! During the war Currie flew out of RAF Wickenby, as did Winkie the carrier pigeon. I seem to recall my father saying that quite a lot of Jack Currie's book was written in his local pub!

64   Vonnegut, K., 1974. *Wampeters, Foma and Granfallons*. Delacorte Press.

65   Eliot, T. S., 1941 (originally published). *Four Quartets*. Harcourt (US).

66   Again, Greene, *Moral Tribes*. 2013.

67   Letter to a group of students. October 1967 in *Solzhenitsyn: A Documentary Record*. 1970.

68   Gelfand, L., 1973. *The Genuine Shona*, Mambo Press.

69   Close, Frank, 2004. *Particle Physics*. A Very Short Introduction. Oxford University Press.

70   I am indebted to my sister Erica for this recollection of long ago (which, when I reminded her recently, she had forgotten) of an opening to a sermon by the late Reverend Henry Thorold, FSA (Fellow of the Society of Antiquaries).

71   Quoted by his son Rob Kenner in an article *Word's Worth* in Poetry magazine, November 2005.

72   Kierkegaard, S., 1844. Journals VA 14.

73   Solzhenitsyn, 1974. *The Gulag Archipelago 1918-1956.* Thomas Whitney. The convoluted history of its publication is worth reading.

74   Again, Greene, *Moral Tribes* 2013.

75   Eliza Cook happens to have been a friend of my brother-in-law Colin McGarrigle's great, great, great aunt, Maria Heath. Through her, he has a portrait of Eliza Cook and three studs that she often wore. When the expression was picked up again in a poem by Frances Shaw in "Who Loves the Rain," first published in *Poetry* March 1914, she refined it to: "look on life with quiet eyes."

76   The ideas here, if not the language, are adapted from Professor Oscar Ces, Imperial College, Imperial/43, page 34, *The Magazine for the Imperial Community*, Winter 2017/18.

77   Essay on the Mission of Poetry, 1942.

78   Again, Gelfand, L., 1973. *The Genuine Shona*, Mambo Press.

ACKNOWLEDGMENTS

I thank my wife Laila and our son Alexander for putting up with all the time I shut them out while writing this. I thank my late parents Eric and Yvonne Nelson, my sister Erica McGarrigle and her husband Colin McGarrigle, my ex-wife Anne and, from that marriage, my daughters Jaime and Antonia and my son Sinclair, and my late uncle Major Ivor Nelson and my cousin Susan Klugman who both gave me help over the years on ancestry. I thank my many friends from days in Africa, Australia, India and elsewhere including: in Africa, Stephen and Anne Carr whose work in Africa has been unparalleled, Julian Blackwood (from whom I may have lifted a story or two), David Pudsey, Ian Rossiter, Isaac Musuva, Joseph Waweru, Vincent Mrisho, Mike Hopper, Gordon Moore, the late Peter Jenkins (in those days Game Warden of Meru Game Park in Kenya), and Hugh Sterling; in India, Balasubramanian, our dear friend Bim Bissell, and many, many, other colleagues and friends from Delhi days; and, in Australia, from my jackarooing days and my years in Wagga Wagga, Tony Dunn, Frank Austin, Ian Horsley, Des Fitzgerald, Peter Blake, Lewis Rowell, Peter Mathews, the late Ken and Joan Palmer, David Palmer, David Mackay, Sinclair Hill and the late Leslie Hill. From Haileybury school days in England, I thank Alan Raymond.

I thank Tom Blinkhorn, who kindly commented on a draft of this book, John Heath and Doug Land, both valued sounding boards on things literary, and Professor Raymond Tallis for his quote on "meaning." I thank my fellow students from Wye College days, Colin Myram and Ursula Thompson (née Hartley), who traveled with me to California to the Cadd Ranch, and Al and Alyce Cadd and their son and daughter Larry and Cindy for introducing us to America and for teaching us more than we ever needed to know about prunes! I thank Larry Kilbourne, my men's coffee group—a fount of knowledge both useful and useless, and all my other friends at The Old Brogue Irish Pub in Great Falls, Virginia. I thank the team at Mascot Books, especially Ben Simpson, Daniel Wheatley, my professional and perceptive editor Kristin Clark Taylor, and Nina Spahn. I'm sure I will kick myself for missing important others who contributed, for which my apologies. And finally, I thank my yellow boy Labrador Nelly, "without whose never-failing sympathy and encouragement this book would have been finished in half the time" to borrow from a P.G. Wodehouse acknowledgment!

ABOUT THE AUTHOR

Ridley Nelson has British and Australian citizenships and lives in America. He has lived in England, Australia, Egypt, India, Tanzania, Kenya, and America and visited ninety-five countries. In his youth, he worked as a jackaroo on sheep properties in Australia and took a working passage on a merchant ship. Over his career he worked as an agriculturalist and agricultural economist for several organizations, including two commercial companies, the World Bank, and a British overseas aid program. Now in semi-retirement, he works as a rural development and project evaluation consultant.

He sails a Laser dinghy, is a fly fisher and surf fisher, and continues an amateur interest in elephants and wildlife management. While he has authored published professional reports and papers, this is his first book. He writes poetry, more for the creative challenge than for publication, but three have been published. He has been a guest lecturer on a cruise ship. He lives in Northern Virginia with his wife Laila, an American citizen originally from Afghanistan.